MW01620775

ACROSS CONTINENTS AND CULTURES

The Art and Life of Henry Ossawa Tanner

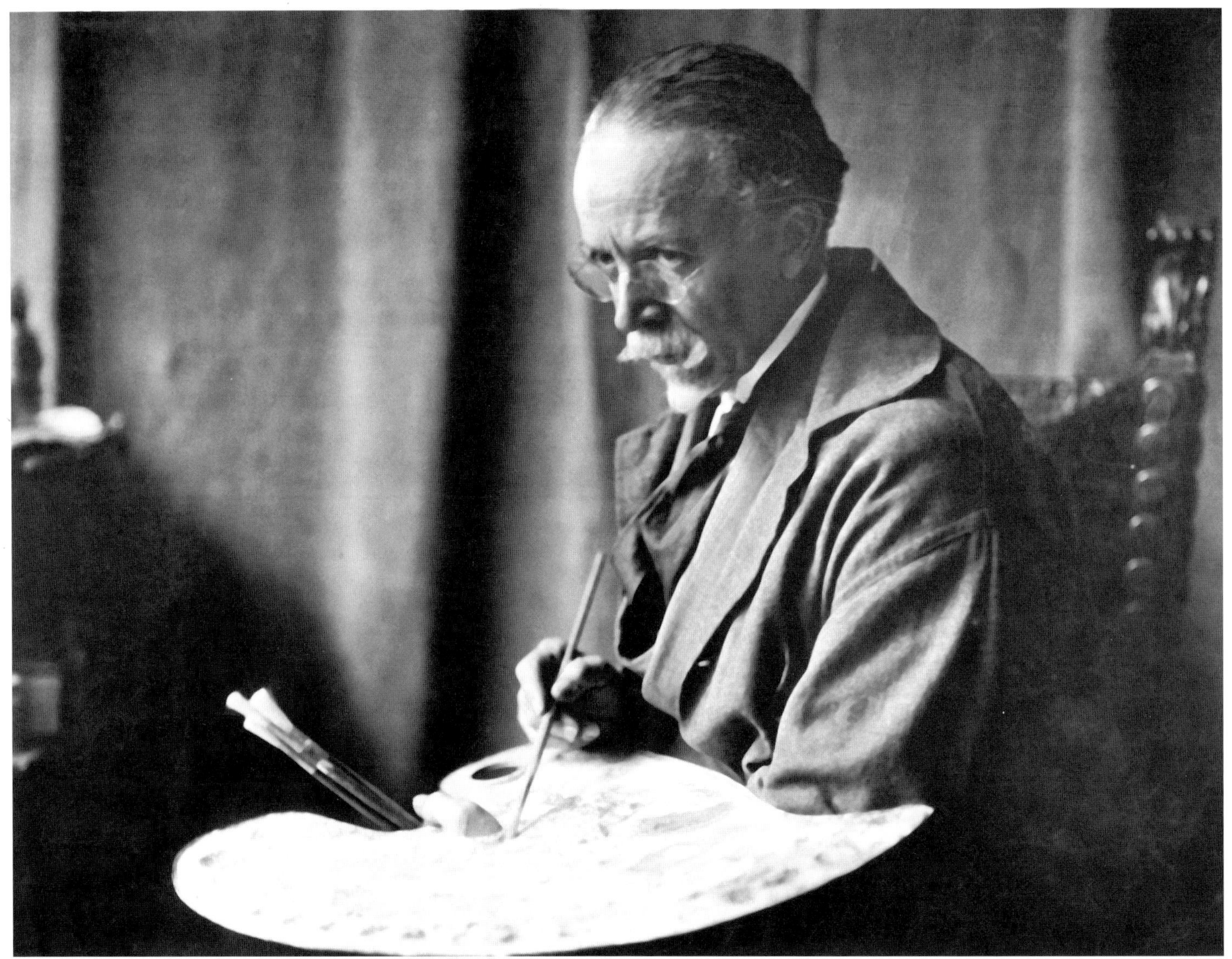

Henry Ossawa Tanner, c. 1935, photograph, Henry O. Tanner Papers, Archives of American Art, Smithsonian Institution, Washington, D.C.

Across Continents and Cultures

The Art and Life of Henry Ossawa Tanner

Dewey F. Mosby

THE NELSON-ATKINS MUSEUM OF ART
KANSAS CITY, MISSOURI

This catalogue was published on the occasion of the exhibition of the same name, on view at:

The Nelson-Atkins Museum of Art
Kansas City, Missouri
June 25-August 20, 1995

Dallas Museum of Art
Dallas, Texas
September 7-December 31, 1995

Terra Museum of American Art
Chicago, Illinois
January 12-April 28, 1996

Project Director: Margaret C. Conrads
Project Assistant: Kevin Moore
Editors: David A. Conrads and Margaret C. Conrads
Design and Printing: Constable-Hodgins Printing Company, Kansas City, Kansas

Library of Congress Cataloging-in-Publication Data

Mosby, Dewey F., 1942-
Across continents and cultures: the art and life of Henry Ossawa Tanner/Dewey F. Mosby. — 1st ed.
Published on the occasion of the exhibition of the same name at The Nelson-Atkins Museum of Art, Kansas City, Mo., June 25-Aug. 20, 1995; the Dallas Museum of Art, Dallas, Tex., Sept. 7-Dec. 31, 1995; and the Terra Museum of American Art, Chicago, Ill., Jan. 12-Apr. 28, 1996.
Includes bibliographical references and index.
ISBN 0-942614-24-0 (pbk. : acid-free paper)
1. Tanner, Henry Ossawa, 1859-1937—Exhibitions. I. Nelson-Atkins Museum of Art. II. Dallas Museum of Art. III. Terra Museum of American Art. IV. Title
ND237.T33A4 1995 759.13—dc20 95-4078 CIP

First Edition

Cover: Henry Ossawa Tanner, *Study for The Thankful Poor,* c.1894, oil on canvas, 12 3/4 x 16 1/4 (32.4 x 41.3), Du Sable Museum of African American History, Inc., Chicago, Illinois

ISBN:0-942614-24-0 (pbk.)

SPONSOR'S STATEMENT

KCPL is proud to support *Across Continents and Cultures: The Art and Life of Henry Ossawa Tanner.* This sponsorship is an outgrowth of our commitment to fostering awareness and understanding of the value of diversity in our communities.

Valuing the talents and contributions of all individuals is key to releasing the creative energy in our communities—energy which enables residents, businesses, and social and cultural agencies to join together to solve common problems and seek opportunities for improvement; energy which enables us to seek the truth and find beauty in our collective culture; energy which enriches all our lives.

As we come together to appreciate Henry Ossawa Tanner's art and life, we come together to appreciate each other and the talents and contributions we can make, individually and collectively, to our community.

Drue Jennings
Chairman of the Board and President
Kansas City Power & Light Company

FRIENDS OF THE EXHIBITION

The exhibition and catalogue are made possible by the generous support of the Kansas City Power & Light Company, the corporate sponsor, and the Carrie J. Loose Trust, an affiliated trust of the Greater Kansas City Community Foundation. Additional funding for the exhibition has been provided by the National Endowment for the Arts, a federal agency, and the Missouri Arts Council, a state agency MAC.

In Kansas City, educational and community outreach programs are made possible by generous grants from The H & R Block Foundation, the Hallmark Corporate Foundation, the Black Community Fund, Kansas City Southern Industries, and Sprint Foundation. Additional funding has been provided by the Earl J. and Leona K. Tranin Special Fund of the Jewish Community Foundation of Greater Kansas City, Suzanne Thompson Knowles, Donald and Sally Tranin, and a group of community friends.

COMMUNITY ADVISORY COMMITTEE

Rose Bryant
William Clark
Paul Copaken
Allan Gray
Donald Hall
Karen T. Haren
Helen Haugh
David H. Hughes, Jr.
Stephanie Jacobson
Dorothy Johnson
Patricia Jordan
Suzanne Thompson Knowles
Alan Kosloff
Sandra A. J. Lawrence
Albert P. Mauro
Donna Nelmes
Victor J. Poirier
Leonard Pryor
Donald Tranin
Sally Tranin
Terrence Ward
William Washington
Mildred L. Watson
David White
Yvonne Wilson

COMMUNITY FRIENDS

Beta Omega Chapter, Alpha Kappa Alpha Sorority
The Book Lovers' Club of Greater Kansas City
Dan and Caryle Carr
Excegis Club
The Greater Kansas City Chapter of Drifters
Les Honneté Mo-Kans Club
The Jackson County Bar Association
Jackson County, Missouri Chapter, Link, Inc.
Herman A. and Dorothy H. Johnson
The Kansas Citians Club
Les Modernes Study Club
Mu Omega Chapter, Alpha Kappa Alpha Sorority, Inc.
P.M. Interlude Club
Virginia L. S. Potter
Sumner High School Alumni Association
Theta Boulé of Sigma Pi Phi Fraternity
Twin Citian Club
Mildred L. Watson

LENDERS TO THE EXHIBITION

Dr. Rae Alexander-Minter
Allentown Art Museum, Pennsylvania
American Red Cross, Washington, D.C.
The Art Institute of Chicago
Berea College, Kentucky
The Brooklyn Museum
Clark Atlanta University Collection of African American Art, Atlanta, Georgia
Dallas Museum of Art
Des Moines Art Center, Iowa
William R. Dorsey
Du Sable Museum of African American History, Inc., Chicago
Fisk University, Nashville, Tennessee
The Frances Lehman Loeb Art Center, Vassar College, Poughkeepsie, New York
Hamilton College, New York
Hampton University, Virginia
High Museum of Art, Atlanta, Georgia
Howard University Gallery of Art, Washington, D.C.
Dr. and Mrs. Dwight L. McKenna
The Menil Collection
Merton D. Simpson
Milwaukee Art Museum
Musée d'Orsay, Paris
Museum of Art, Rhode Island School of Design, Providence
Muskegon Museum of Art, Michigan
National Academy of Design, New York
National Museum of American Art, Smithsonian Institution, Washington, D.C.
New Britain Museum of American Art, Connecticut
New Orleans Museum of Art
Pennsylvania Academy of the Fine Arts, Philadelphia
Philadelphia Museum of Art
Schomburg Center for Research in Black Culture, The New York Public Library
The Springfield Museum of Art, Ohio
State Historical Society of Iowa, Des Moines
George and Joyce Wein
Willkie House, Inc., Des Moines, Iowa
Private collections

TABLE OF CONTENTS

FOREWORD

As a project, the Tanner exhibition epitomizes the adage that mighty trees spring from small seeds. An innocent telephone call sparked an enterprise that brought together an entire community. Partnerships grew up where none existed and crossed political boundaries, bridged cultural differences, and knocked down color lines.

In 1897, Henry Ossawa Tanner came west to visit his family shortly after his father, Benjamin Tanner, had taken up residence in Kansas City, Kansas, as Bishop of the Fifth District of the African Methodist Episcopal church. His mother, Sarah Miller Tanner, and his sister, Bertha, had already joined the Pierian Club, a study society founded in 1894 by a group of African-American women.

Nearly a century later, Pierian member Suzanne Knowles placed an unassuming phone call to the Nelson: "Did we know that Henry Tanner had a connection to Kansas City?" "Did we know of the Pierian Club and the contributions of Tanner's family to the cultural and religious life of Kansas City?" "Would the Museum consider doing something modest to help the Pierian Club observe its upcoming centennial?"

From this small spark grew a grand alliance of individuals, schools, churches, businesses, foundations, community centers, and governmental agencies. An entire community has been electrified by the possibility of a major exhibition of Tanner's work.

An advisory committee was formed to organize fundraising and to stimulate community participation in a rich array of educational programs that would soon be developed. The energy and intelligence the committee brought to their charges are clearly evidenced in the exhibition and accompanying programs which reach every corner of the greater Kansas City community. All who enjoy this exhibition or partake of the accompanying programs in Kansas City will surely join me in expressing our admiration and gratitude for their achievement. All are deserving of recognition, but only a few can be named.

Mildred Watson ably led the advisory committee and exhibited a keen sense of personal relationships that kept everyone working smoothly toward a common goal. Rose Bryant, Bill Clark, Suzanne Knowles, Stephanie Jacobson, Terry Ward, and Bill Washington served as her lieutenants.

I am especially grateful to Drue Jennings and Vic Poirier of the Kansas City Power & Light Company for the insight and concern for community that led their company to undertake the role of corporate sponsor.

The Carrie J. Loose Trust, an affiliated trust of the Greater Kansas City Community Foundation, joined them in providing major funding for organizational costs.

The Missouri Arts Council has continued its ongoing support for exhibition projects such as this one.

Those in Kansas City who avail themselves of the educational and community programs will no doubt want to recognize the generosity of contributors who made them possible: The H & R Block Foundation; Hallmark Corporate Foundation; Black Community Fund; Kansas City Southern Industries; Sprint Foundation; the Earl J. and Leona K. Tranin Special Fund of the Jewish Community Foundation of Greater Kansas City; Suzanne Thompson Knowles; and Donald and Sally Tranin.

The number of community friends who stepped forward to contribute to the project demonstrates a remarkable breadth of support that is a source of special satisfaction. Listed elsewhere in this catalogue, each should be assured of my heartfelt gratitude.

I extend my thanks to my colleagues Jay Gates, Director of the Dallas Museum of Art, and D. Scott Atkinson, Curator of the Terra Museum of American Art, for recognizing that there is much new to consider about Tanner as recent research and thinking really demand broader interpretive perspectives on his work.

The credit for the expanded views of Tanner posited in this exhibition and its accompanying catalogue goes with thanks to Dr. Dewey F. Mosby who served as the exhibition's guest curator and the catalogue's author.

An exhibition of this sort is a complicated undertaking. So many different threads need to be woven into a coherent whole, while chaos threatens every step. I applaud the extraordinarily effective leadership Margaret Conrads, our Samuel Sosland Curator of American Art, has shown throughout this project. Her masterful direction of the project has been aided by the very effective efforts of Kevin Moore, Project Assistant. Ann Brubaker, Director of Education, has wisely shaped the educational and community programs. Associate Registrar Cindy Cart made the complications of shipping the works seem effortless.

Finally, to the lenders go deepest thanks, not only on behalf of the exhibiting institutions, but also on behalf of the thousands of Americans who will enjoy and learn from this exhibition. We are beholden.

Marc F. Wilson
Director

ACKNOWLEDGMENTS

The generous and unfailing support the Museum has received from all fronts for this project has been truly extraordinary. For the success of this exhibition, catalogue, and its accompanying programs, we owe a great debt to many. As Marc Wilson has indicated in the foreword, the Kansas City communities of both Missouri and Kansas have been wonderfully active participants. To Dr. Dewey F. Mosby, our guest curator, I extend warm thanks for his thoughtful work and guidance. We have all benefited from his broad thinking and wide range of expertise. To the lenders to the exhibition, who are listed at the beginning of this volume, we thank you for your generosity and cooperation.

Dr. Mosby and I would like to acknowledge our many colleagues who assisted us in our work: Jerold Pepper, The Adirondack Museum, Blue Mountain Lake, New York; Dr. Rae Alexander-Minter; Joan Wardner Allen; Nancy Allyn; Philippe Fleury and Yveline Cantarel-Besson, Archives des Musées Nationaux, Paris; the staff of the Archives of American Art; Mary Doering, American Red Cross; Barry Bauman; Robert Boyce, Berea College, Kentucky; Mary Curtis Bok; Barbara Dayer Gallati and Guillermo Ovalle, The Brooklyn Museum; Douglas C. Dolan, Bucks County Historical Society; Sally Gibson, Sterling and Francine Clark Art Institute; Eleanor Jones Harvey, Dallas Museum of Art; Eugene C. Daymude; Deborah Leveton, Des Moines Art Center; Dan DuBois; Ramon Price and Theresa Christopher, Du Sable Museum of African American History; Karen C. C. Dalton, Harvard University; Judy Larson, High Museum of Art; Lynn Moody Igoe; Larry Hancks, Kansas City, Kansas Landmarks Commission; Dr. Kathleen James; Ilene S. Fort and Quincy Houghton, Los Angeles County Museum of Art; Carol Lowery; Miki Marku, Merton Simpson Collection; David Dearinger, National Academy of Design; Earl A. Powell, III, National Gallery of Art; Elizabeth Broun, Kimberly Cody, Linda Hartigan, and Quentin Rankin, National Museum of American Art, Smithsonian Institution; Chester Owens; Suzanne Penn; Barbara Katus and Sylvia Yount, Pennsylvania Academy of the Fine Arts; Caroline Demaree and Mike Hammer, Philadelphia Museum of Art; Dr. Gerald Ackerman, Pomona College; Leni Potoff; Sally Wardner Richards; Michael Rosenfeld and Halley Harrisburg, Michael Rosenfeld Gallery; Grace Scull Sawyer; Dr. Merle Schipper; Candy Schock; Laurel Tucker Duplessis, Tammy Lawson, and Malcolm Sweet, Schomburg Center for Research in Black Culture, New York; Margaret Stenz; Debra Dandridge, University of Kansas; Pat Soden, University of Washington Press; Richard D. White; Jacqueline Brown, Wilberforce University; the late Michael Willoughby; and Robert Woterstorff.

At Colgate University, the home institution of Dr. Mosby, we thank the staffs of the Everett Needham Case Library, especially David Hughes and Mary Jane Walsh; and with special appreciation to Jeanie Newlun, secretary to Dr. Mosby.

At the Nelson-Atkins, many staff members have played essential roles in this project, including Ellen Goheen, Administrator for Special Exhibitions; Briane Lawler and Julie Aronson of the American Art Department; Forrest Bailey and Steve Bonham of the Conservation Department; Antoine Leriche, Jennifer Segale, and Mark Hughey of the Design Department; Dawn Biegelson, Joann Duncan, Ann Kaufmann, Boots Leiter, and Mary Ellen Young of the Development Office; Ann Brubaker, Carol Inge, Debbie Brooks, and Kate Livers of the Education Department; Greg Olson and the Installation Department; Brent Powell and the Packing and Storage Department; Robert Newcombe and the Photography Department; and Gina Kelley and Margaret Keough, Public Information Office.

Special recognition is due those people without whom this project would have been impossible: Suzanne Knowles of the Pierian Club, who provided the initial spark for the project and offered continual support;

Mildred Watson of the Community Advisory Committee and Michael Churchman of the Museum's Development Office for their cheerful guidance and persuasive powers; Rebecca Ofiesh for her careful shepherding of all the educational materials and programs; Cindy Cart for her meticulous handling of all registration matters; David Conrads for his editorial expertise; and John Elliott for his graceful book design and the first-rate production of all printed materials affiliated with the exhibition. Finally, to Kevin Moore, my assistant for the project, we extend our most heartfelt gratitude for his keen abilities and good humor.

Margaret C. Conrads
Samuel Sosland Curator of American Art

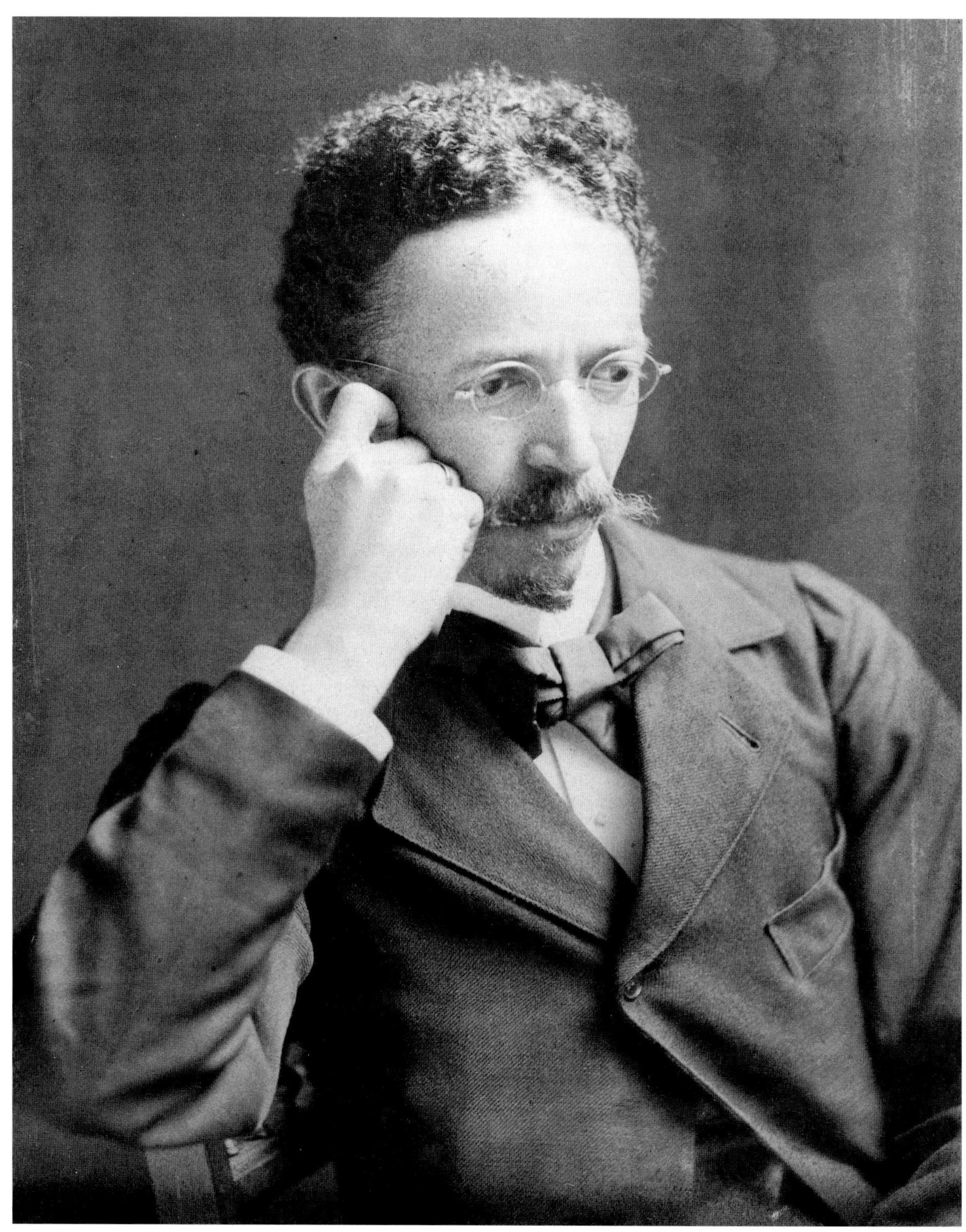

Henry Ossawa Tanner, c. 1900, photograph, Dr. Rae Alexander-Minter

Across Continents and Cultures

The Art and Life of Henry Ossawa Tanner

Dewey F. Mosby

Introduction: Henry Ossawa Tanner and Questions of Race

The issue of race was important to Henry Ossawa Tanner (1859-1937), as it was to the period in which he lived. Tanner's seemingly ambivalent attitude toward race often elicited conflicting responses during his lifetime, and continues to do so today. To fully understand this complex issue, a close examination of the relation between Tanner's life as an African American and the nature of his artistic production is essential.[1] *Across Continents and Cultures: The Art and Life of Henry Ossawa Tanner* surveys Tanner's life and art, with special consideration given to the question of how the artist engaged his racial heritage in his work. He is discussed as an African-American artist, rather than as simply an artist.

Today, with many critics wanting to leave behind the baggage of the first two-thirds of the twentieth century, the question is raised: why cannot Henry Tanner be appreciated simply as an artist, without bringing up the tiresome issue of race.[2] The simple answer is that Tanner was inspired in his art by his cultural heritage. In order to address issues of concern for African Americans, Tanner drew from the wide range of experiences he encountered, and employed models from several cultures. As a result, the histories of both American and French art are richer for it. Moreover, Tanner has been placed on the side of his race in this study because, as the artist's father wrote in regard to the 1900 World's Fair: "our only protection against robbery of proper credit is to claim credit for what we do, resting assured that everything to our discredit is cheerfully placarded and always will be."[3]

The distinguished African-American scholar W. E. B. Du Bois (1868-1963) reflected on the situation for blacks in general when he wrote in 1903: "The problem of the twentieth century is the problem of the color-line...."[4] In reference to Tanner's career, Du Bois's notion seems to have been supported by an anonymous art critic in 1908: "In America, public recognition of Tanner's greatness has been somewhat retarded by the fact that he is a Negro.... It has pleased them to slight his art in the exploitation of his race."[5] Yet, the high quality of Tanner's art could dissolve the barrier of color. For example, the renowned educator Booker T. Washington noted: "Few people ever stopped, I found, when looking at his pictures, to inquire whether Mr. Tanner was a Negro painter, a French painter, a German painter. They simply knew that he was able to produce something which the world wanted—a great painting—and the matter of his color did not enter into their minds."[6]

———— ♦ ————

Henry Tanner spent over half his life in France. There he found an expansive and more accepting environment, free from the racial strife found in much of the United States. He wrote in 1908: "There is a breadth, a generosity, an obsolete cosmopolitanism about her recognition of the fine arts, which bars no nationality, no race, no school, or variation of artistic method. All she asks is that the art shall be true, in other words that it shall set forth life."[7] It should be emphasized that the artist mentioned race in this passage, a clear indication that it was something on his mind even in France. Prejudice against different races was not absent in French culture. E. Azalia Hackley reported in 1907, at the height of Tanner's popularity: "The French call all dark people 'negre,' no matter what the race may be.... It always gives me a chill to hear the French say 'negre'.... I believe that 'down in their hearts' the French people despise black people.... They also say that if a 'savant' of any nation comes to France, he is accorded the honor due him, and this I believe to be true."[8] Tanner acquired "savant" status, and was accorded special privileges as a result of his great talent.

Rev. William E. Barton shed further light on Tanner's life in France and the artist's ambivalence about the United States. Barton recalled in 1913: "In Paris his color never counted against him in the least, and he and his [Caucasian] wife...moved freely in such society as they chose. It was not quite so in America, but he intended to win fame and return to his own land. He has returned from time to time and the recognition he was seeking has come to him, but still he lives in France. I have never asked him why, but I think perhaps I can guess."[9]

If ever there was a time when Tanner might have decided to live permanently in the U.S., it should have been during an extended visit to New York in 1908, when the artist was at the height of his reputation in his native land. Yet at the time, America was still recovering from the impact of the 1906 Brownsville Affair, in which members of a black battalion stationed at Fort Brown, Texas, were accused of going on a shooting spree in nearby Brownsville that left one resident dead. Although no witnesses could identify the black soldiers as the culprits, President Theodore Roosevelt ordered their dishonorable discharge, incurring the outrage of blacks across the country. Two years later, during Tanner's visit, the Brownsville Affair was still an open wound and the U.S. Senate was conducting hearings on the incident.[10]

The hostile climate produced by such events helps explain why the artist wrote a few years later: "This condition has driven me out of the country, but still the best friends I have are 'White' Americans and while I cannot sing our National Hymn, 'Land of Liberty,' etc., still deep down in my heart I love it and am sometimes sad that I cannot live where my heart is."[11] The dilemma Tanner faced is reinforced by the fact that he never renounced his American citizenship and served in the American Red Cross during World War I.

———— ♦ ————

The heart of the question of race and Henry Ossawa Tanner lies neither in what other people thought nor in where the artist chose to live, but in what Tanner himself believed. Some modern black critics believe that Tanner denied his own blackness.[12] Others thought that Tanner saw himself as an "expatriate phenomenon in search of artistic truth rather than a black artist bound to the heritage of his people."[13] Tanner's son, who denied the black part of his ancestry,[14] fueled these beliefs by writing: "My father was...a fourth-generation American of Negro extraction. But he always felt himself to be an American first and a Negro second. This was quite natural, as our family was of mixed blood with Red Indian, Negro, and White ancestors."[15] These views concur with a racially volatile question Tanner himself posed: "Now am I a Negro? Does not the three-fourths of English blood in my veins...count for anything?"[16] He went on to say that his best friends were "White Americans" while lamenting that his blond, curly-headed little boy would be a "Negro" in Tanner's native land.[17]

Several details need to be examined before drawing conclusions from Tanner's words. As a boy, he received solid grounding in racial pride from his father, who wrote in 1869: "No people now exists who can trace more clearly their paternity than the Negro. The genealogical table of the Negro, written in his own flesh remains. Ages of scouring have not sufficed to erase it. Written by the finger of God, it is more enduring than the stones of Sinai. It remains, and will remain the badge of our suffering, the triumph of our courage."[18] The artist's middle name, also from his parents, was a tribute to the abolitionist John Brown (1800-1859), whose nickname was "old Brown of Osawatomie," a reference to his activities in that Kansas town.[19] Tanner gave Brown's sobriquet to his own son, Jesse Ossawa Tanner. Most importantly, the published account of his letter quoted above left off the last paragraph: "I am glad I am what I am, for the same reason that a Swede hates to be called a Norwegian, and a Dane to be called a Swede, a Scotchman to be called an Englishman, etc., etc."[20] Tanner made it clear that he wished to be identified ethnically as black, but not to be judged solely on that account.

What Tanner did object to was the use of the word Negro. By 1903, that appellation had come under attack: Du Bois equated it with the institution of slavery.[21] Later, around the very time that Tanner was voicing concern about being labeled a "Negro," an acquaintance, the black intellectual W. H. Ferris, expounded on the issue: "Scholars and scientists are in despair as to what term will best classify the hybrid and ostracized group of individuals who are known as 'Negros,' 'colored people,' 'African-Americans.' 'Negro' will not do because that ethnologically refers to the full-blooded Negro in Africa, or of African descent living elsewhere, whereas more than fifty percent of the colored population in America has more or less of Anglo-Saxon blood in its veins."[22] It is evident that Tanner, being a man of his times, objected to a term rather than to his own black American heritage.

Tanner's sense of racial identity and pride is further demonstrated in his unpublished letters among the recently released Alexander Papers in the Archives of the University of Pennsylvania. In a letter of 1936, he expressed admiration for the beautiful voice of contralto Marian Anderson, but, in spite of many years in France and characteristic of black on black racism, he noted she was "a rather dark girl...who did not know how to dress."[23] In the same letter he expressed hope that Zora N. Hurston's *Mules and Men* was as good as "they say" and that the book would be a credit to the race. Tanner's actions, too, reflect the importance he placed on his racial identity. During the height of his fame, the artist's door was always open to young black artists studying in France and to African Americans vacationing there.

Tanner was also involved financially in contemporary African-American causes. The author James Weldon Johnson (1871-1938), secretary of the NAACP Legal Defense Fund, wrote to him on New Year's Eve 1925: "It was especially gratifying to us to receive your contribution of twenty-five dollars to the Legal Defense Fund which we are establishing. I think that the published report of your contribution stimulated others to give."[24] During the Depression, Du Bois put out an appeal for funds in support of the *Crisis*, the NAACP journal, of which he was the editor. Tanner, as a member of the "talented tenth," sent a ten-dollar contribution.[25] The artist put his purse in the service of the two most aggressive civil rights organizations of his time. These contributions alone should silence anyone inclined to call him an Uncle Tom.

All of these details confirm that Tanner did not deny his ancestry, but involved himself in racial matters. They also offer an introduction to the environment in which Tanner constructed the points about race he made in his art. Henry Ossawa Tanner never turned his back on his race, and so the story of his life and art must reflect his relationship with his heritage. Shortly before his death, in 1937, Tanner himself provided a summation of the issues of race and the pressure it placed on him: "[The African-American stranger I met in Paris] has very probably never heard of me, as have not many hundreds and thousands of our people whom you might expect would know of my work, but it was not all for myself that I have tried in the measure of my ability to make a success of my life."[26]

Family Background, Early Years, and Struggling to Become an Artist, 1859-1879

Henry Ossawa Tanner was born in Pittsburgh, Pennsylvania, on June 21, 1859. His early childhood was spent in a society where human bondage was widespread. Tanner's birth occurred three and one-half years before the Emancipation Proclamation was issued, on January 1, 1863, by President Abraham Lincoln. This decree granted *de jure* freedom to all slaves in any state or district then in rebellion against the United States government: slavery had already been abolished "on a gradual level" in Pennsylvania on March 1, 1780.[27] The American Civil War ended on April 11, 1865, when Tanner was just under six years old.

The future artist's father, Benjamin Tucker Tanner (1835-1923), was a second-generation freedman and third-generation resident of Pittsburgh. He was educated at Avery College and the Western Theological Seminary, both in Allegheny City, Pennsylvania. He rose rapidly through the ranks of the African Methodist Episcopal church, holding posts in Washington, D.C., and Frederick and Baltimore, Maryland, before moving the family permanently to Philadelphia in 1868. There he was editor of the *Christian Recorder*, a weekly journal of the A.M.E. church containing news about national political events. He became bishop of the diocese in 1888.[28] The Reverend Tanner's numerous books show that he used his writings to deliver messages not strictly on religion but also on civil rights for his emancipated flock. For example, he wrote at the outset of *The Negro's Origin and Is the Negro Cursed*: "This little pamphlet is dedicated to the Negro whose Manhood can neither be destroyed by the rust of Barbarism nor the fires of persecution."[29]

Henry Tanner's mother, Sarah Elizabeth Miller (1840-1914), was born in Winchester, Virginia, where her family was freed from slavery in 1841; she eventually moved to Pittsburgh. Sarah Miller attended Avery College and conducted a private school in her home. She married Rev. Benjamin Tanner on August 19, 1858, and from this union came nine children, of whom Henry was the first born.[30] Many of the Tanner children went on to have extraordinary careers. For example, Tanner's younger sister, Halle (1864-1901), became a physician and colleague of the esteemed educator Booker T. Washington (1856-1915); she was the first woman of any race to pass the Alabama medical boards.[31]

The family owned a three-story, eight-room house and the grounds at 2908 Diamond Street in North Philadelphia. Rev. Tanner's salary was probably in the range of that of the pastor of the Bethel A.M.E. Church, or one thousand dollars per year. An annual wage of fifteen hundred dollars ranked with the richest of his race.[32] Education, religion, racial pride, and good citizenship were important ingredients in the daily lives of the Tanner household.

Henry Ossawa Tanner was enrolled in the Lombard Street School for Colored Students soon after the family moved to Philadelphia in 1868. He transferred to the Roberts Vaux Consolidated School for Colored Students in 1870, where the missionary minister Jacob C. White, Jr., was principal. This school provided a secondary education with a liberal arts curriculum, and so it did not discourage students with art interests as did most schools of the day.[33]

———— ♦ ————

In the summer of 1872, thirteen-year-old Henry Tanner was walking with his father in Fairmount Park when they saw an artist at work. He recalled vividly that "the subject the artist had chosen was a middle distance hillside with a magnificent elm in bold relief."[34] After watching the artist at work for an hour, the teenager decided on the spot to become an artist himself. With encouragement from his mother and fifteen cents from the family, Henry acquired basic art supplies and embarked upon a phase of self-training as a landscape painter. The compositional elements used by that artist in the park—a middle-distance landscape with a prominent foreground object—would remain with Tanner over the whole of his career.

During the ensuing school year Tanner's enthusiasm for art did not wane in spite of the taunts from classmates that an artist is always poor and dies in a garret. In addition to what must have been crude attempts at painting, he studied works by professional artists exhibited on Chestnut Street at James S. Earle and Sons Gallery and in the window of Bailey's Jewelry Store. Tanner was impressed by *A Foggy Morning* by William Wilson Cowell (1856-1920) and *A Morning at Long Beach* by Prosper Louis Senat (1852-1925). He was taken particularly with the numerous stormy sea images by James Hamilton (1819-1878) and still more numerous renderings of the seacoast off Dieppe, France, by Franklin D. Briscoe (1844-1903). Upon returning home, he would make renditions from memory of the pictures that he had seen.

Unfortunately, no works survive that might shed light on Tanner's youthful output of the early 1870s. We do know that his self-training included perusing art journals, because he wrote in his autobiography that he had read that America needed a great marine painter.[35] He decided to fulfill this need in spite of the fact that the artists he could see at Earle's and Bailey's devoted much of their careers to marine subjects. This youthful arrogance had to do with his unwavering desire not to be "one of your every day kind" of artists.[36] He continued in this mode over the next year, but by the summer of 1874 he recognized that he needed formal training in art. He worked during summer vacation—most likely in Atlantic City, New Jersey—and saved fifty dollars for art lessons.

During the fall of 1874 Tanner made the rounds of the studios in Philadelphia looking for a teacher who would accept at once a neophyte with little money and an African American. He recalled: "No man or boy to whom this country is a land of 'equal chances' can realize what heartaches this question caused me."[37] Tanner's worst fears were realized when "Mr. M.-" informed him that he "had other pupils!"[38] However, Isaac L. Williams (1817-1895), a painter of landscapes and interiors, agreed to teach him for two dollars a session. Tanner thought this sum for a lesson would "ruin even a Rothschild," since a family of four adults and two children could eat for one week on $2.16.[39] He paid the two dollars, but to his dismay he spent three hours simply drawing straight lines. He quit Williams's studio after one lesson and continued to work on his own instruction.

Around 1874 or 1875 a young artist named James N. Hess (1859-1890) informed Tanner that animal painters were even less numerous in America than good marine painters. Tanner noted: "I determined that my country should not be left longer in this deplorable situation. I renounced the inviting field of marine painting to become the great American Landseer."[40] An early writer on the artist pointed out that Tanner studied animals at the Philadelphia Zoo while a mere boy.[41] One work that might belong to this period is the canvas known as *"Pomp" at the Zoo* (fig. 1). (The Zoo acquired a lion named Pompeii in 1874.[42]) Tanner inscribed the painting "African Lion." Could Tanner have intended this sad-faced lion as a metaphor for the large number of African men and women who were enslaved? Even as a teenager he seems to have been sophisticated enough to ponder such subtle issues. Tanner also introduced here the theme of age instructing youth, depicted by the woman and child in the foreground. This motif will appear time and again in his work. Despite the high ideals and precocious themes, the painting shows Tanner's lack of training. The composition is not based on a system of scientific perspective. Here figures are rendered shorter or taller as needed and the recession of the floor into space does not match that of the cage. Yet the figures themselves are well-grounded and have convincing attitudes, as do the straight vertical and horizontal lines—perhaps lingering memories of the one lesson with Isaac L. Williams in the fall of 1874. Finally, the multiple touches

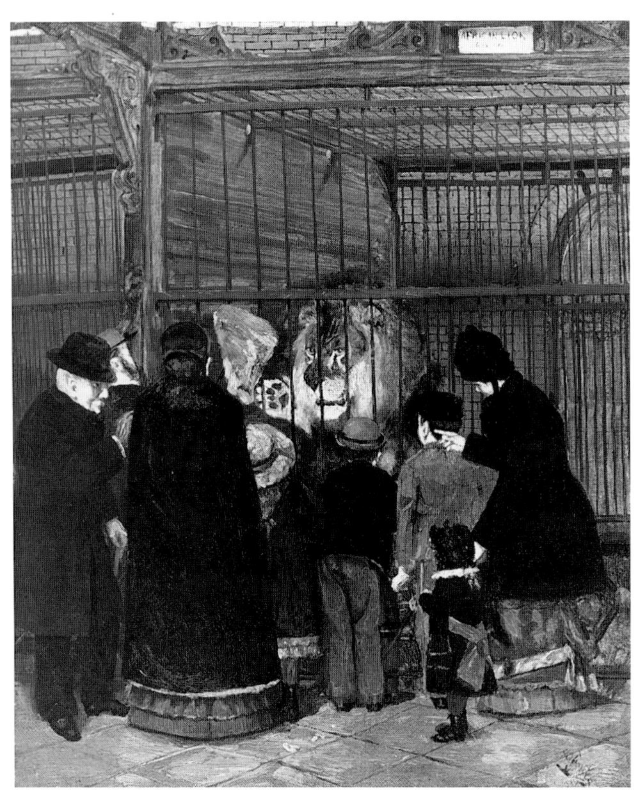

FIGURE 1
"Pomp" at the Zoo, c. 1880
Oil on canvas
20 x 16 (50.8 x 40.6)
Private collection

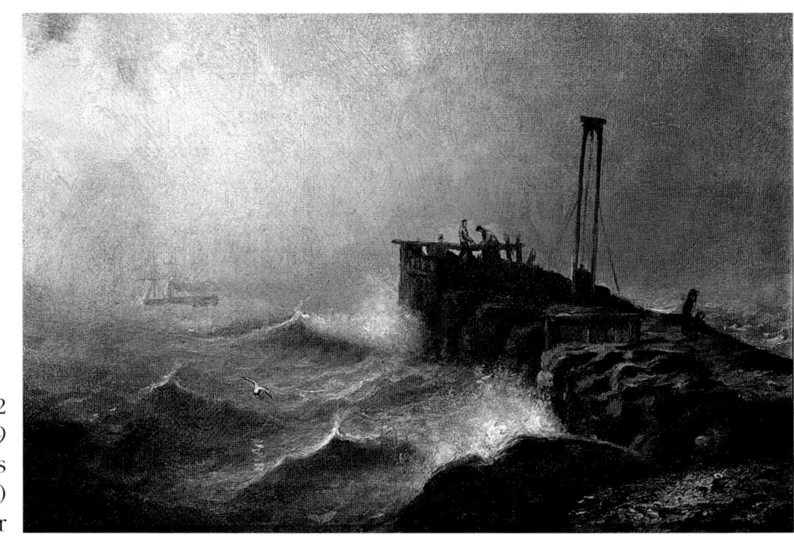

FIGURE 2
Seascape—Jetty, c. 1876-79
Oil on canvas
12 x 17 (30.5 x 43.2)
Dr. Rae Alexander-Minter

of colors in this essentially limited palette point to his later, characteristic blue-green palette full of different color accents.

Tanner's interest in animal subjects was short-lived: during the summer of 1876 he returned to marine subjects and his career as an artist began in earnest. He was in Atlantic City, New Jersey, where a black resort industry, with many seasonal employees, was developing.[43] A Tanner sketch of a wrecked schooner driven ashore during a great storm (location unknown) caught the attention of Henry Price, an amateur artist spending the summer there. Price befriended Tanner and took him into his home in Philadelphia to live and work for over a year. Kind but erratic in his likes and dislikes, Price discouraged Tanner from his interest in attending the Pennsylvania Academy of the Fine Arts, which had just reopened in a new building. Under Price's tutelage Tanner produced *Seascape—Jetty* (fig. 2), in which there is a sense of expansive space, atmospheric perspective, and wetness of the foam-capped water. However, the overall technique is somewhat tentative, with limited color range and lack of detail, as might be expected from a self-trained artist. Also noteworthy is the drybrush technique in the sky, which was probably the result of his misunderstanding of how to build up glazes, or translucent color applied in layers, to modify the effect of the painted surface. Other works from this period, including *Harbor Scene* (1876; John Quincy Johnson), share these characteristics, which were the hallmarks of Tanner's developing style.

Tanner continued his general education during this period. He was valedictorian of his class, graduating on July 6, 1877, from the Roberts Vaux Consolidated School. The subject of his valedictory address was compulsory education. He argued it was the means for expelling ignorance and vice from the land, and that with it "many diamonds in the rough...would become lustrous stars in the crown of America's glory."[44] About this time, the mercurial Henry Price abruptly ended his relationship with the young painter. Tanner recalled: "For some reason, I went home that evening, and upon my return the next morning I found all my belongings with my little canvases tied together, outside his locked studio door."[45] The aspiring artist remained undaunted. His inspiration was likely bolstered by the great success of the black painter Edward Mitchell Bannister (1828-1901) and black sculptor Edmonia Lewis (1845-after 1911) at the 1876 Centennial Exhibition held in Philadelphia. Bannister's painting *Under the Oaks* (location unknown) received one of the four first-prize medals and was considered the best effort possible from an American artist.[46] Edmonia Lewis, too, received praise at the Centennial and former President Ulysses S. Grant sat for her the following year.[47] Rev. Benjamin Tanner also would have been aware of both Bannister's and Lewis's triumphs through the writings of the Philadelphia African-American artist and collector William Henry Dorsey (1837-1923) and their coverage in the *Christian Recorder*.[48] Still, the artist's father was reluctant to allow his son to pursue a career in art because such a life was fraught with insecurity and young Henry had yet to demonstrate any special artistic talent. In addition, he was aware that local Philadelphia black artist Robert Douglass, Jr. (1809-1887) did not have a particularly distinguished career in spite of study at the Pennsylvania Academy of the Fine Arts and travel to Europe. The multi-talented Douglass supported himself in part through private shorthand lessons, but mostly as a teacher at the Institute for Colored Youth.[49] Rev. Tanner would not have wanted a similar career for his son.

Perhaps the overriding reason for Benjamin Tanner's reluctance about art as a career for an African American was based on an exchange of letters published in the Washington, D.C., *People's Advocate* in 1877, the winter before Henry's high school graduation. A certain "Blackibus" of Richmond, Virginia, initiated correspondence on black subjects and black artists. William Henry Dorsey's response covered several important points on the topic. He noted that the black populace was generally aware that taste and, even more so, financial commitment were necessary to become a patron of the arts. He continued that Blackibus perhaps did not appreciate "the obstacles a painter or sculptor has to contend with." He further pointed out that anyone faced with these challenges discovered that he had the "unending prejudice of the dominant race to buffet him from place to place, for only a few years have elapsed since we have been admitted, even as visitors, to...art exhibitions."[50]

Thus recognizing the double burden of being black and an artist in American society, Rev. Tanner placed Henry with a friend to learn the flour business, an unusual occupation for blacks in nineteenth-century Philadelphia.[51] However, Tanner's determination to become an artist did not wane. He rose at dawn so he could paint before going to his job selling flour, but the effort proved to be too strenuous and he became severely ill. As a result, his parents acquiesced and supported his efforts to become an artist, even assisting him financially, as they would do for the next fifteen years. Benjamin Tanner was surely impressed by the tenacity of his son's quest to make art. He wrote later: "All men who have amounted to much or even a little in this world, have had as it were a guiding star—some omnipresent object, which has been their thought by day and dream by night. In the eyes of some it has been money; in others medicine [i.e., his daughter Dr. Halle Tanner Dillon Johnson]; and in others art."[52]

———— ♦ ————

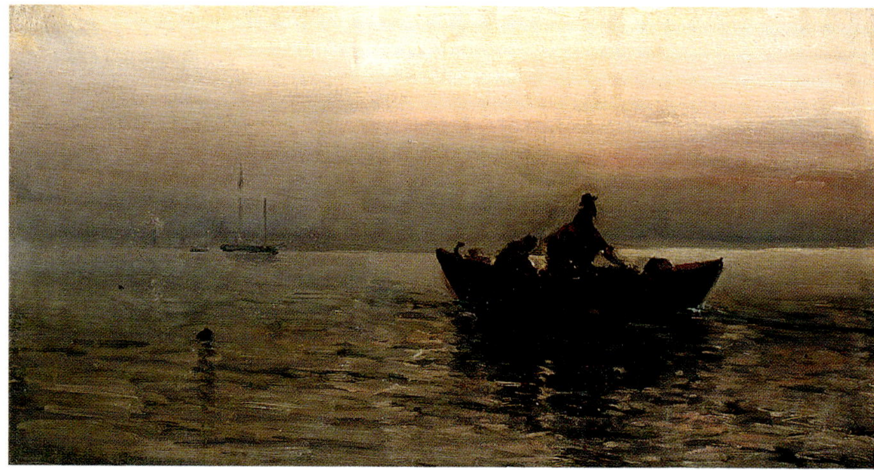

Plate 1
Seascape: Three Men in a Boat, c. 1880
Oil on canvas
17 1/2 x 28 (44.5 x 71.1)
Dr. Rae Alexander-Minter

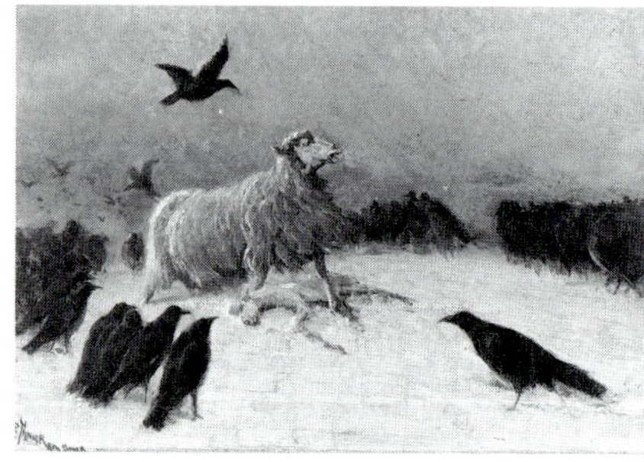

Figure 3
Ewe with Dead Lamb and Crows, c. 1878-79
Oil on fabric
13 x 18 (33 x 45.7)
Dr. Rae Alexander-Minter

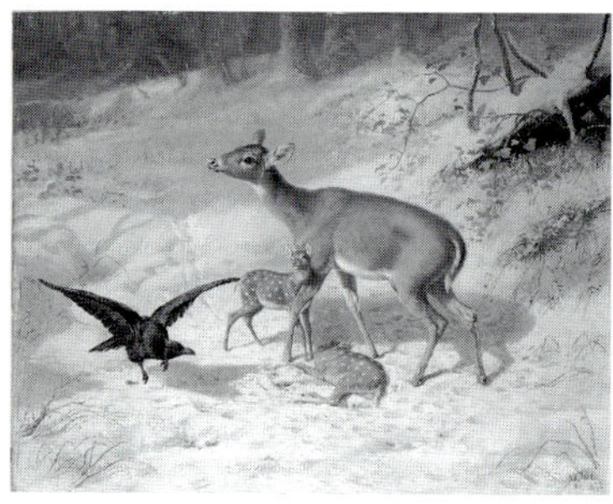

Figure 4
Arthur Fitzwilliam Tait
Maternal Solicitude, 1873
Oil on panel
19 1/2 x 24 (49.5 x 61)
The Cleveland Museum of Art; the Hinman B. Hurlbut Collection

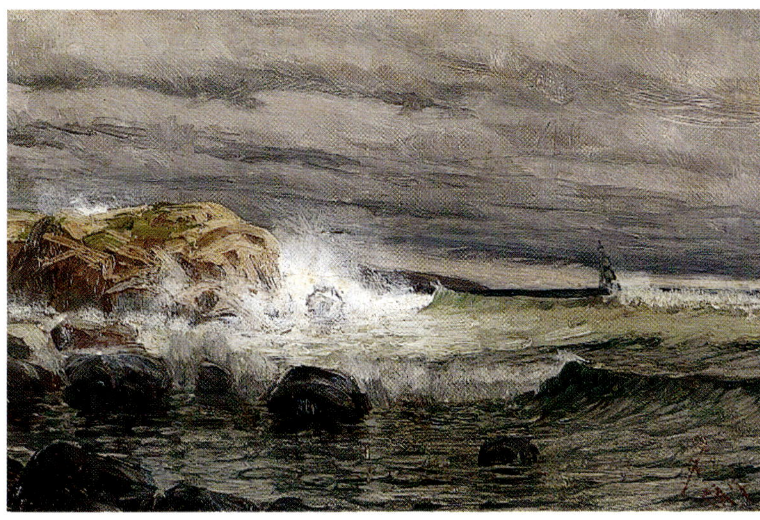

PLATE 2
Point Judith, c. 1880
Oil on canvas board
8 x 12 (20.3 x 30.5)
Private collection

Tanner recuperated from his illness at Wardner's Rainbow Lake Inn in the Adirondack Mountains just northwest of Lake Placid, New York. The region was widely advertised as an inexpensive haven for health-seekers.[53] The resort area did not have an African-American population at the time, but it had strong ties to abolition history. Gerrit Smith, a Peterboro, New York, abolitionist, took occasion on August 1, 1846, to celebrate the twelfth anniversary of the British emancipation of the West Indies by offering free blacks 100,000 acres of his land on easy terms.[54] John Brown had also been given land there and he established his farm amid the black colony at North Elba (Keane, New York), not far from Rainbow Lake.[55] Tanner would have been aware of the region's connections to these famed abolitionists, most likely due to his father's devotion to the legend of John Brown. Rev. Tanner had been an officer in a group that, just days before Brown's hanging, had proclaimed the abolitionist "a hero, patriot and Christian" and called for the annual observance of his death.[56]

During his stay at Wardner's Rainbow Lake Inn, Tanner saw the work of the artist Arthur Fitzwilliam Tait (1819-1905), a number of whose paintings hung in the Inn.[57] Some of the paintings made by Tanner during 1878-79 show a predilection for the sheep and hunting themes favored by Tait. For example, Tanner's *Ewe With Dead Lamb and Crows* (fig. 3) borrowed directly from Tait's *Maternal Solicitude* (fig. 4) the theme of a mother protecting her young and the inclusion of scavenger birds.[58]

Tanner ended his stay at Rainbow Lake sometime in 1879 and then may have traveled to Narragansett and Point Judith in Rhode Island. *Hazy Morning at Narragansett*, probably the work now known as *Seascape: Three Men in a Boat* (pl. 1), and *Point Judith* (pl. 2), two paintings exhibited the next year, suggest this itinerary. The reason for this trip could have been to make the acquaintance of Edward Mitchell Bannister, an original board member of the newly established Rhode Island School of Design. Bannister sailed Narragansett Bay during the summers.[59] About this time, Tanner also made a trip to Florida, again in quest of good health.

Tanner was back in Philadelphia by November 1879, when he inscribed *Ship in a Storm* (1879; Mr. and Mrs. E. T. Williams, Jr.) to Bishop Daniel A. Payne. The trip to the Adirondacks worked wonders for the young artist's health. He wrote: "When my dear mother, who was used to my more or less delicate health, finally saw me off on my journey, she never expected, as she afterward told me, to see me return alive. But I did get there and return alive, and I must always believe that it was the good God who opened the way and gave me good friends, thus filling me with confidence in the future which never deserted me in those darkest days."[60]

Probably around this time, Tanner made the acquaintance of Christopher High Shearer (1840-1926), a landscape painter from Reading, Pennsylvania, who became a close friend, confidant, and a source of professional inspiration. Shearer also fired his desire to visit Europe.[61] Perhaps through Shearer, or vice versa, Tanner met William Wilson Cowell, whose works he had admired some years before. Cowell's studio provided Tanner with his first experience of a regular professional artistic ambience, although he was not Cowell's pupil in any formal sense. This close proximity to a bona fide student of the Pennsylvania Academy of the Fine Arts seems to have rekindled Tanner's desire to study there. The Academy may also have been on the artist's mind because of a long article illustrated with works by Academy students that appeared in an 1879 issue of *Scribner's Monthly*.[62]

Tanner applied for admission to the Pennsylvania Academy of the Fine Arts by submitting a drawing (location unknown). He gave no indication of his race. He was accepted on merit and registered as a student in the antique class on December 4, 1879. However, the specter of racism reared its ugly head. In spite of the fact that Robert Douglass, Jr., had been a student there around mid-century, and the Academy hierarchy had affirmed in September 1878 that the "time has passed for such distinctions to be recognized," Tanner's acceptance was put to a vote of the students.[63] There was not a dissenting voice.[64] The professional career of Henry Ossawa Tanner was launched.

Study at the Pennsylvania Academy of the Fine Arts, Overcoming Racism, and Embarking on a Profession, 1880-1890

Henry O. Tanner's tenure at the Pennsylvania Academy of the Fine Arts, although not continuous, was quite successful. After his initial registration on December 4, 1879, his name appears again in Academy records on January 4, 1881, on the list of students in the life drawing class of the charismatic teacher Thomas Eakins (1844-1914). Tanner apparently dropped out later that year due to illness. The minutes of the Committee on Instruction for January 30, 1884, show that Eakins successfully petitioned the committee to admit Tanner as a free student in the life class, and he probably stayed until classes ended in the spring. During his stints at the Academy, Tanner learned sculpture, printmaking, and photography, in addition to painting.

When Tanner first entered the Pennsylvania Academy, tuition was free once a student passed the entrance examination. The curriculum was divided into antique, life, modeling, and composition classes, plus lectures.[65] Eakins, named director in 1880, was in charge of the courses where students drew from antique casts and painted from live models, including animals. Pennsylvania Academy students did not face any initiation rites; in the life class, for example, "one just went in at the beginning of the pose, drew a number, sat down and began to work."[66] The professors did not attend classes every day but appeared intermittently to provide critiques and demonstrations for the fledgling artists. Tanner recounted one of these sessions, which had a profound impact on his artistic formation:

> About this time Mr. Thomas Eakins, under whom I was studying in the Pennsylvania Academy of the Fine Arts, gave me a criticism which aided me much. I had made a start on a study which was not altogether bad; indeed, I think it was the best thing which up to that time I had ever done. He encouraged me to go on with it, but I was so afraid I should destroy what I had done that I really did nothing the rest of

> the week. He was disgusted and gave me emphatic orders to work it over. "Get it better or get it worse," he said; "no middle ground compromise." This advice has helped me ever since. Mediocrity is the foe of real excellence.[67]

A work which might relate to the kind of assignment completed in Eakins's class on painting from live models is *Sister Sarah* (pl. 3). It is a portrait of the young artist's sister Sarah Elizabeth Tanner (1873-1900), who later taught at the Downington Industrial School before she married Dr. Lewis B. Moore, who organized the Teachers College at Howard University. The direct "drawing in paint" Tanner employed is consistent with the methods taught at the Academy under the aegis of Eakins.[68]

Although Eakins had an enormous impact on Tanner, Thomas Hovenden (1840-1895) also played a pivotal role in his formation at the Pennsylvania Academy. In fact, an early biographer of Tanner went so far as to say that Hovenden was his primary instructor.[69] A family friend, W. S. Scarborough, pointed out in an article of 1902 that Hovenden infused in Tanner "a comprehension of and sympathy with the broader and deeper things of life and art."[70] Hovenden's genre paintings of the 1880s would have intrigued the racially conscious Tanner, especially in light of their sympathetic and dignified treatment of African Americans. Tanner would have been attracted in particular to Hovenden's *The Last Moments of John Brown* (1884; Metropolitan Museum of Art, New York), in which the abolitionist is seen kissing a black child in route to his execution. Others of

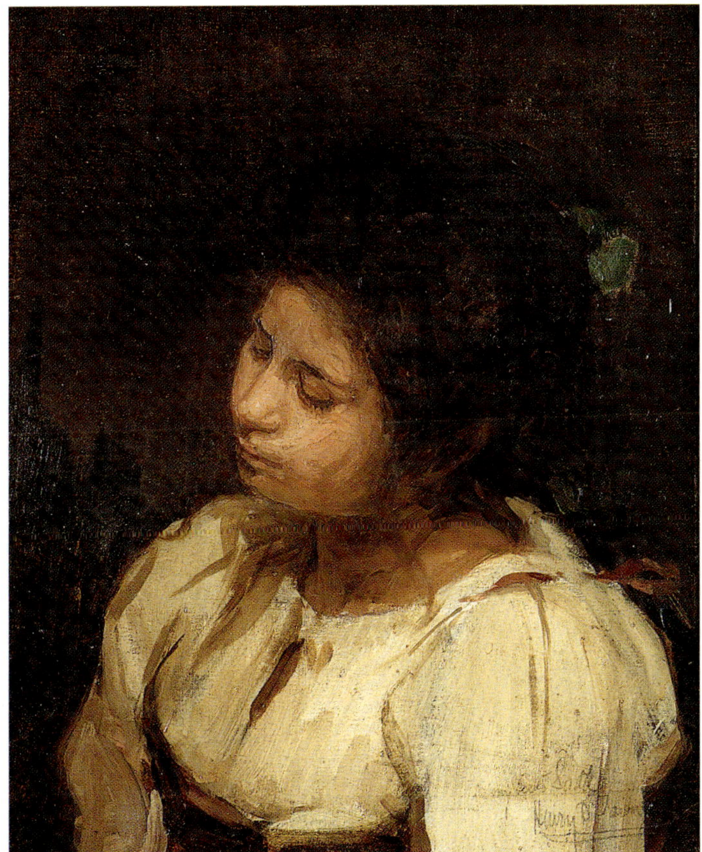

PLATE 3
Sister Sarah, c. 1881-82
Oil on canvas
16 x 13 (40.6 x 33)
Private collection

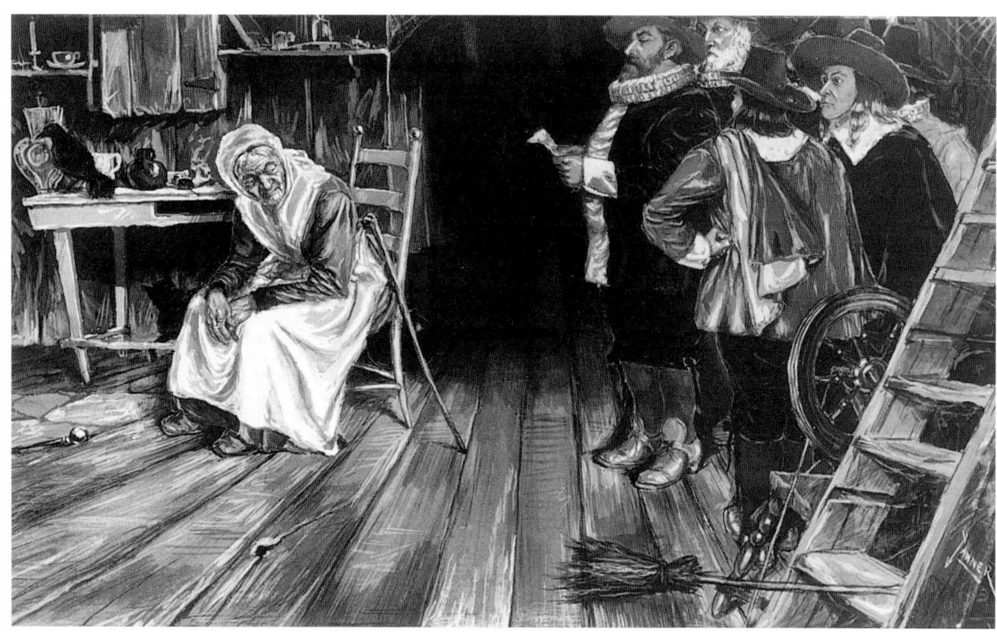

FIGURE 5
The Witch Hunt, c. 1882-88
Gouache on board
13 x 20 (33 x 50.8)
Sheldon Ross Gallery, Birmingham, Michigan

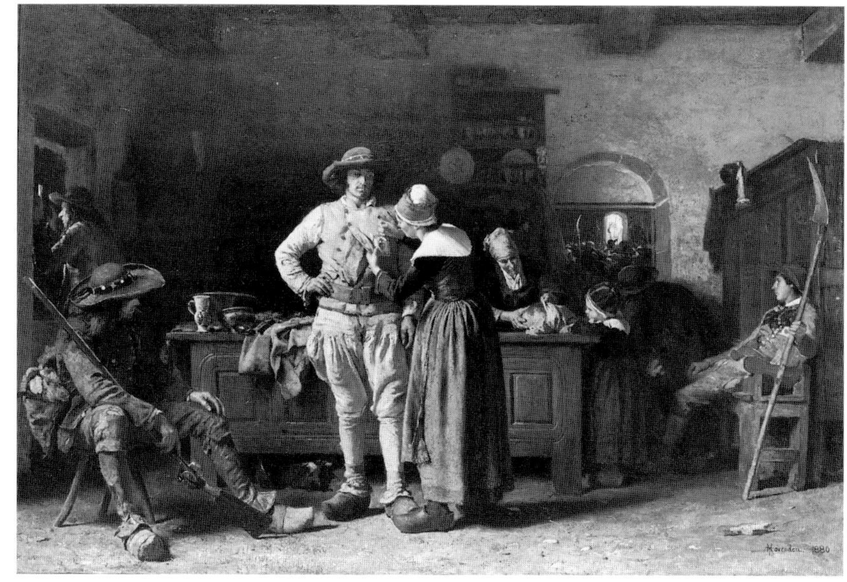

FIGURE 6
Thomas Hovenden,
In Hoc Signo Vinces, 1880
Oil on canvas
39 x 54 (99.1 x 137.2)
The Detroit Institute of Arts; gift of Mr. and Mrs. Harold O. Love

Hovenden's images, too, help us to understand apparent anomalies in Tanner's pictures of the early 1880s. For example Tanner's *The Witch Hunt* (fig. 5), a work quite different from his marine, animal, and landscape scenes, is reminiscent of Hovenden's *In Hoc Signo Vinces* (fig. 6), in spite of the stumpy standing figures.

The Witch Hunt also presents another side of Tanner's study at the Pennsylvania Academy: his growing familiarity with Rembrandt (1606-1669). For example, the figure with his back to the viewer in *The Witch Hunt,* who directs our gaze towards the principal action, recalls the seventeenth-century Dutch master's compositional devices. The collars on the costumes and right-most figure of the painting call to mind Rembrandt's *The Anatomy Lesson of Dr. Tulp* (1632; Maritshuis, The Hague), while the prominent positioning of the staircase echoes *The Philosopher* (1632; Musée du Louvre, Paris). Rembrandt was highly esteemed at the Academy.[71] Tanner himself noted: "Rembrandt...was a true portrayer of man."[72]

While Tanner gained control over the tools of his trade at the Pennsylvania Academy and absorbed the work of Rembrandt, his path was laden with racial strife. The printmaker Joseph Pennell (1860-1926) and a group of devious friends were expelled from the Pennsylvania Museum and School of Industrial Art in Philadelphia in late November 1879 and enrolled in the Pennsylvania Academy. Pennell, a self-described "conceited prig," shed light on Tanner's talent as well as his reception:

> He came, he was young, an octoroon, very well dressed, far better than most of us.... He worked at night in the Antique, and last of all, he drew very well. I do not think that he stopped long in the Antique—the faintest glimmer of any artistic sense in a student, and he was run right into the Life. He was quiet and modest, and he "painted too," it seemed, "among his other accomplishments." We were interested at first, but he soon passed almost unnoticed, though the room was hot.[73]

Tanner's presence did not always go so unnoted by Pennell and his gang of thugs. The life-long racist wrote:

> One night we were walking down Broad Street, he with us, when from a crowd of people of his color who were walking up the street, came a greeting, "Hullo, George Washington, howse yer gettin on wid yer White fren's?" Then he began to assert himself and, to cut a long story short, one night his easel was carried out into the middle of Broad Street and, though not painfully crucified, he was firmly tied to it and left there. And this is my only experience of my colored brothers in a White school; but it was enough. Curiously, there never has been a great Negro or Jew artist in the history of the world.[74]

This horrific account helps us to understand the proud black artist's profound anguish: "I was extremely timid, and to be made to feel that I was not wanted, although in a place where I had every right to be, even months afterward caused me sometimes weeks of pain. Every time any one of these disagreeable incidents came into my mind, my heart sank, and I was anew tortured by the thought of what I had endured, almost as much by the incident itself."[75]

By November 1881 Tanner was "lying very ill, suffering from hemorrhage of the nose."[76] He remained in that state until the spring of 1882, but the good care of his mother and the vigilance of many friends aided his recovery.[77] He convalesced again at Rainbow Lake in the Adirondack Mountains of New York State. Christopher High Shearer, the antithesis of Pennell, was among Tanner's cherished friends and helped Tanner through this difficult period. The artist noted: "He gave me personal advice and helped me to reduce the bitterness which at this time had crept into my life, and gave me a hopeful view of my individual situation.... He encouraged me to put bitterness out of my soul and to cultivate the best within me."[78]

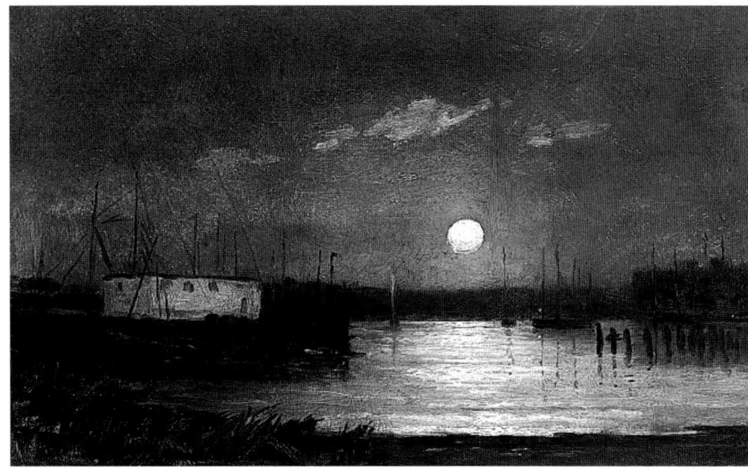

FIGURE 7
Edward Mitchell Bannister
Untitled (Moon Over Harbor), c. 1868
Oil on fiberboard
9 5/8 x 15 1/4 (24.5 x 38.7)
National Museum of American Art, Smithsonian Institution; gift of H. Alan and Melvin Frank

Tanner's debut as a professional artist was intertwined with his study at the Pennsylvania Academy of the Fine Arts. Academy students could send two works to its prestigious annual exhibition and Tanner wasted no time in seizing this perquisite. He sent two paintings—*Pursuing Cavalry* (location unknown) and *Hazy Morning at Narragansett*—to the 1880 show.[79] The overall composition and brushwork of *Seascape: Three Men in a Boat*, which may be the Narragansett canvas, call to mind works by Bannister, such as *Untitled (Moon Over Harbor)* (fig. 7). Thus, to Tanner's artistic development, Bannister's influence was added to that of Tait, Eakins, Hovenden, and Rembrandt. Tanner's progress is evident in *Seascape* in its atmospheric effects and the convincing manner in which the rower is slumped forward in the rear of the boat, preparing to make a pull. The other Rhode Island inspired scene, *Point Judith*, was exhibited at the World's Industrial and Cotton States Centennial Exposition in October 1880. The name Point Judith was known to all mariners as one of the most dangerous spots along the Atlantic coast, which is evident in the threatening water and rocks of Tanner's picture.[80] The painting is quite sophisticated technically. The artist simply used brushstrokes to indicate the essence of water, rocks, and sky. Moreover, he loaded his brush to make a myriad of colors and effects of light. Again, Bannister comes to mind: a work such as his wave-swept *Bass Rock* (c. 1860; Kenkeleba House, New York) could have been a source for *Point Judith*.

Tanner exhibited another marine subject, *Atlantic City Inlet* (location unknown), at the Progressive Working Mens' Club in Philadelphia from October to November 1880.[81] This exhibition was the first ever of African-American artists organized by African Americans. It included Bannister and several artists who are now forgotten. Tanner received his first review: "Our boy artist, H. O. Tanner, has sent a very fine oil, 'Atlantic City Inlet.' This young gentleman is a hard and conscientious worker, and his future is filled with promise."[82]

Side by side with the marine subjects, Tanner painted scenes inspired by his stay at Rainbow Lake. The recently discovered *Camping Scene: Adirondack Reminiscence* (pl. 4) is the only known signed and dated work of the early 1880s. Camps of the sort shown in the painting were used by guides for tourist groups and hunting parties. Tanner depicted a typical camp, including the sleeping tents and kitchen shed.[83] Another local image was *Burnt Pines: Adirondacks* (*Flora*) (pl. 5). In May of 1877 there was a major fire at McColloms, one of the communities abutting Rainbow Lake. Afterwards, McColloms was called "the burnt land."[84] In both works, the compositions are straightforward, conceived as a series of horizontal bands or overlapping horizontal areas to achieve recession into space. Diagonal accents are provided by the logs and fallen trees in order to achieve further depth. Hints of sparkling light throughout both pictures enliven the surfaces.

Tanner was interested in depicting a variety of subjects. He wrote: "I did all sorts of things. I purchased a goose, and from it made a picture. In fact, I became the owner of a sheep also and made a sheep picture."[85] *Boy and Sheep Lying Under a Tree* (fig. 8), or one nearly like it, may be the painting Tanner described. It has the middle-distance composition that had so impressed Tanner the day he decided to become an artist. The tree itself and the nearly panoramic view seem to acknowledge, at once, Rembrandt's famous etching *The Three Trees* (1643; Lugt no. 1692) and Eakins's *Mending the Net* (1881; Philadelphia Museum of Art). *Boy and Sheep* also shows a budding interest in light as an element in itself, and the figure and animals are firmly drawn.

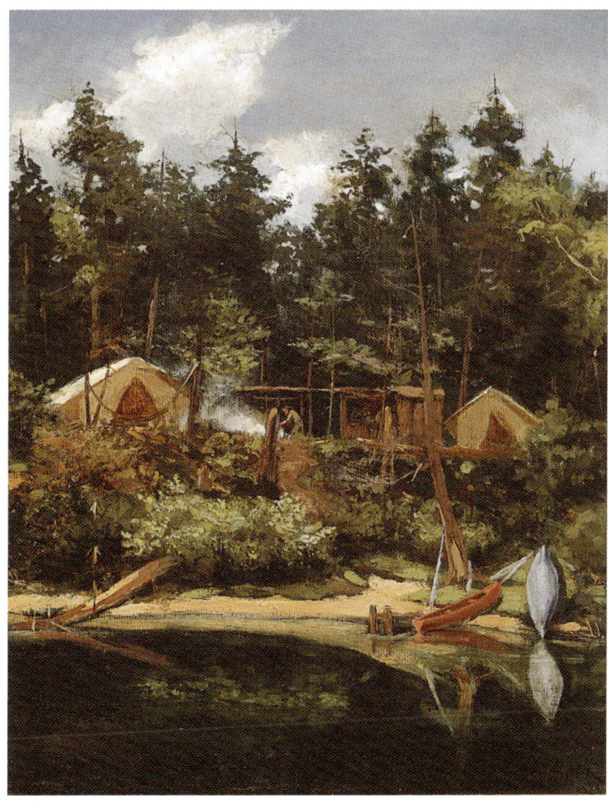

PLATE 4
Camping Scene: Adirondack Reminiscence, 1880
Oil on canvas
18 1/4 x 14 1/4 (46.4 x 36.2)
Dr. and Mrs. Dwight L. McKenna, New Orleans, Louisiana

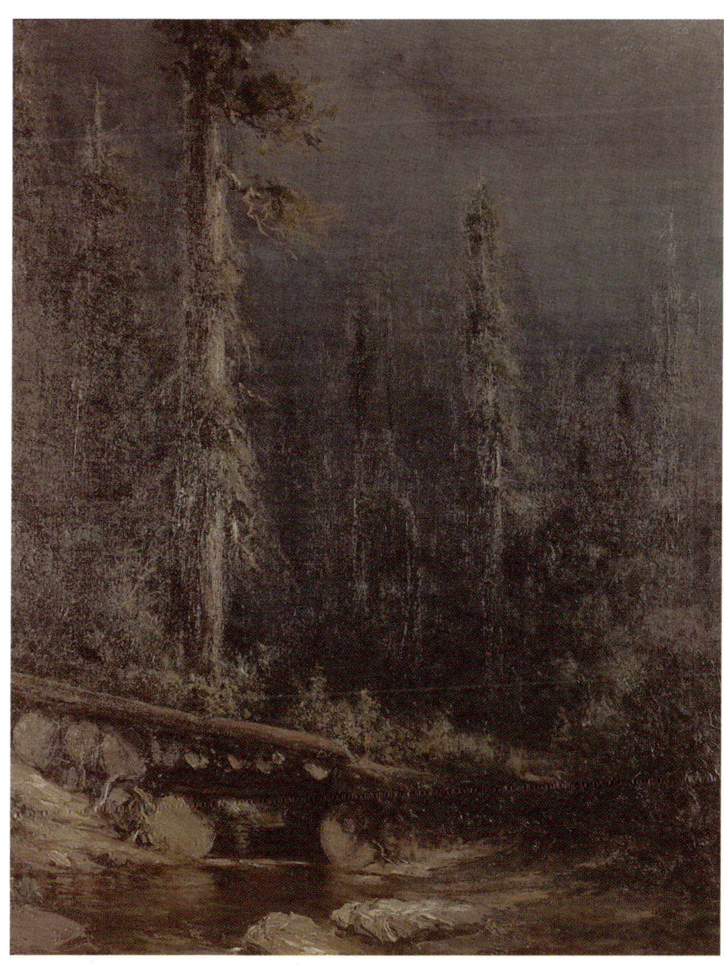

PLATE 5
Burnt Pines: Adirondacks (Flora), c. 1880
Oil on canvas
39 3/4 x 31 1/2 (101 x 80)
Hampton University Museum, Virginia

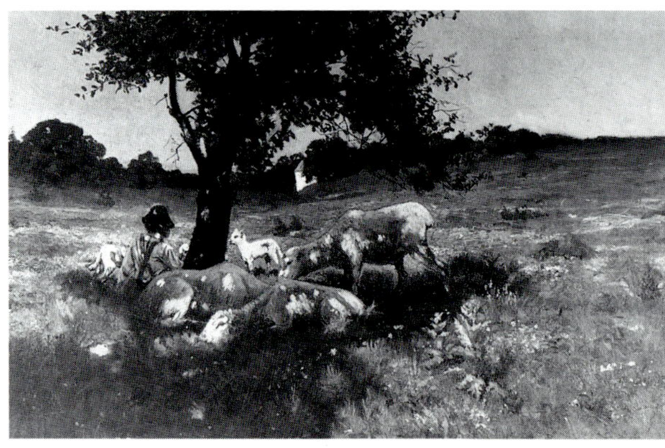

FIGURE 8
Boy and Sheep Lying Under a Tree, 1881
Oil on canvas
17 3/8 x 27 (44.1 x 68.6)
Grace Scull Sawyer, Philadelphia

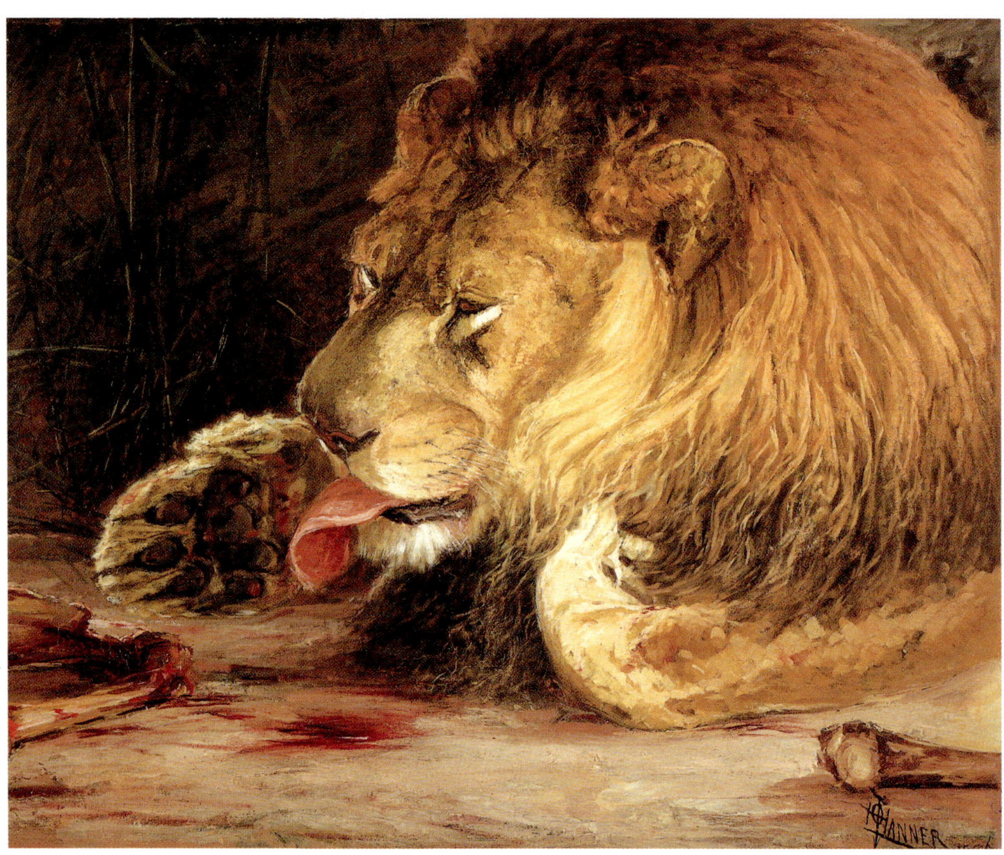

PLATE 6
Lion Licking Its Paw, 1886
Oil on canvas
30 x 36 (76.2 x 91.4)
Allentown Art Museum, Pennsylvania; gift of Mr. and Mrs. Philip Berman, 1962 (62.05)

The artist also tried his hand at illustration: "I was sending black and white drawings every month or so to New York publishers. As fast as they would be returned with thanks by one, they were off to another. Very few stayed, but I remember the first one that did, and the check for forty dollars that came with the letter of acceptance made me wonder how they could pay such 'big prices.'"[86] It is unlikely that Tanner's earliest-known illustrations were random submissions. Wood engravings based on three gouache drawings appeared in *Our Continent* for August 30, 1882. These sheets, commissioned by Judge Albion Tourgee, were illustrations for a story entitled "In the Days of Witchcraft," by Louise Stockton. In the story an impoverished old woman struggles against temptations and mockeries of the devil and longs for a peaceful death in bed as salvation.[87] *The Witch Hunt* is related to this group but was not illustrated.

In early 1884 Tanner's subject matter reverted to the one of his youth: "It is his ambition, and he thinks his forte, to become an animal painter, and he is certainly making good progress."[88] These comments were prompted by a review in the *Philadelphia Press* of *The Battle of Life* (location unknown), a picture of an elk attacked by wolves, based on studies at the zoo. That reviewer also said: "The painting is attracting attention, not only for its real merit, but for the fact that it was painted by a young colored man.... Mr. Tanner thinks that his race has an adaptability to art, if only it is given an opportunity."[89] The reason for these defensive remarks had to do with the black community's sensitivity to a twenty-year-old comment in the *New York Herald*, in which it was said "that the Negro seems to have an appreciation of art, but is manifestly unable to produce it."[90]

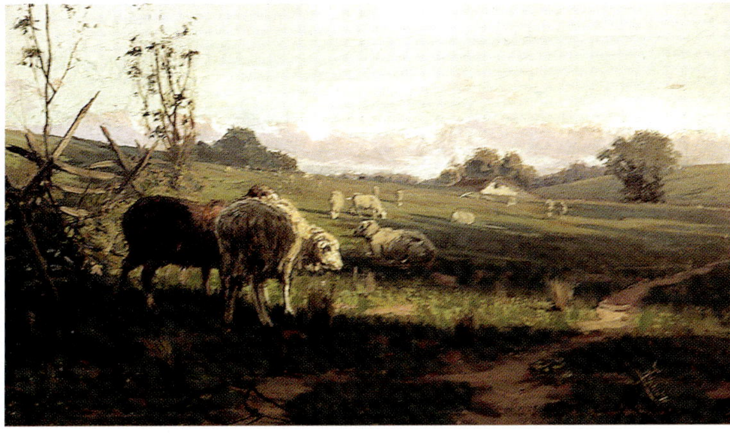

PLATE 7
Adirondack Landscape, 1886
Oil on canvas
16 x 25 (40.6 x 63.5)
The Springfield Museum of Art, Ohio

Tanner made his New York debut with *Lions at Home* (location unknown) in April 1885 at the National Academy of Design; the painting quickly sold. A related canvas, *Lion Licking Its Paw* (pl. 6), shows the tremendous progress that Tanner had made by the middle of the decade. He confidently rendered the anatomy and volume of the lion through deft, liquescent passages of the brush in the mane, sophisticated use of lights and darks, and highlights in the face. This work was seen by Rev. Dr. William J. Simmons in Tanner's studio, which he opened in September 1886 at 927 Chestnut Street, not far from Thomas Eakins's studio and the Philadelphia Art Students' League. Simmons, author of *Men of Mark*, which chronicled notable African-American males including Tanner, shed light on the overall impact of the painting: "A lion in his den...was truly life-like and the lion's head with all its fierceness, seemed so natural that one would almost feel like looking toward the door for egress."[91]

Tanner returned to Rainbow Lake in New York's Adirondack Mountains during the summer of 1886.[92] While there, he painted another animal scene. Signed and dated 1886, *Adirondack Landscape* (pl. 7) has been misidentified as a Georgia landscape, an area that Tanner did not visit until 1889. In this painting, Tanner used the rolling hills for the composition's recession into space. The animals are solid, firmly grounded, and believably represented. Lights and darks, with varied brushstrokes, are used to distinguish the various elements of the painting. The subdued harmonies of color create a serene effect in spite of the fact that Tanner thought a sheep was "the most stubborn, balky, run-away, befuddled animal you can imagine."[93]

William J. Simmons saw Tanner's animal pictures in a religious sense, presaging what would become the artist's special field of interest. Simmons wrote: "His talent is somewhat on the order of that of Landseer and Bonheur, who love animals. These artists did not look upon them simply as so many bones, with hide, horns and other necessary parts thrown in, but they delighted to portray their nature, habits, affections, symmetry and beauty. This is indeed an exaltation of their Maker and the dignifying of God on canvas, by employing their genius in portraying the characteristics mentioned."[94]

Although Tanner's professed forte was animal painting, it did not prevent him from treating other subjects. One of his largest, most artistically ambitious, and most beautifully pure landscapes, *Sand Dunes at Sunset, Atlantic City* (pl. 8), belongs to this period. The hills of sand piled up by the wind in this painting suggest a mid-Atlantic setting and, in fact, Tanner visited Atlantic City, New Jersey, off and on during the summers of the 1870s and 1880s because of the seasonal employment opportunities. The painting is probably the one known originally as *Back from the Beach*, a work Tanner exhibited at the Pennsylvania Academy in 1885 and again at the National Academy in 1886. Indeed, the scene indicates an area remote from the beach at water's edge. The undulating terrain in this work, and in *Adirondack Landscape*, is characteristic of Tanner's landscapes of the mid- and late 1880s, and a white textured horizon line, created here by the foam on the waves, is a mainstay of his style.

The image of Henry O. Tanner that emerges by the mid-1880s is one of an individualist. He had gained control over the tools of his profession as taught at the Pennsylvania Academy of the Fine Arts. He had absorbed the art of Arthur Fitzwilliam Tait, Edward Mitchell Bannister, Thomas Eakins, Thomas Hovenden, and Rembrandt without becoming an imitator of either their styles or subject matter. Moreover, he had overcome racism, to a great extent, by rising above the pain and bitterness caused by racial bigotry, believing firmly and correctly that his race had an adaptability to art. Tanner was so inspired by his successes up to this point that he decided to take on a historical subject, a category which was recognized as the most challenging for an artist.

In keeping with his interest in animals, he opted for the story of Androcles. According to legend, Androcles, a Roman slave, escaped and took refuge in a cave. A lion entered, in obvious pain, and Androcles extracted a large thorn from its paw. Later the slave was captured and thrown to the beasts in a Roman arena, whereupon he was recognized by the same lion, who caressed rather than attacked him.[95] Tanner mentioned this painting in his autobiography: "I spent all my money on models, and did not finish the picture."[96] He only completed a study for the ambitious scheme (pl. 9). In it, the model's striking pose suggests that the idea inspiring the picture was more than a simple study of the male body, although the foot support in the foreground, the stool, and the easel in the background indicate a studio setting.[97] Nudes are unusual among Tanner's surviving body of work in spite of the fact that the study of anatomy from the live model was an important part of the curriculum at the Pennsylvania Academy. Tanner did not emphasize the carnal nature of the nude, probably in keeping with his father's idea that "the body is sanctified."[98]

Tanner could draw upon more than one closely connected issue when he decided to attempt his first history painting. His religious upbringing, which emphasized human rights, was certainly a contributing factor. The relevance of the issue of slavery is obvious and it is worth recalling that his mother was born a slave. Aulus Gelluis's tale of Androcles dealt with public execution, as did the story of John Brown. Tanner's ambitious plans for a picture did not go beyond this eloquent oil sketch and, perhaps, *Lion Licking Its Paw*, although he noted: "I learned some things in my failures."[99]

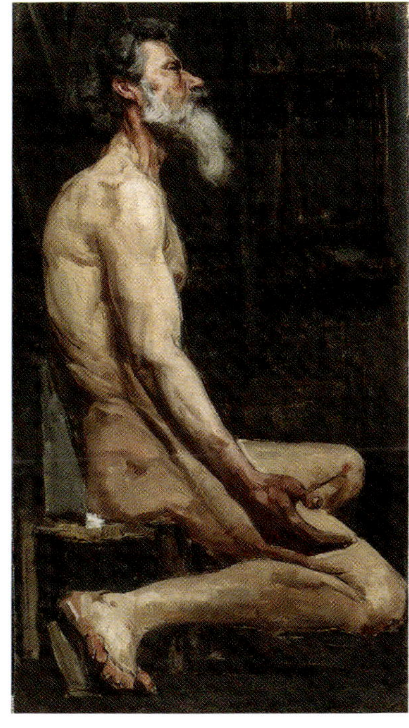

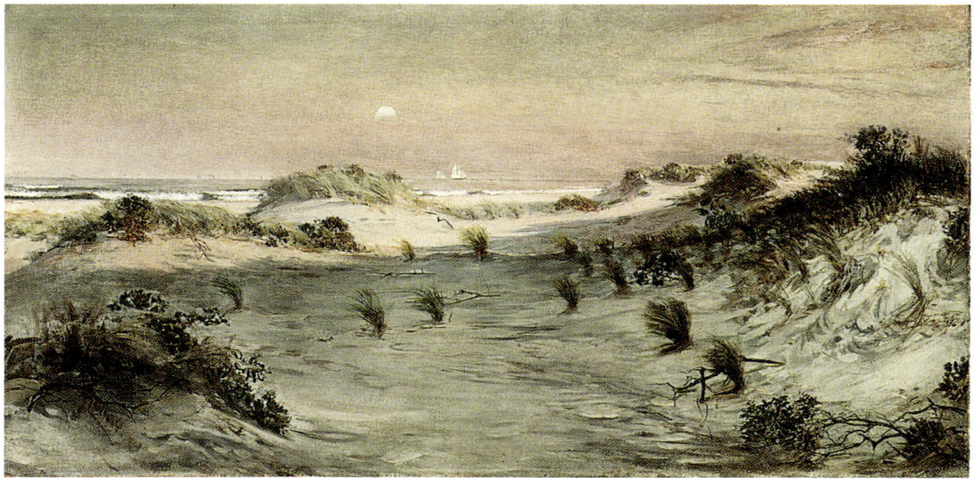

PLATE 8
Sand Dunes at Sunset, Atlantic City, c. 1885
Oil on canvas
29 1/4 x 58 3/4 (74.3 x 149.2)
Dr. Rae Alexander-Minter

PLATE 9
Study for Androcles, c. 1885-86
Oil on canvas
31 x 18 (78.7 x 45.7)
Private collection

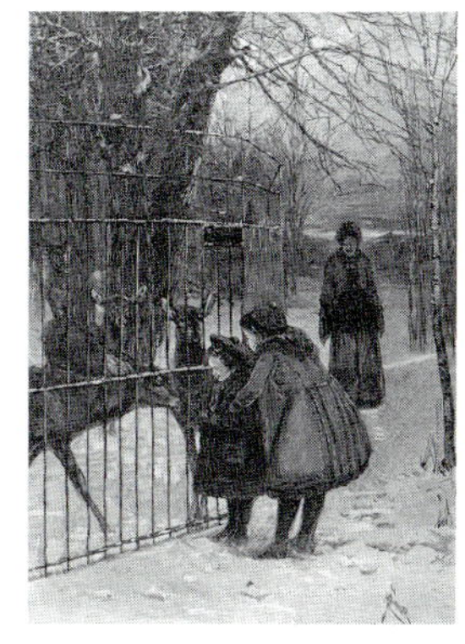

FIGURE 9
It Must Be My Very Star, Come Down to Brooklyn, After All
from "Old Win-ne-wan's Star," by Kate Upson Clark, in *Harper's Young People*, vol. 9 (January 10, 1888)
Wood engraving
6 1/2 x 9 1/4 (16.5 x 23.5)
The Free Library of Philadelphia

In early 1887, Tanner produced another drawing for illustration (fig. 9).[100] Published as a wood engraving in *Harper's Young People* in January 1888, this piece was likely commissioned, rather than submitted unsolicited. Harper and Brother encouraged black artists in the late 1880s.[101] This sheet, titled *It Must Be My Very Star, Come Down to Brooklyn, After All,* illustrated Kate Upson Clark's "Old Win-ne-Wan's Star." The story deals with a young girl, Roselle, and her little brother, Roger, who are given a fawn by an old Native American, Win-ne-Wan, while vacationing in New York's Catskill Mountains. Not allowed to take the gift home, they discover it later while visiting the zoo at Brooklyn's Prospect Park. Tanner seems to have had his age-instructing-youth theme in mind as he pictured Roselle exclaiming: "Coax her with your bun, Roger."[102] The old woman in the background is the ultimate mentor and recalls the figure at the right of the cage in the earlier *"Pomp" at the Zoo.* Even in this illustration, Tanner used the characteristic white highlight on the horizon.

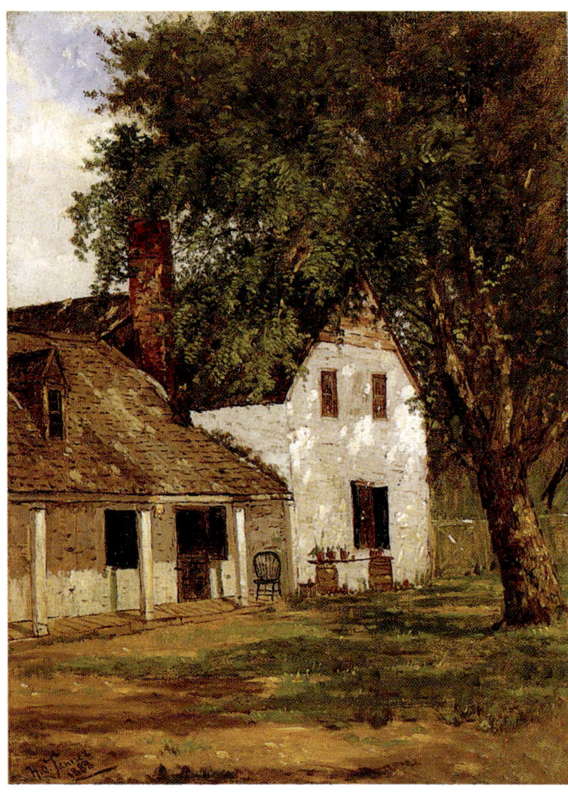

Plate 10
Wynkoop House, Old Haarlem, 1888
Oil on canvas
18 1/2 x 13 1/2 (47 x 34.3)
New Britain Museum of American Art; John Butler Talcott Fund

In November 1887 Tanner attended the African Methodist Episcopal Church Conference in Jacksonville, Florida, and stayed on with Bishop Daniel A. Payne, a family friend and early supporter of his career.[103] He painted several marine subjects while in Florida, then returned to Philadelphia by February 1888.[104] He painted what may have been his first commission: *Wynkoop House, Old Haarlem* (pl. 10). Wynkoop House, also known as "Vredens Hof," was located in Northampton Township, in Bucks County, Pennsylvania, not far from Tanner's home in Philadelphia. It was the residence of Henry Wynkoop (1736-1816), an abolitionist judge who freed his own slaves. Most of the freed slaves elected to remain on the farm, and upon their deaths they were buried under a tree near the mansion.[105] Tanner emphasized a tree in the foreground of the painting and cleverly called attention to a comfortable human presence through the empty chair, which we suppose will be occupied again once the shade of the tree reaches it. The dappled but sparkling light that falls on the building and ground presage one of the most beautiful aspects of Tanner's mature style.

———— ♦ ————

At some point in 1888 Tanner came up with the seemingly brilliant idea of uniting business with art and decided to move to Atlanta to try his hand as a professional photographer. Photography was not an entirely new endeavor for Tanner. He had made photographs, such as *Log Cabin Birthplace of Bishop Wayman* (location unknown), in Atlantic City during the summer of 1887.[106] The choice of the Georgia capitol followed a trend of migration by blacks back to the South from the North. Atlanta, particularly, had a history of attracting blacks due to its forward-looking attitudes.[107]

The artist opened a photography studio in January 1889 in Atlanta with the idea that this business would give him time to paint. However, he said: "I had so much more leisure than I had calculated upon, and this so distressed me, that I could not work."[108] Tanner was able to meet expenses with his photography studio and eventually sold it with great satisfaction. The most significant result of his venture into the world of business was meeting Bishop and Mrs. Joseph C. Hartzell, who provided moral support and eventually became his patrons.[109]

In the summers of 1889 and 1890 Tanner traveled from Atlanta to Highlands, in the Smoky Mountains of North Carolina, with the thought that he could make a living with his camera and that the mountain air would be good for his health. He had very little money and subsisted on a diet of corn meal and applesauce. His situation improved when he accepted a commission to photograph a small cottage. He also made a series of photographs of the Smoky Mountain region, which was successful due to the fact that no photographer had ever recorded it. Tanner's activities as a photographer account for the paucity of his drawn and painted sketches of the area. When he did paint, however, the results were beautiful, as in the watercolor *Mountain Landscape, Highlands, North Carolina* (pl. 11). The scenic region yielded a few finished oils, such as the one in the collection of Berea College (pl. 12).[110] This canvas shows Tanner's artistic development in his use of atmospheric perspective, as well as an ability to render changes in tone and color values on the horizon.

While in Highlands, Tanner made the acquaintance of the family of Wesley N. Clifford, with whom he became friends.[111] Clifford taught at Clark University and might have worked with Bishop Hartzell to secure a post there for the artist. Tanner taught drawing at Clark when he returned to Atlanta in the fall. While it has been suggested that the artist remained at the black Methodist institution until 1893, there is no documentation that outlines Tanner's stay at the college. It is known that Professor William Crogman commissioned Tanner to paint his portrait, an opportunity that led the artist to explore a new genre.[112]

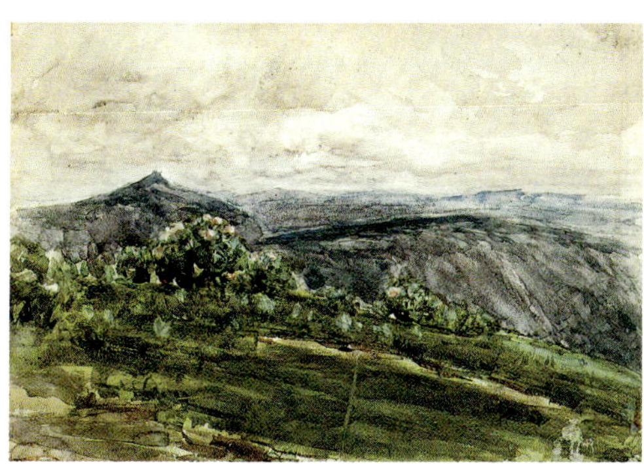

PLATE 11
Mountain Landscape, Highlands, North Carolina, c. 1889
Watercolor, pencil and colored pencil on paper
10 13/16 x 15 (27.5 x 38.1)
National Museum of American Art, Smithsonian Institution; gift of Mr. and Mrs. Norman B. Robbins

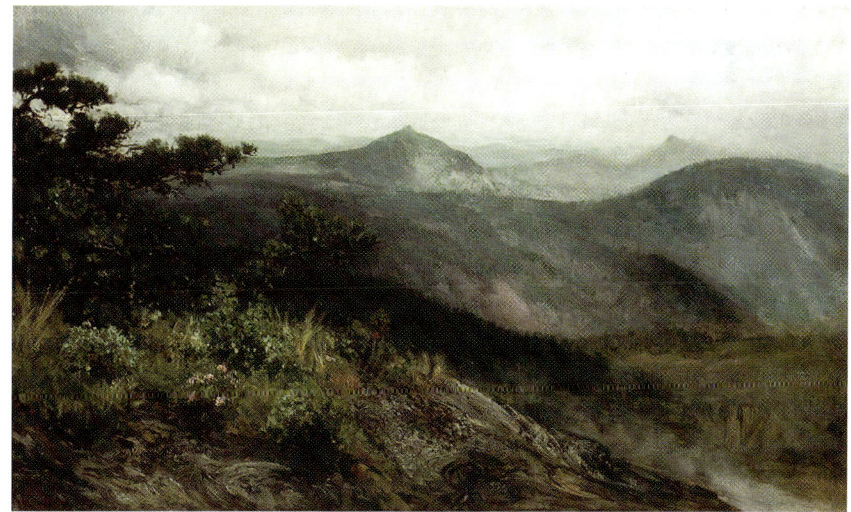

PLATE 12
Mountain Landscape, Highlands, North Carolina, c. 1889
Oil on canvas
24 x 36 (61 x 91.4)
Berea College Art Department, Kentucky

Tanner seems to have had only occasional contact with Atlanta artists and his style evolved little while there. Bishop Hartzell wrote: "While Tanner was in Atlanta he encountered [Henry Wilson Barnitz (1863-1914)] a former schoolmate and personal friend from the days of the Pennsylvania Academy. He was the leading White artist in Atlanta. Unfortunately, however, since the southern mores rigidly prohibited any social intercourse between Whites and Negroes, the two surreptitiously arranged to meet secretly in the room of the White artist whereupon he eagerly sought Tanner's criticism of his works."[113] Tanner also was acquainted with James Field, the successful portrait painter in Atlanta.[114] When Field left for Europe in 1890 to study at the Académie Julian in Paris, his departure must have rekindled Tanner's own desire for European travel, which had been first fired by Christopher H. Shearer in 1879.

Tanner's decade-old desire for study in Europe turned into a goal. In order to raise funds for this venture, Mrs. Hartzell suggested having an exhibition of his art in Cincinnati, her hometown and the headquarters of the board of education of the Methodist church.[115] The show, Tanner's first one-man exhibition, was arranged for two or three weeks in the fall of 1890.

In spite of a favorable review, Tanner did not sell anything from the exhibition.[116] However, his dream of study in Europe was not shattered: Bishop and Mrs. Hartzell bought out the entire show for a sum sufficient for Tanner to realize his plan. It is not known if Tanner traveled to Cincinnati for his opening, nor when he left Atlanta. He was certainly back in Philadelphia before the end of the year because a photograph of Tanner with his family (fig. 10) was made in late 1890. Equally important, he was paid seventy-five dollars for a commission from a "Mr. E.-" in order to help with European expenses. It is difficult to resist speculating that Thomas Eakins was the source of this commission: Eakins was known for aiding his students financially in exchange for work rendered.[117]

December 1890 marked the end of the formative American period of Henry Ossawa Tanner. He was a well-trained artist who enjoyed a modicum of public acclaim. As was the case with numerous American artists before and after him, he was attracted by the lure of European study and the glamour that surrounded it. With the money in hand from the sale to Bishop and Mrs. Hartzell and the commission from "Mr. E.-," Tanner set sail for Rome, via Liverpool and Paris, on January 4, 1891, headed for another continent and culture.

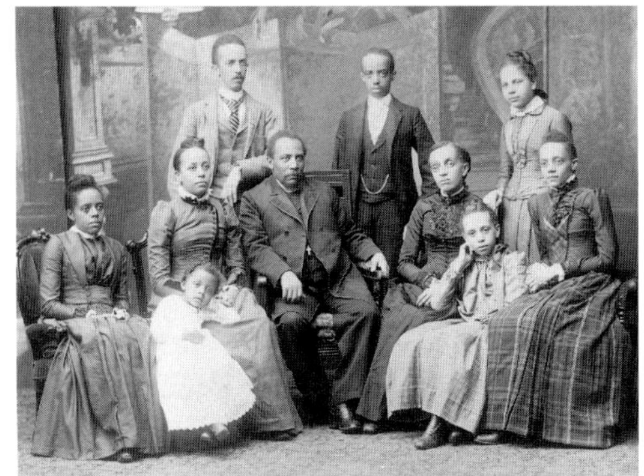

FIGURE 10
Gilbert and Bacon Photographers
The Tanner Family, c. 1890
Albumen photograph on printed photographer's mount
7 5/8 x 9 1/4 (19.4 x 23.5)
Dr. Rae Alexander-Minter

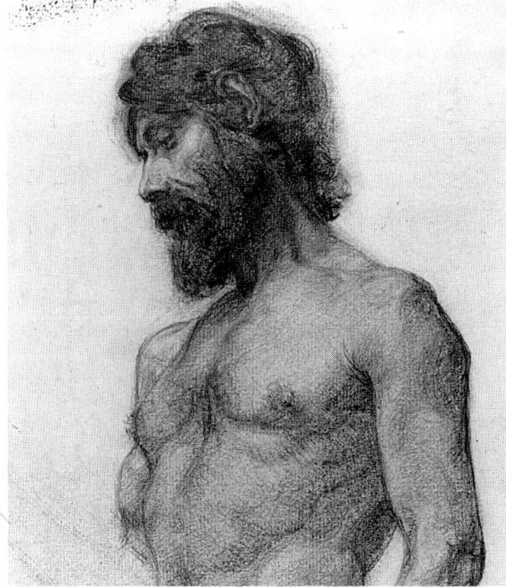

PLATE 13
Bust-Length Study of a Bearded Man with Short Hair, c. 1891-93
Charcoal on paper
12 x 9 1/2 (30.5 x 24.1)
Schomburg Center for Research in Black Culture, Art and Artifacts Division, The New York Public Library, Astor, Lenox and Tilden Foundation

France, The Holy Land, and America: Success, Symbolism and the Circle of Paul Gauguin, and Greater Racial Awareness, 1891-1897

Henry Ossawa Tanner arrived in Liverpool, England, on January 18, 1891. His stay there was brief and uneventful. The artist soon set out for Rome via Paris, where he was welcomed by good friends, who probably included his cohort from Atlanta, James Field. Yet at first, Tanner was depressingly lonely and felt like an outsider: "How strange it was to have the power of understanding and being understood suddenly withdrawn!" In addition, he did not speak fondly of his hotel room at 12 rue de Seine in the Latin Quarter; the weather was disagreeable; the continental breakfast was far removed from his American fare; noises, such as "the clatter of the wooden shoes on the stone pavement," were unbearable; and the French custom of taking wine with meals was threatening. However, after just one week, Tanner found Paris so to his liking that he abandoned his previous plan to study in Rome.[118]

Tanner enrolled at the Académie Julian, founded by Rodolphe Julian in 1868. Julian had earned the Legion of Honor for teaching in 1881.[119] The curriculum at Julian's included drawing from live models, weekly critiques, and visits from celebrated artists who were always members of the Institut Nationale des Sciences et des Arts, the government agency for art. Julian himself supervised the day-to-day activities of the studio.[120]

Study at the Académie Julian was an invaluable start for a career as an artist, and there were numerous American students in attendance. The school had no entrance requirement, guaranteed a model, and provided experience and important contacts.[121] Tanner was assigned to Julian's Institut team of tutors, Jean-Paul Laurens (1838-1921) and Jean-Joseph Benjamin Constant (1845-1902).[122] He became closest to Constant, a painter of portraits and themes depicting North African and Near Eastern life.[123]

Samples of Tanner's *académies*, or drawings after the live model (pl. 13), show that he was already a superb draughtsman when he arrived in Paris. They also reveal how studiously he avoided depicting male and female genitals, in keeping with his religious persuasion and his avoidance of the carnal.[124] Tanner also found his church-going at odds with the studio practice of having a weekly *concours*, or competitive examination, on Sundays. The studio secretary allowed him to complete the assignments on Mondays. Tanner thrived in the nurturing atmosphere of Julian's; one of his *concours*, *The Deluge* (location unknown), was awarded a prize.

Around this time and as a result of friendships formed at Julian's, Tanner joined the American Art Club. There he made the acquaintance of Lewis Rodman Wanamaker (1863-1928), a member of a wealthy family of merchants who owned an international chain of clothing stores. Wanamaker, who would figure prominently in Tanner's future, was not only interested in art, but in the lot and conditions of Native Americans and African Americans.[125]

While Tanner's choice for academic training followed a typical route, he did not, as was common for artists during this period, supplement his formal training with making copies of old master paintings at the Louvre.[126] Eakins, Carolus-Duran (1838-1917), Pierre-Auguste Renoir (1841-1919), and Stéphane Mallarmé (1842-1898), to name just a few, had all complemented their academic pursuits by copying.[127] Tanner, however, was an individualist and direct copying was anathema to him.

Tanner soon learned that it was the custom for art students in Paris to spend the summer in the country. He took up this practice beginning in the summer of 1891. That year he chose the physically isolated district of Pont-Aven, on the Brittany coast, to economize and to improve his French. Pont-Aven was inexpensive, and also provided suitable models for the painting of peasant figures in the landscape—a most popular subject for American artists abroad at the time.[128] To Tanner's dismay, however, it had a large English-speaking colony.

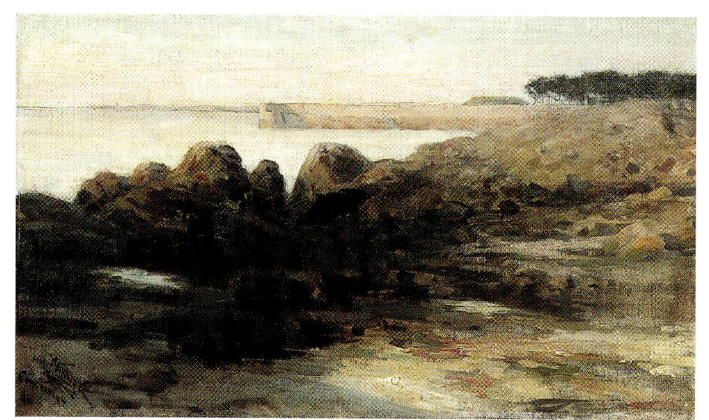

Plate 14
Concarneau, 1891
Oil on canvas
10 x 17 (25.4 x 43.2)
Mr. William R. Dorsey

Tanner spent the summer of 1892 in Concarneau, also in Brittany, rather than returning to Pont-Aven. This choice was probably made on the advice of fellow Académie Julian student Armand Séguin (1869-1903), a native of the region. Séguin was one of many artists in the orbit of the painter Paul Gauguin (1848-1903), who was something of a cult figure among artists who summered in Brittany.[129] Tanner came to Concarneau with a new aim: to exhibit at the Paris Salon, the official annual exhibition held each spring.[130] The artist's discovery of the Salon ranks, along with his desire to become a painter in 1872, as a seminal event in his career. With the knowledge of the Salon, Tanner began to think like an artist instead of merely wanting to be one.

Paintings that resulted from Tanner's 1891 and 1892 Brittany sojourns essentially continued his pre-Paris style. *Concarneau* (pl. 14) is site-specific and is arranged around rocks placed in the middle distance. *The Bagpipe Lesson* (c. 1892; Hampton University Museum, Virginia), the subject of which could have been inspired by an old man and boy of *chanteurs populaires*, who roamed the area providing impromptu entertainment in 1892, continued his earlier compositional approach to landscape painting.[131] However, Tanner's palette became noticeably brighter and more akin to the Impressionist aesthetic. Tanner conceived another Brittany-subject picture during this summer, *The Young Sabot Maker*, but he would not complete it until 1895. At the time of these Brittany sojourns, Tanner's signature changed from the decorative monogram of previous years to a straight forward "H. O. Tanner." Never again would it be possible to date his work based on a signature.

By 1893 Tanner was renting a studio at 15 rue de Seine with the American sculptor Hermon A. MacNeil (1866-1947), and was friends with the painter Hermann D. Murphy (1867-1945).[132] Tanner's *Apple Orchard*, which may have been the original title of *The Bagpipe Lesson*, was rejected by the Salon jury and, even more daunting, he came down with typhoid fever. When he was well enough to travel, he returned to Philadelphia for convalescence, and "to 'recoup' a depleted treasury."[133] An evaluation of his first three years in France gave him a greater sense of personal freedom, greater self-confidence, and a consciousness of self-responsibility that fed his innate ambition and energy.[134]

———— ♦ ————

Henry O. Tanner's return to the United States in 1893 was eventful. While most of the artist's time was spent in Philadelphia, he was an invited speaker at the Congress on Africa held in August at the World's Columbian Exposition in Chicago. This symposium addressed African-American life some thirty years after the Emancipation Proclamation, and provided the first real overview of black leadership and African-American aspirations across the nation.[135] The text of Tanner's talk was not published, but he returned to a theme from nearly a decade earlier: that black artists have the talent and ability to compete with white artists.[136]

The Chicago conference had a profound impact on the artist's racial awareness and his choice of subject matter. He wrote about himself:

> Since his return from Europe he has painted mostly Negro subjects, he feels drawn to such subjects on account of the newness of the field and because of a desire to represent the serious, and pathetic side of life among them, and it is his thought that other things being equal, he who has most sympathy with his subjects will obtain the best results. To his mind many of the artists who have represented Negro life have only seen the comic, the ludicrous side of it, and have lacked sympathy with and appreciation for the warm big heart that dwells within such a rough exterior.[137]

The first work that can be ascribed to this new dedication is the famous *Banjo Lesson* (fig. 11). It shows an older black man teaching his beloved art to a young lad. Again, Tanner chose the age-instructing-youth theme. The man's hat on the floor, rather than among the clothes hung in the corner, suggests that he is an itinerant teacher, not a member of the household. The image might have been inspired by a poem by Paul Laurence Dunbar (1872-1906), who read from his work at the World's Columbian Exposition. It is not known whether he recited "A Banjo Song," but it had been published in 1892 in a volume called *Oak and Ivy* and included the lines: "An' it seems we're so nigh heaben/We kin hyeah de angels sing/When de music o'dat banjo/Sets my cabin all er-ring."[138] As well as presenting a theme he used throughout his career, the painting announced Tanner's mature approach to light, which often included the suggestion of unseen sources. In *The Banjo Lesson*, the unseen cabin fire, whose light plays on the faces and forms of the figures, is contrasted with that of an unseen window behind them.

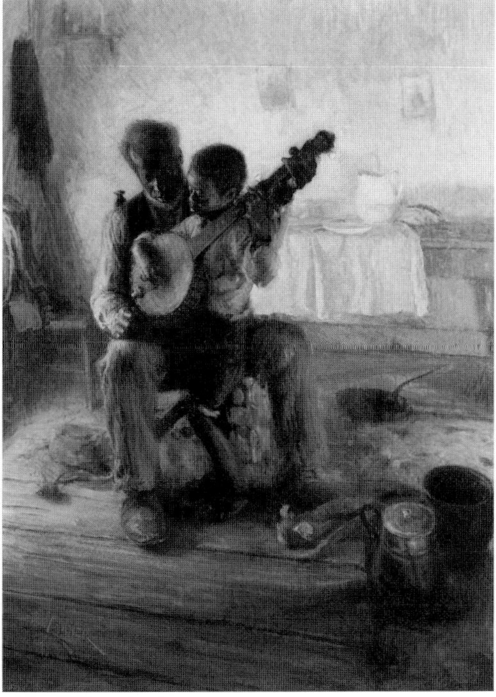

Figure 11
The Banjo Lesson, 1893
Oil on canvas
49 x 35 1/2 (124.5 x 90.2)
Hampton University Museum, Virginia

Tanner continued the theme of youth and age in African-American life in *Study for The Thankful Poor* (pl. 15). Here, age instructs youth in saying grace over a meager meal. The artist illustrated "the warm big heart that dwells within a rough exterior." The empty plate and unoccupied space at the table invite the viewer to partake of the scant meal. Stylistically, Tanner set for himself a difficult problem: the composition had the potential for being mundane because of its symmetry and shallow space. Tanner circumvented the problem by adding counterpoints to its regularity. For example, in addition to the older man with two hands raised juxtaposed by a young boy with one hand raised, the tablecloth, with its browns, whites, and lime greens, is echoed in the window curtains. Lively brush strokes and thick paint are used to model the figures and still life of vessels, but it is all depicted in very even light.

In between *The Banjo Lesson* and *Study for The Thankful Poor,* Tanner turned to sculpture.[139] Tanner modeled a plaster *Portrait of Bishop Payne* (1893; Wilberforce University, Ohio).[140] Daniel A. Payne (1811-1893), a Tanner family friend and abolitionist, obtained Wilberforce University as an educational arm of the A.M.E. church and also established its museum. He served as president of the college from 1863 to 1876, which made him the first African-American president of a university in the western world.[141] Although the sculpture seems to have remained unrealized in bronze, numerous casts were to be made and an editorial in the *Christian Recorder* urged: "Every Negro lover of education should have it on his desk or table as an inspiration."[142]

Another critical factor in Tanner's increased sense of racial identity was the influence of his father's *Theological Lectures,* delivered in 1893 at Tuskegee Institute and published in 1894. Bishop Tanner wrote, drawing upon the text of Xenophanes of Colophon (570-480 B.C.): "If oxen or lions had hands and could work in men's fashions, and trace out with chisel and brush their conception of Godhead, then would horses depict gods like horses and oxen like oxen, each kind the divine with its own form and nature endowing."[143] This passage supports the artist's feeling that "he who has most sympathy with his subjects will obtain the best results." Tanner, too, understood—as his father had pointed out in *Theological Lectures*—that the representation of all races was heavily dependent on the European or Japhetic viewpoint.[144] In art, Tanner would have been familiar with such an approach to the images of blacks by his teachers Eakins and Hovenden,[145] as well as Winslow Homer (1836-1910), whose work he admired.

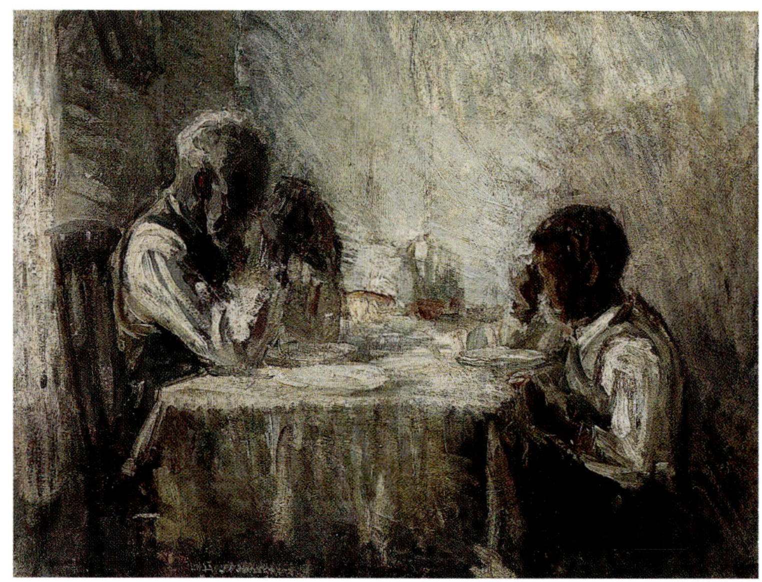

PLATE 15
Study for The Thankful Poor, c. 1894
Oil on canvas
12 3/4 x 16 1/4 (32.4 x 41.3)
Du Sable Museum of African American History, Inc., Chicago, Illinois

While Henry Ossawa Tanner was painting African-American subjects, he was also pondering another aspect of his working method: "[W]hether it was better to do a few things—one picture, for instance—and bring it to a fairly successful conclusion, or to do many pictures, trusting to some chance that one of them would be better than any continued and more or less labored effort could be."[146] This quandary accounts in part for the relatively few black images that Tanner completed during this period of avowed commitment to the theme. At the same time, he continued to dabble in other subjects, some of which originated during a trip to Florida in February 1894.[147]

During his prolonged stay in Philadelphia, Tanner was visited by his French professor, Jean-Joseph Benjamin Constant, and made the acquaintances of Robert C. Ogden (1836-1913) and Harrison S. Morris (1856-1948). Ogden was a partner in the Wanamaker dry-goods business and an advocate of African-American public education.[148] Morris was the managing director of the Pennsylvania Academy of the Fine Arts. Both men would figure prominently in Tanner's career over the next ten years.

Tanner also shared an exhibition from April 28 to May 5, 1894, with Thomas Hovenden at James S. Earle and Sons Gallery on Chestnut Street.[149] Earle's was the very establishment at whose windows the teenaged Tanner had eagerly studied pictures in the 1870s. The exhibition included a variety of subjects, both old and recent works. When the exhibition was reviewed in the *Daily Evening Telegraph*, one of Tanner's new black subjects was singled out for special praise: *The Thankful Poor* (1894; William and Camille Cosby) was called "an important work" and its manner of execution was praised.[150] *The Banjo Lesson* had received similar acclaim a few months earlier in the same newspaper.[151]

While still in Philadelphia, Tanner submitted *The Banjo Lesson* to the Paris Salon. It was accepted by the jury for the 1894 exhibition. The importance of acceptance into the Salon should not be underestimated. The *vernissage* (or varnishing day for artists) was a great social event in Paris for the smart crowd. For European and American artists, it was an immense marketplace with many thousands of visitors. In spite of the difficulty of making an impact among the thousands of paintings, sculptures, drawings, and prints, artists were provided an entrée to art critics and opportunities for public success.[152] Although Tanner did not attract the attention of art critics, he achieved a goal, set two years earlier, "to be able to make a picture that should be admitted here."[153]

In the light of this success, Tanner seemed eager to return to France. He wrote: "An auction sale of all the pictures I could lay my hands upon furnished a few hundred dollars, and with this and 'promises' (never fulfilled) I returned again to Paris."[154] Roger Lane has recently uncovered what Tanner meant by "promises never fulfilled" and has shed light on the extent of his support from within the black community.[155] The *Item,* a Philadelphia newspaper, proposed a plan in June 1894 to link black and local pride by buying *The Bagpipe Lesson* for the permanent collection of the Pennsylvania Academy of the Fine Arts. Tanner was apparently an active participant in the plan: he suggested a price of one thousand dollars, many times the few hundred dollars gained at the auction sale and enough to finance nearly three years in Paris. The Board of Ministers of Bishop Tanner's church was to buy the painting and present it to the Pennsylvania Academy "on behalf of the colored people of Philadelphia."[156] (Perhaps the participation of the *Item* was aimed at dispelling any thought that this was merely a sectarian or, worse, family affair.)[157] The Board planned to recoup the purchase price of the painting by reproducing it in levytype and selling copies to blacks all over the United States, capitalizing on Tanner's growing reputation and the honor this reflected on his race. The plan fell through when the Board was able to raise only three hundred dollars.[158] Evidently, Tanner did not accept this money. With the funds raised from his auction sale, he returned to France.

———— ♦ ————

Tanner spent the summer of 1894 at Pont-Aven in Brittany in the company of his old acquaintances Armand Séguin and Paul Sérusier (1863-1927). Gauguin was there from April to November. Tanner formed close links with Gauguin's group, which included Louis Roy (1862-1907), Roderic O'Conor (1860-1940), Charles Filiger (1863-1928), Séguin, Sérusier, Jan Verkade (active 1880s-1890s), and the author Alfred Jarry (1873-1907).[159]

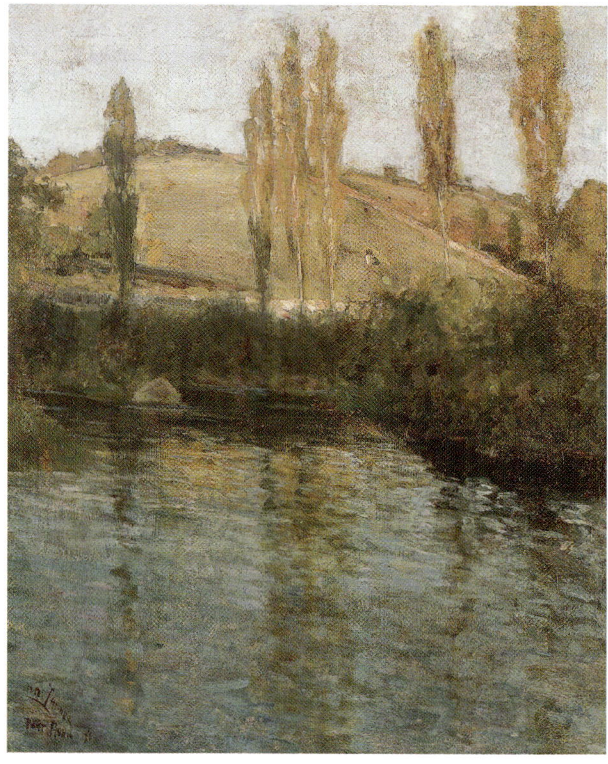

PLATE 16
Pont-Aven Landscape, 1894
Oil on canvas
18 1/2 x 14 3/4 (47 x 37.5)
Du Sable Museum of African American History, Inc., Chicago, Illinois

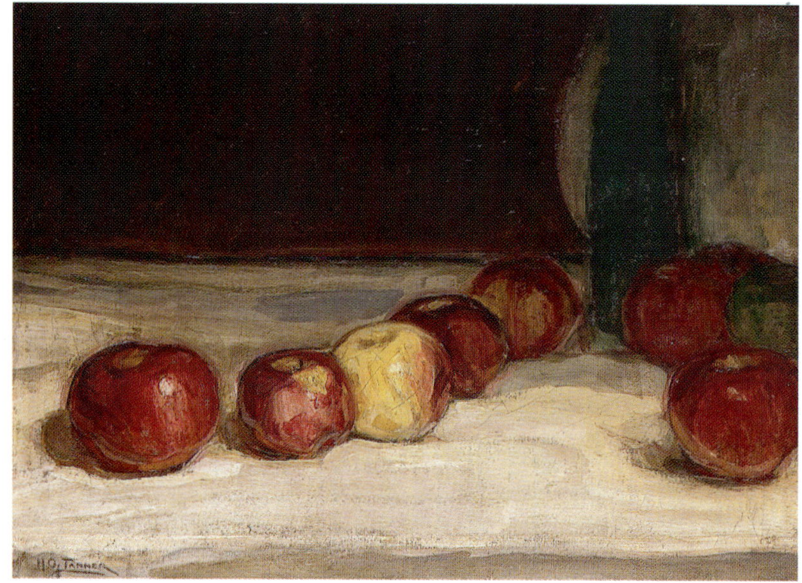

PLATE 17
Still Life With Fruit, c. 1894
Oil on canvas
19 x 25 (48.3 x 63.5)
Schomburg Center for Research in Black Culture, Art and Artifacts Division, The New York Public Library, Astor, Lenox and Tilden Foundation

Tanner seems to have been closest to Séguin, whose biographer described him as very shy and always in poor health,[160] traits that would have made him sympathetic with Tanner. The African-American artist sat for a portrait (location unknown) by Séguin during this period.[161] Séguin wrote on February 11, 1898: "I saw the same [unhappy expression] in Tanner, the celebrated Negro-American of Pont-Aven whose appearance frightened me but whose paintings left me awestruck."[162] (Tanner apparently wore a woolen overcoat in the summer.)

The group of artists at Pont-Aven was bound together by common interests in art and religion. Tanner's religious upbringing is well known. Verkade was baptized in August 1892, became a novice in the Benedictine Order in April 1894, and was ordained in 1902 with the name Dom Willibrord.[163] The other artists, especially Sérusier, went on retreats with him. All of the group, including Gauguin himself, rendered pictures either with religious subjects or religious overtones.[164] In this environment, Tanner painted his first known Biblical subject—*Expulsion from the Garden of Eden* (c. 1894; Du Sable Museum of African American History, Chicago).

The changes in Tanner's painting reflected his absorption of the principles of Gauguin and his circle. This group had become known as "Synthetists" in 1889, when the Café Volpini, a gathering place for artists and intellectuals in Paris, held an exhibition of paintings by Pont-Aven artists.[165] Dubbed Synthetism, or Symbolism, this aesthetic sought to express ideas, moods, and emotions without particular attention to naturalistic representation. Space was flattened, and colors were often bright and separated by black lines. Paintings in this mode tend to be both decorative and abstract—a synthesis, or symbolic rendering, of the subjects that inspired them.

Tanner embraced Symbolism in *Pont-Aven Landscape* (pl. 16) and *Still Life With Fruit* (pl. 17). The fruits depicted in the still life seem to be apples or pomegranates or both. As symbols, apples stand for the Christian notion of original sin—the subject Tanner had explored in *Expulsion from the Garden of Eden*—while pomegranates represent the Resurrection; together they symbolize rebirth, a theme that recurred over the rest of the artist's career.

Tanner adopted Symbolism's method of artistically expressing underlying ideas, moods, and emotions while using his own, individual version of Symbolist style and technique. *Still Life With Fruit* is composed much like paintings by numerous Pont-Aven artists. Tanner used black lines to separate the shapes, but he refused to sacrifice volume for the flatness associated with the Symbolists. In *Pont-Aven Landscape* Tanner rendered a composition based on subtle, complex artistic choices. For example, the trees move diagonally into space, but their placement in the same horizontal band is reinforced by their reflections in the water. He used the prevailing French tilted-up perspective and turned the horizon line into an irregular diagonal rather than his usual separation of land and sky. Tanner also employed a palette with vivid pinks, greens, and yellows set off by a pearly purple, with bold daubs of color as highlights. He even adopted the Gauguinesque practice of emphasizing contours for the purple trees. Where previous Tanner landscapes were rendered according to mid nineteenth century American traditions, here he broke with the American penchant for specificity and adopted modern French approaches to landscape painting.

Although clearly influenced by Symbolism, Tanner never abandoned all academic rules. He wrote at this time: "Impressionism, at least that kind which uses violent blues, reds and purples is disappearing for which we ought to be thankful."[166] As the artist Gustave Loisseau (1865-1935) remembered the summer of 1894 in Pont-Aven, it was the religious and mystic elements of Symbolism that influenced Tanner the most.[167] Indeed the artist became a Symbolist in spirit without wholly embracing their artistic technique.

———— ♦ ————

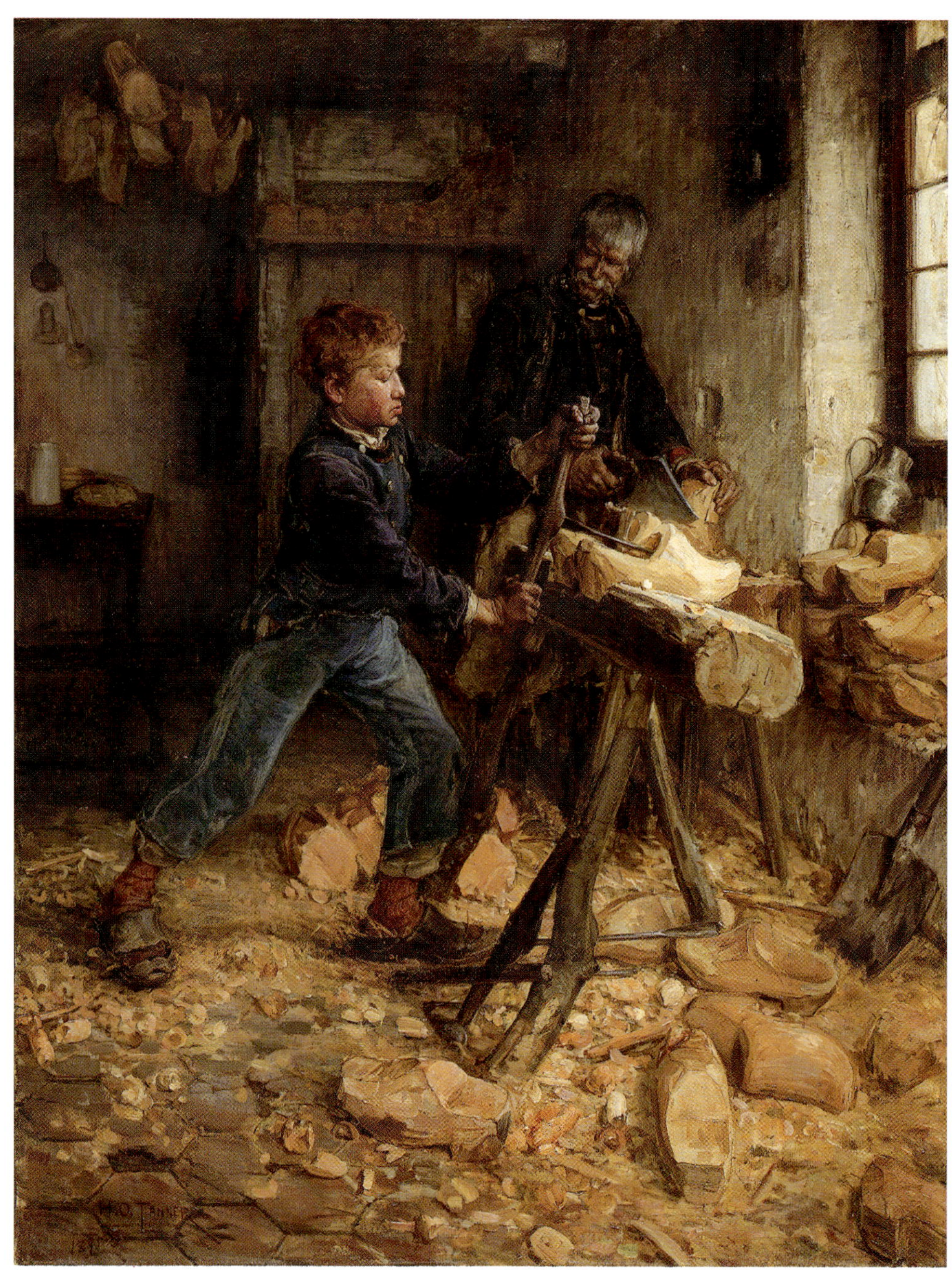

PLATE 18
The Young Sabot Maker, 1895
Oil on canvas
41 x 35 (104.1 x 88.9)
Private collection; courtesy of Michael Rosenfeld Gallery, New York

Tanner returned to Paris in the fall and rented an atelier at 51 boulevard Saint-Jacques, in a district where many artists lived and worked. His personal brand of Symbolism was manifested in *The Young Sabot Maker* (pl. 18), the initial idea of which had appeared in a study around 1891. In the painting, a young boy works hard on a pair of sabot—the traditional wooden shoes of Brittany—as an older craftsman takes a break from his own work to assess the boy's progress. Moving beyond a simple scene of everyday life in Brittany, Tanner again highlighted the theme of age instructing youth. The combination of the theme and workshop setting suggest the story of Jesus learning in the carpentry shop of Joseph. Connections to his African-American images surfaced in this context. While the first studies for the painting depict a white youth, Tanner finally rendered the young sabot maker as a lad of mixed heritage.

Tanner enlivened the composition with strategically placed still lifes and crisp light. The predominantly green and brown palette was applied with clean, descriptive brushstrokes. *The Young Sabot Maker* was accepted into the Salon and received a favorable review in the *New York Times*.[168] As was the case with previous phases of his career, Tanner did not limit himself artistically: he painted the straightforward portrait of the *Bagpipe Player* (pl. 19) at the same time.

In March 1895 Tanner was visited by Henry McNeal Turner (1833-1915), an A.M.E. bishop and the first of numerous famous African Americans to pay calls on him.[169] After this visit, the artist continued to draw inspiration from the Bible with *Daniel in the Lions' Den* (fig. 12). This subject deals with the same issues he had attempted to address in *Androcles* in 1886: slavery, false accusation, execution, and martyrdom (see Daniel 6:16-24). The highly controversial Dreyfus affair might have fanned the painter's interest in issues of race and persecution. In 1894, Alfred Dreyfus, a young French military officer of Jewish descent, was found guilty of spying and sentenced to life imprisonment in a degrading trial based on meager evidence. Tinged with virulent anti-Semitism, the affair was frequently discussed in the media, including the *Christian Recorder*, the journal of the A.M.E. church.[170] The Daniel story was also one that bore some of the sentiments inherent in Tanner's African-American scenes, and Bishop Tanner identified Daniel as the one prophet who recognized the children of

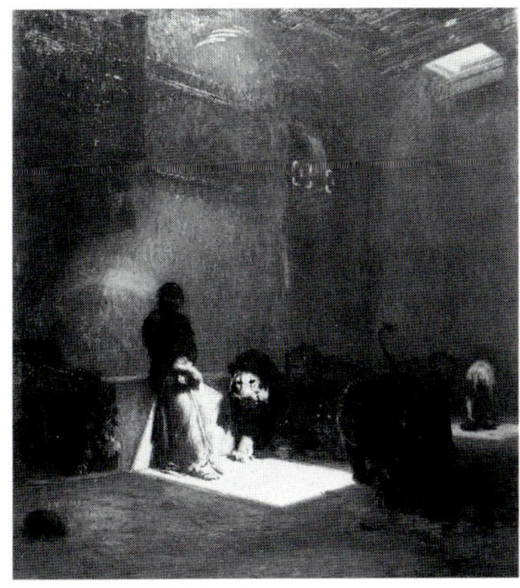

FIGURE 12
Daniel in the Lion's Den, 1895
Oil on canvas
Location unknown; photograph courtesy of the Pennsylvania Academy of the Fine Arts Archives, Philadelphia

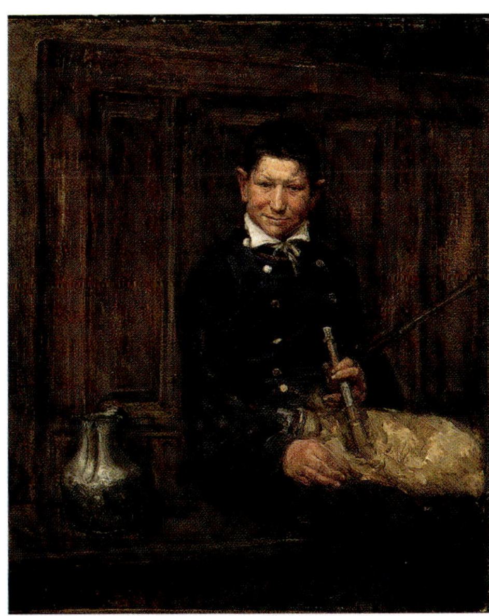

PLATE 19
Bagpipe Player, 1895
Oil on canvas
21 1/2 x 18 (54.6 x 45.7)
Private collection

Ham—the black race.[171] Of *Daniel*, Tanner family friend W. S. Scarborough pointed out: "Mr. Tanner studied to put race in it."[172] Tanner's approach to the subject, which also deals with the rebirth theme, is a clear example of the manner in which he used double and even triple layers of meaning in his individualized Symbolism.

Tanner stayed in Paris during the summer of 1895, working on *Daniel in the Lions' Den* rather than going to Brittany. He studied lions at the Jardin des Plantes under the direction of the sculptor Emmanuel Frémièt (1824-1910). The beautiful nocturnal effects in *Daniel in the Lions' Den* are characteristic of other works of this period and would become a favorite technique of the artist.

Daniel in the Lions' Den was not only accepted for the 1896 Salon, but it secured Tanner's first Salon award (an Honorable Mention) and was nearly purchased by the French government.[173] After 1880 only eighty-five prizes were awarded annually among the thousands of paintings accepted by the Salon jury.[174] Tanner was highly motivated by this official notice:

> True it was but a "mention honorable," but it was an "honor." I could have all the confidence in myself possible. I could believe that I might do something some day, but I verified however small a part of that belief, that day was new hope given to me that I might also reach other "day dreams" which I would never have confessed even to my most intimate friend. So it was that this first little "mention honorable" gave me a courage and a power for hard work, and also a hope that I had never before possessed.[175]

The press also noticed the painting favorably, mentioning especially Tanner's use of light.[176]

These experiences must have been particularly sweet to Tanner in light of events that had transpired the previous fall. The Cotton States Exposition was held in Atlanta, where Booker T. Washington gave an inaugural speech that was hailed as "the beginning of a moral revolution in America."[177] The art show was a star-studded event with Thomas Eakins, Mary Cassatt (1844-1926), and Winslow Homer winning medals.[178] Tanner's friend and Académie Julian compatriot James Field also won a medal. Tanner himself had three paintings at the Cotton States; only *The Bagpipe Lesson* can be identified for certain, and it won a medal.[179] However, the artist did not show with his peers as he was accustomed to doing at the Paris Salon. Instead his work was relegated to the Negro Building. Tanner's works were placed there at the urging of his patron Robert Curtis Ogden, who rationalized in a letter of October 17, 1895, to Professor Washington: "They would lose their distinctive race influence and character if placed in the general art exhibit. My purpose was to get the influence of Mr. Tanner's genius on the side of the race he represents and at the same time I did not want it degraded by inharmonious associations with inferior work."[180]

In spite of the explanation and good intentions of Robert Ogden, Tanner must have felt that his exclusion from the Exposition proper was a racial affront from his native country. Moreover, during this period of Tanner's heightened race consciousness, he certainly recognized that his *Bagpipe Lesson*, with Brittany denizens, was given a medal, while paintings with a "distinctive race influence and character" were ignored. Conversely, in France he was not only treated equally with his peers at the Salon, but he could even solicit advice from someone like the sculptor Frémièt, who was both a stranger and well-regarded in his field.

Following the success of *Daniel in the Lions' Den*, Tanner embarked on his most famous religious painting, *The Resurrection of Lazarus* (fig. 13). Again, instead of his usual summer sojourn to Brittany, Tanner stayed in Paris in 1896 to work on his painting. He took advantage of the fact that models, who were not in high demand during the summer months, were available to artists on favorable terms. He finished *The Resurrection of Lazarus* in early winter, but not before trying unsuccessfully, at the urging of a friend, to render the same design on a much larger canvas than the one on which he started. After working on the new six-by-ten-foot

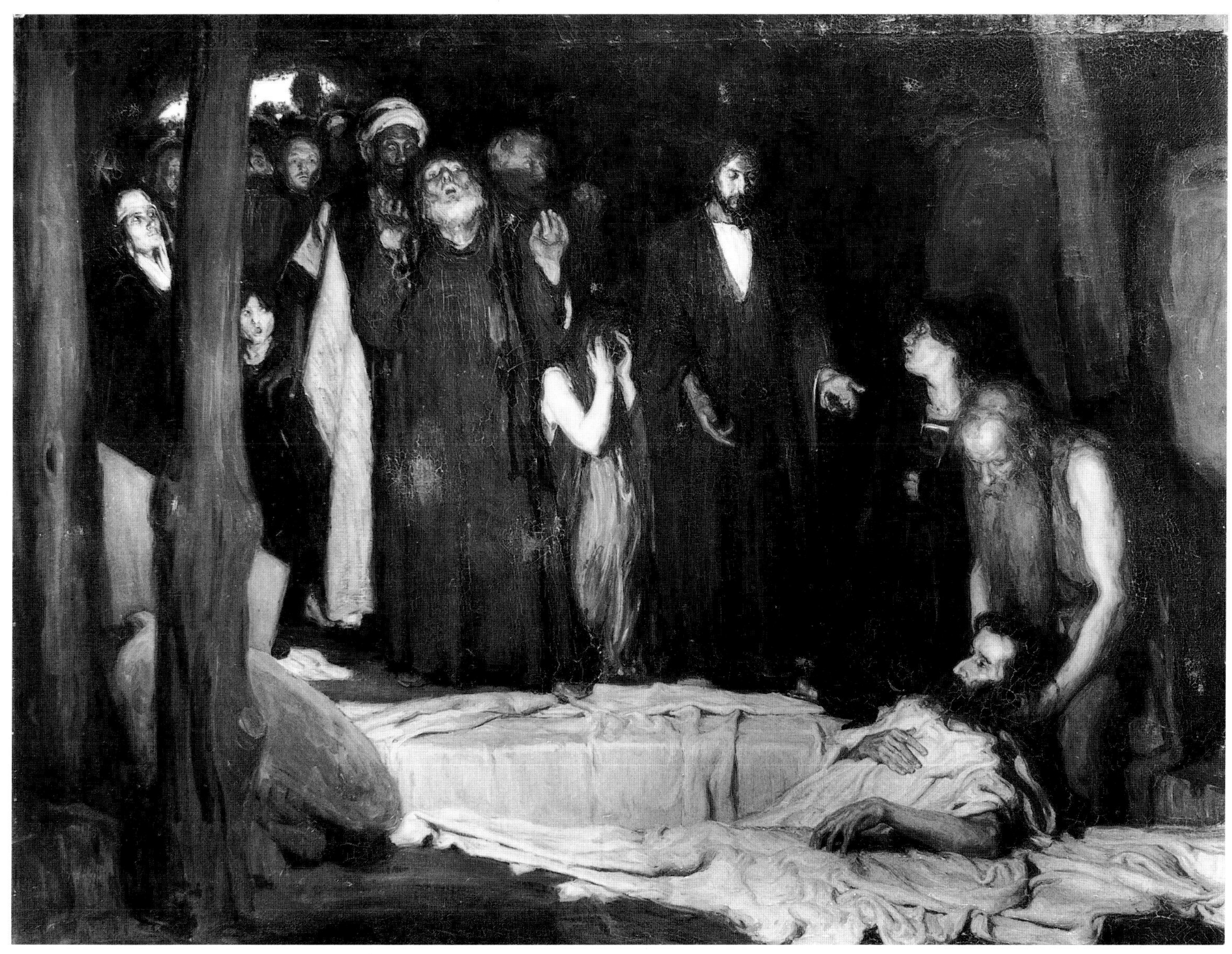

FIGURE 13
The Resurrection of Lazarus, 1896
Oil on canvas
37 3/8 x 47 13/16 (94.9 x 121.4)
Musée d'Orsay, Paris

canvas for some time, Tanner abandoned it in favor of his original, smaller one. Thereafter, he found himself "accepting radical criticism with more caution."[181]

The story of Lazarus held themes important to African Americans in the era between the Civil War and the turn of the century. The stories of the raised Lazarus (John 11:1-44) and the beggar Lazarus (Luke 16:19-31), sometimes linked by commentators, touch on ideas of new life and redemption, as did the Emancipation Proclamation of 1863, which provided a rebirth for black slaves. In choosing the Lazarus story, with its pertinence to contemporary black life, Tanner reflected what had been a common thread in black churches. W. E. B. Du Bois noted in 1903: "For fifty years Negro religion...transformed itself with the dream of abolition, until that which was a radical fad in the White North and an anarchistic plot in the White South had become a religion to the black world. Thus, when Emancipation finally came, it seemed to freedmen a literal Coming of the Lord."[182] Furthermore, in using the Lazarus subject Tanner followed the African-American pulpit tradition that Henry H. Mitchell characterized as one in which black preachers "simply engage in interpretation which unites ancient biblical insights with modern experience to give some firm word about God's will for today."[183]

Tanner put his message across in a carefully balanced composition that owes a debt to Thomas Hovenden's *The Last Moments of John Brown.* Tanner created groups of figures with subtle pyramidal configurations. These devices link all the participants to the main event both in arrangement and emotion. The figures are united further through richly textured surfaces, in the manner of Rembrandt, and the somewhat monochromatic palette so appropriate for the interior of a cave. The reddish light, coming from unseen lanterns, also unifies these witnesses in this vivid recognition that the raising of Lazarus was indeed a miracle. W. S. Scarborough summed up the overall impact of the work: "There was race in it, a quality that one critic avers to be new to Biblical painting."[184]

Lazarus was met with a superb reception when it was shown at the Paris Salon of 1897. Reviewers for such noted periodicals as the *Gazette des Beaux-Arts* and *Harper's Weekly* were impressed.[185] More importantly, the painting was purchased by the French government for the Musée du Luxembourg, where it would join other celebrated works by living artists, such as *Arrangement in Grey and Black: Portrait of the Painter's Mother* (1872; Musée d'Orsay, Paris) by James McNeill Whistler (1834-1903). Almost overnight, Tanner became an artist of international renown.

———— ♦ ————

Toward the end of 1896, Tanner's supporter Rodman Wanamaker paid a visit to the artist's studio to see the completed *Resurrection of Lazarus.* He was impressed by the work, but found its pleasing "Orientalism" to be "a fortunate accident." He offered to send Tanner to the Holy Land for his own firsthand glimpse: "One should go there every two or three years, at least, to keep in touch with the Oriental spirit."[186] Orientalism in nineteenth-century art and literature was largely inspired by North Africa, Albania, Turkey, and the Holy Land. Interest in it had been expanded through the 1894 founding of the Société des Peintres Orientalists Français, which held regular exhibitions.[187]

Tanner spent six weeks, beginning in January 1897, in Egypt and Palestine. His impressions of the landscape were not immediately reflected in his work other than *The Road to Jerusalem* (1897; private collection). Tanner's fascination with the Near Eastern people and their customs surfaced quickly. Works such as *Study of an Arab* (c. 1897; private collection) show that the artist made a concerted effort to understand the features of the local inhabitants. The Wailing Wall in Jerusalem, where Orthodox Jews traditionally go to pray and bewail the capture of their city by the Romans and their dispersion, made a profound impression on him. Tanner noted: "Nor do I forget the deep pathos of the 'Jews Wailing Place'—those tremendous foundation stones of that glorious temple

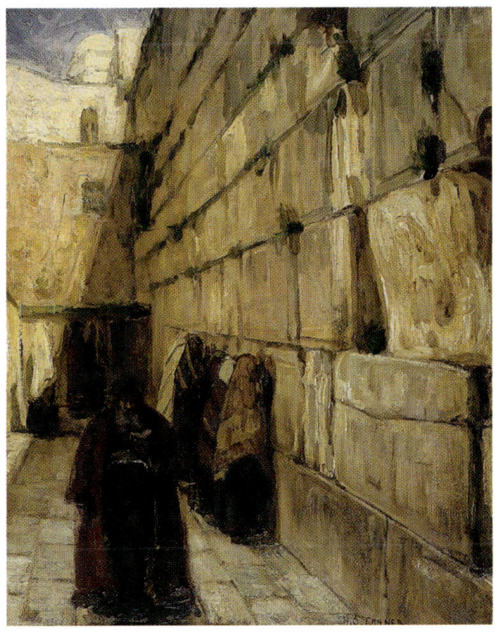

PLATE 20
The Wailing Wall, c. 1897
Oil on canvas
25 1/2 x 19 1/4 (64.8 x 48.9)
Museum of Art, Rhode Island School of Design; gift of Mr. and Mrs. Leonard Granoff

that stood upon Mt. Moriah, worn smooth by the loving touch of tearful and devout worshippers from all over the world."[188] His response to this powerful experience was *The Wailing Wall* (pl. 20). In it, Tanner continued his manner of choosing subjects with more than one possible meaning. Bishop Tanner had drawn similarities between Jews and African Americans: "Like our great precedent the Jewish nation, under the galling bondage of the yoke of Egyptian slavery, we have increased and grown to a fearful strength in the sight of our enemies."[189] Stylistically, Tanner used a plunging perspective, unlike his usual panoramic approach to space; an intense light; characteristic handling of paint; and varied costumes. These features altogether present a fairly realistic view of the Wall and the universal nature of the worshippers in this sacred place.

Tanner returned from the Orient in April 1897 with a stopover in Italy. While there, he learned about the great success of *The Resurrection of Lazarus* and returned to Paris in May with hero status. He was the first African-American artist to achieve international acclaim and was among only a handful of American artists of any race to reach this level by the late nineteenth century.

Following these heady experiences, Henry Tanner planned a three-month, triumphal return to the United States to commence on June 18, 1897.[190] His primary destination was Kansas City, Kansas, where his family had lived since January, when Rev. Tanner began his term as Bishop for the midwestern district of the A.M.E. church. The senior Tanner's household and circle of friends provided the artist with an intellectually rich summer. Kansas City, Kansas, due to its proximity to the Missouri border, had a long abolition and pro-civil rights history. The city was also the home of Western University, an affiliate of the A.M.E. church, which attracted a number of important religious scholars.[191] The women of the community were also active in its intellectual life. Sarah Miller Tanner, the artist's mother, and Bertha Tanner, his sister, were members of the Pierian Club, a women's study group that explored topics ranging from art to science.[192] In this supportive atmosphere, Tanner painted his new surroundings. Two watercolors of Kansas City, Kansas (pls. 21 and 22), may depict women returning from domestic service in the city's affluent Jersey Creek section, just north of downtown. In one of the sheets, the lights of downtown are seen in the distance. With watercolors like this one, Tanner solidified an interest in nocturnal effects, which would last over the rest of his career.

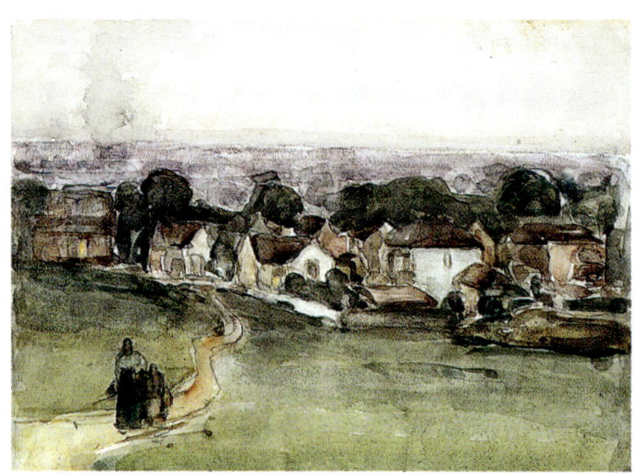

PLATE 21
Kansas City, Kansas, 1897
Watercolor and pencil on paper
9 3/16 x 13 7/8 (24.9 x 35.3)
National Museum of American Art, Smithsonian Institution; gift of Mr. and Mrs. Norman B. Robbins

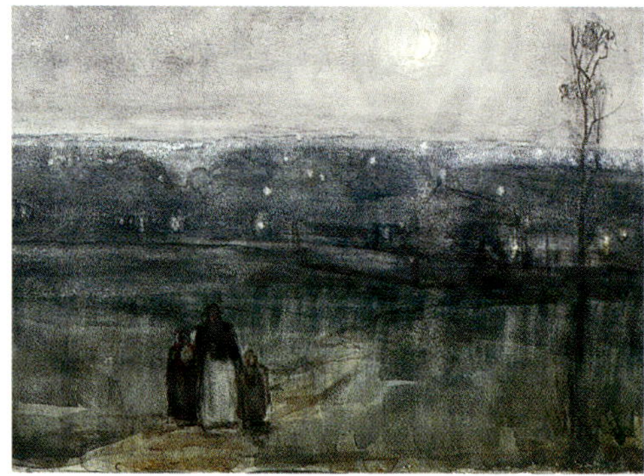

PLATE 22
Kansas City, Kansas, 1897
Watercolor and pencil on paper
9 7/8 x 13 7/8 (25.1 x 35.3)
National Museum of American Art, Smithsonian Institution; gift of Mr. and Mrs. Norman B. Robbins

The artist also painted two small portraits of his parents (pls. 23 and 24), which echo the handling of *The Bagpipe Player* in their shallow spaces, frontal presentations, and purplish-brown backgrounds. He kept the one of his mother in his personal collection and referred to it affectionately in correspondence.[193] His major undertaking during the summer was the tender *Portrait of the Artist's Mother* (pl. 25).[194] The composition calls to mind Whistler's famous mother and Paul Gauguin's *Faaturuma, (Melancholic)* (1891; The Nelson-Atkins Museum of Art). Tanner did not glamorize his mother, but portrayed her realistically, as a woman who had endured a great deal from slavery to nurturing nearly a dozen children. He also acknowledged contemporary art by including a fan, a device used often by the Impressionists. The flowing shawl helps to establish the space and light patterns while calling attention to the fact that, by contemporary Philadelphia standards of fashion in the black community, she was an upper-middle-class lady.[195] Tanner also bared her head so that the highlight on her forehead suggests her intelligence.

PLATE 23
Bishop Benjamin Tucker Tanner, 1897
Oil on canvas
13 x 9 1/4 (33 x 23.5)
Dr. Rae Alexander-Minter

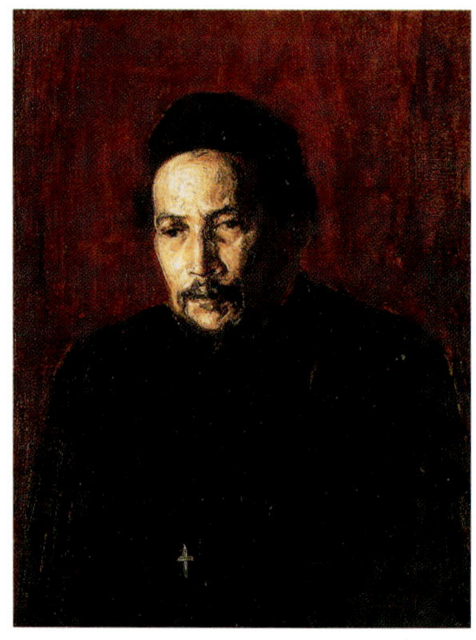

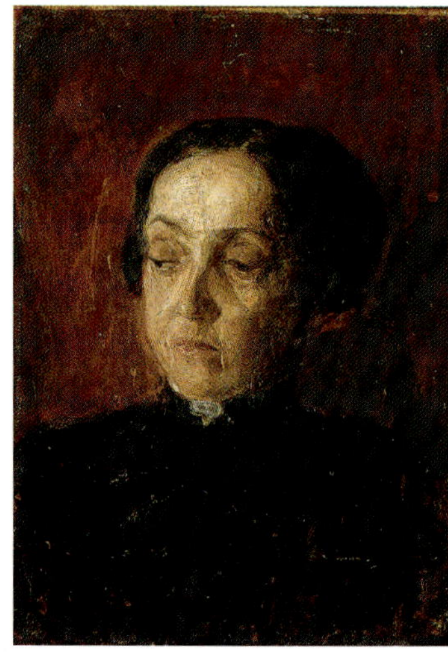

PLATE 24
Mother of Henry O. Tanner, 1897
Oil on wood
13 x 9 1/4 (30 x 23.5)
National Museum of American Art, Smithsonian Institution; gift of Dr. Nicholas Zervas

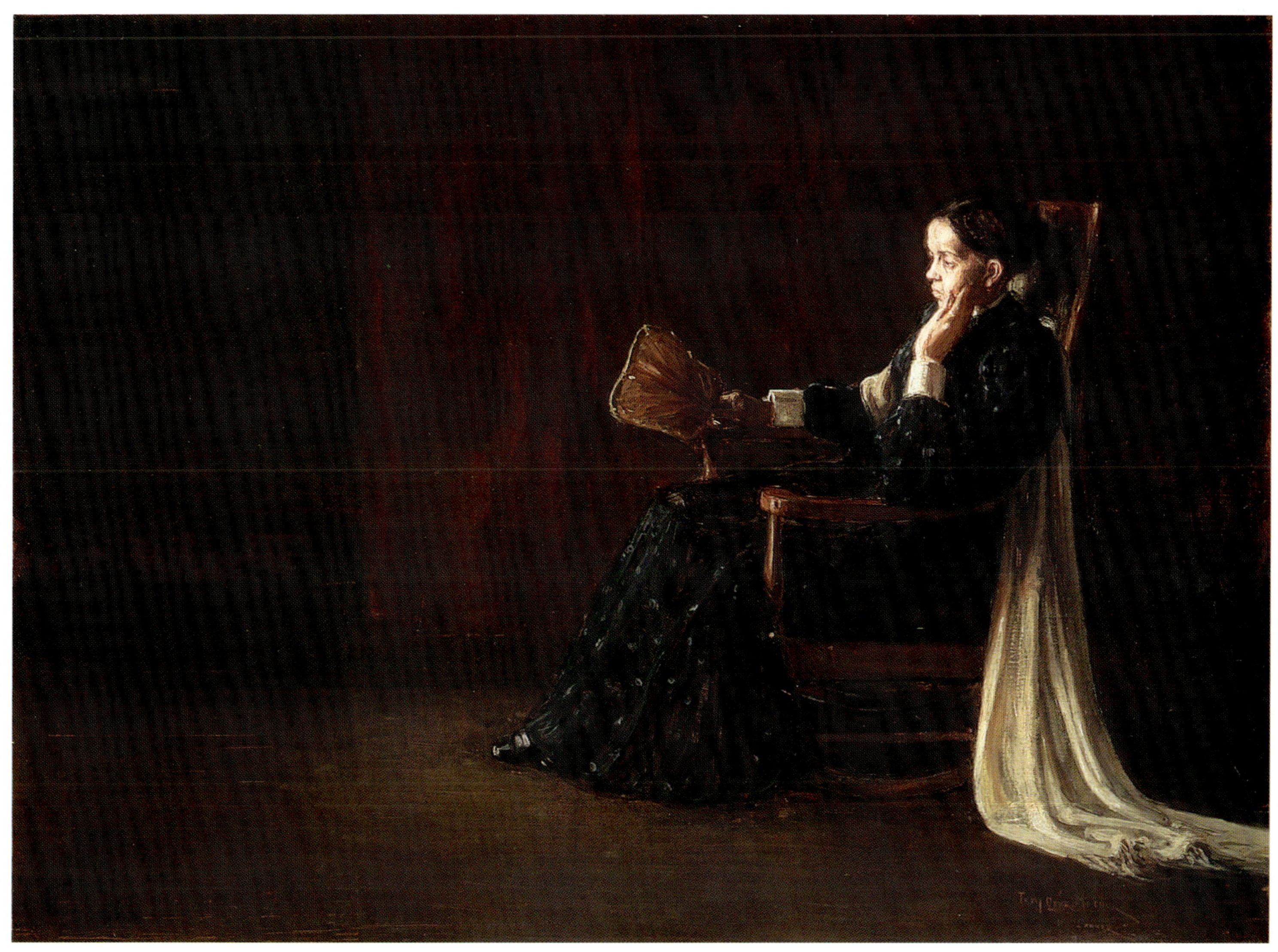

PLATE 25
Portrait of the Artist's Mother, 1897
Oil on canvas
29 1/4 x 39 1/2 (74.3 x 100.3)
Philadelphia Museum of Art; partial gift of Dr. Rae Alexander-Minter and purchased with the W. P. Wilstach Fund, the George W. Elkins Fund, and funds contributed by the Dietrich Foundation and a private donor

The *Portrait of the Artist's Mother* is not a copy of Whistler's work and might be seen as a challenge to him. As early as the eighteenth century, theorists in French art suggested to young artists the practice of competition: by surpassing recognized works, challengers demonstrated their imaginative powers and proclaimed their own genius.[196] Tanner noted at the Chicago World's Fair in 1893 "that actual achievement proves Negroes to possess ability and talent for successful competition with White artists."[197] Tanner's newfound fame with the success of *The Resurrection of Lazarus* could have encouraged his competitive spirit; a few months later, he apologized to Harrison S. Morris for sounding egotistical about his paintings.[198] Tanner's allusion to Whistler's painting in his own *Portrait of the Artist's Mother* could have also reflected another aspect of French tradition. During the nineteenth century, a premium was placed on originality, but with an approach that acknowledged existing works without servile imitation.[199] Tanner was certainly aware of this tradition because Albert Maignon pointed out in his review of the 1897 Salon that Lazarus contained a "recollection of Rembrandt," but that it "does not displease us because it does not obscure the personal sensibility of the artist."[200]

Tanner returned to France during the fall of 1897. On December 6, he met Atherton Curtis (1863-1943), a wealthy collector, historian of old master prints, and an advocate of animal rights.[201] Curtis would become Tanner's closest lifelong friend and, beginning in 1904, a regular financial benefactor.[202] Back at his easel, Tanner began to work on *The Annunciation.* The picture, conceived in Kansas City, reflected his total confidence in his abilities that he had gained during his Midwest interlude and was central to the next phase of his career.[203]

The Evolution of a Personal Style: Religious Painting, Images of Women, and the Influence of Spanish Art, 1898-1907

The great success of *Daniel in the Lions' Den* in 1896 and especially *The Resurrection of Lazarus* in 1897 set the course that Tanner followed for the rest of his career: he devoted himself almost exclusively to the rendition of religious themes. Much speculation has been made about his reason for this decision.[204] However, Tanner wrote at length on the subject and gave precise reasons for his choice:

> It is not by accident that I have chosen to be a religious painter.... I have no doubt an inheritance of religious feeling, and for this I am glad, but I have also a decided and I hope an intelligent religious faith not due to inheritance but to my own convictions. I choose religious subjects not primarily because I believe they will interest people, nor because I consider them most salable. I am very glad if they do interest the people, and certainly am glad to sell them. Yet, I have chosen the character of my art because it conveys my message and tells what I want to tell to my own generation and leave to the future.... [I] hope to continue for many years to come in my work of interpreting through my brush the holiest and greatest theme that belongs to the literature and hope of the world.[205]

The majority of Tanner's biblical themes are taken from the Gospels of the four Evangelists. They favor miracles over martyrs, and focus on the events of the nativity, crucifixion, and resurrection. The notions of birth and rebirth inherent in these subjects are easily linked to messages of human rights and social equality, and they relate to issues of equality in African-American churches.[206] Another of the artist's aims was to present the simple domestic side of biblical personages. He was never interested in merely illustrating the Bible, but in providing that "quiet suggestion of character as we might imagine them to be"—a reflection of his personal brand of Symbolism.[207]

The perfect example of Tanner's approach to religious painting is *The Annunciation* (pl. 26). This beautiful and emotionally compelling work was the artist's primary undertaking during late 1897 and early 1898. His choice of subject matter was inspired by a trip to Italy earlier in 1897: "I made a wise choice when I saw Fra Angelico's *Annunciation* in Florence. I refused to buy even a photograph of it preferring to live with the impressions I had."[208] Tanner's impression of the subject was aptly described by a contemporary writer: "The

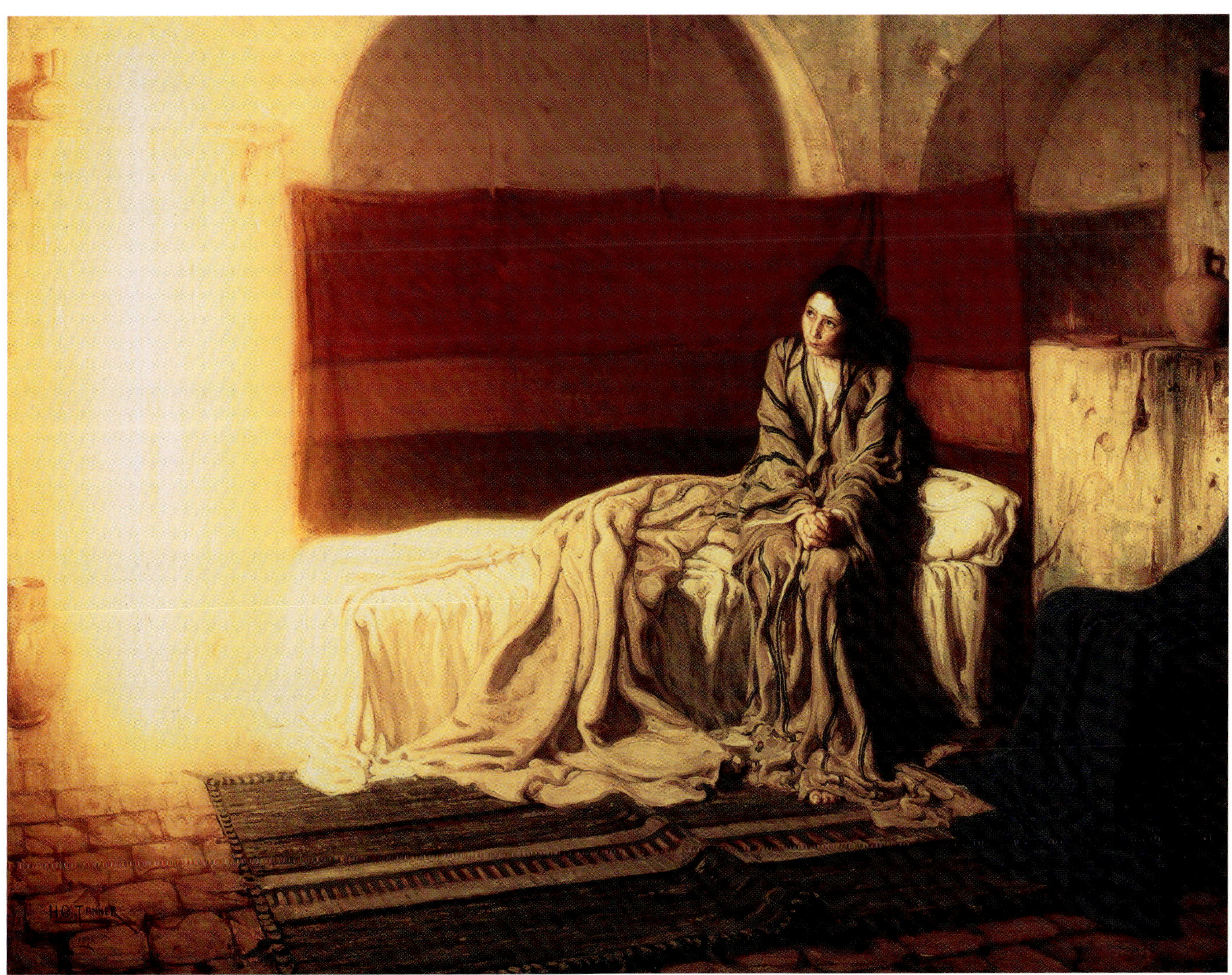

PLATE 26
The Annunciation, 1898
Oil on canvas
57 x 71 1/2 (144.8 x 181.6)
Philadelphia Museum of Art; purchased with the W. P. Wilstach Fund

young Jewish peasant sits on the edge of a couch, wearing the common striped cotton of the Eastern women of the poorer class, a costume which they have kept to the present day, no halo or celestial attributes about her, and only the flood of golden light to herald the approach of the angel."[209] Indeed, the light is an integral part of the scene's message and an element of definition throughout the composition.

The Annunciation was novel among religious paintings executed during the last years of the nineteenth century, being happily devoid of the photographic historicism found in the late works of James Tissot (1836-1902) and the heavy-handed symbolism found in the religious paintings of the Swiss-born, American painter Carl Gutherz (1844-1907).[210] Tanner's domestic treatment of the Virgin annunciate captured the imagination of both art critics and fellow painters.[211] Harrison S. Morris wrote to the artist: "I have been hearing unbound praise of your Salon picture. Mr. Alexander Harrison was here last week and said 'Tanner has made another ten-strike.' Walter Gay tells me that not since Sargent's early triumphs has there been anything like it."[212] The success of *The Annunciation* resulted in the artist's first sale to a major public collection in his native land. It was bought by the Wilstach Collection, the forerunner of today's Philadelphia Museum of Art.

Tanner still would not be pinned down to a single subject of painting. During the summer of 1898 he painted landscapes at Cernay-la-Ville, northwest of Fontainbleau Forest, where he met his future wife, Jessie Macauley Olssen (1873-1925) and her sister Elna, in the company of the artists Joseph-Maurice Avy (1871-?) and Roy H. Brown (1879-1956).[213] Along with landscapes and religious themes, he continued his interest in animals in works like *Lions in the Desert* (1897-98; National Museum of American Art). It should be mentioned, too, that at this time Morris employed Tanner to select and make annotated comments on the best pictures by American artists in the Paris Salon as guidance in choosing works for the Pennsylvania Academy of the Fine Arts annual shows. He continued to do so until 1905. Also, in the winter of 1898 Tanner was elected Corresponding Member of the American Negro Academy in the category of "Foreigner of Great Distinction."

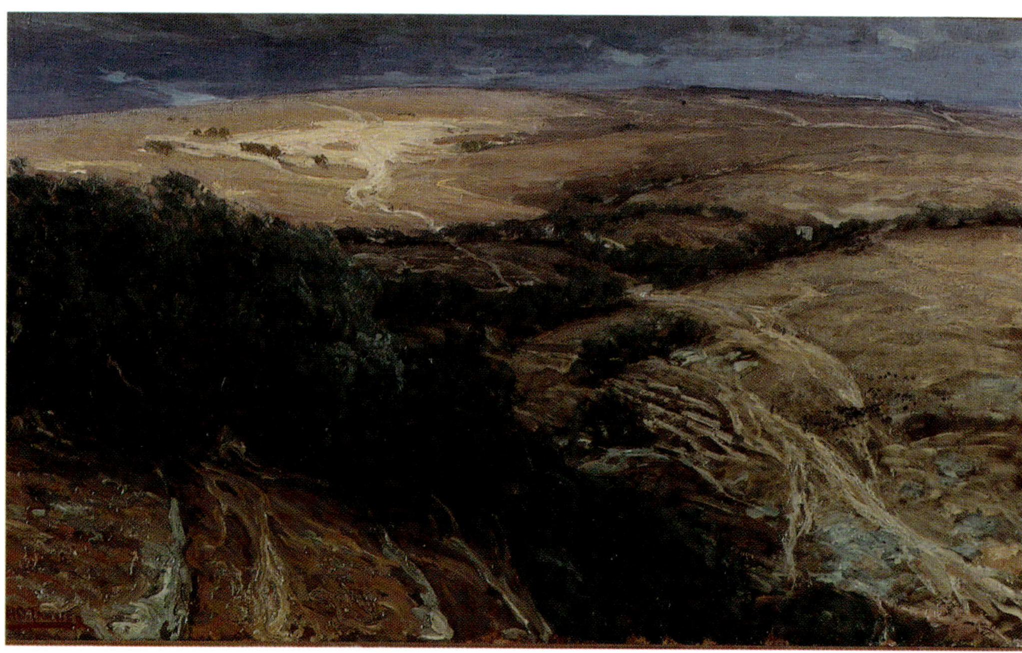

PLATE 27
A View in Palestine, c. 1898-99
Oil on canvas
22 1/2 x 37 (57.2 x 94)
The Frances Lehman Loeb Art Center, Vassar College, Poughkeepsie, New York; gift of Mrs. Walter Driscoll (Margaret L. Weyerhaeuser, class of 1923), Mrs. F. Rodman Titcomb (Elizabeth L. Weyerhaeuser, class of 1915) and Mrs. Robert J. Sivertsen (Sarah Weyerhaeuser, ex class of 1930)

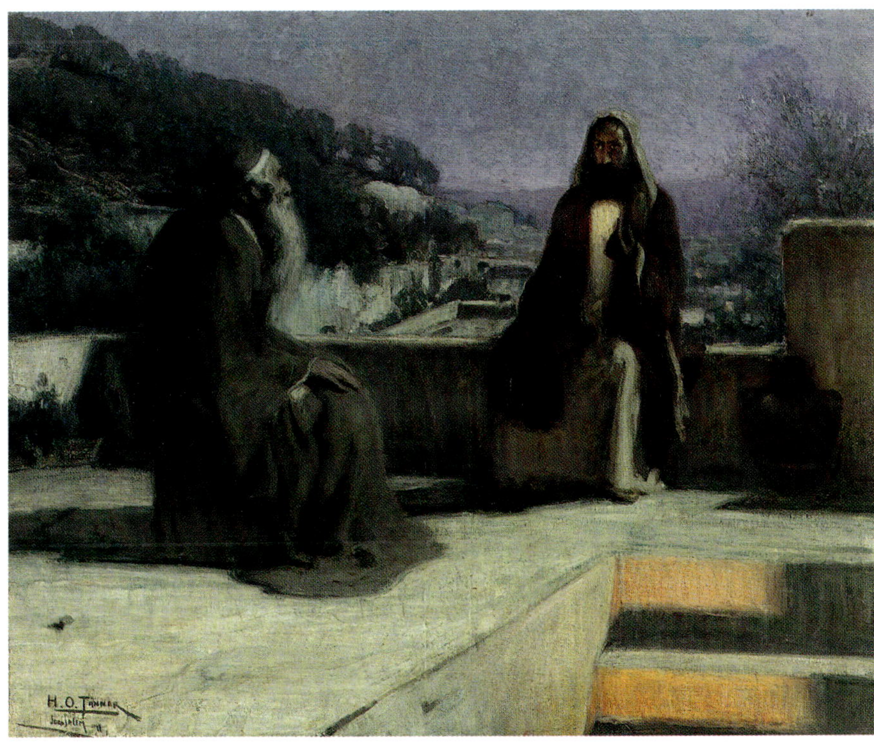

Plate 28
Nicodemus, 1899
Oil on canvas
33 11/16 x 39 1/2 (85.6 x 100.3)
Pennsylvania Academy of the Fine Arts, Philadelphia; Joseph E. Temple Fund, 1900.1

In the fall of 1898, Rodman Wanamaker planned a second trip for Tanner to the Holy Land to coincide with a visit there by German Emperor William II and Empress Augusta Victoria. Tanner was accompanied on his trip by the Hungarian-born painter Sandor Landeau (1864-?), who had been a fellow student at the Académie Julian. The journey by the emperor and empress to Palestine to inaugurate new foreign policies began in the middle of October 1898.[214] Tanner had hoped the visit would result in scenes of great pageantry and an opportunity for making an interesting painting. He was disappointed and lamented later that "our hoped-for picturesqueness of the entry of the Emperor into Jerusalem did not materialize. The police regulations were too severe, the whole affair was, as it were, at a gallop, and at no time was it in any way an event of any beauty."[215] Tanner and Landeau remained in the Near East throughout the winter of 1899, painting around Jerusalem and the region of the Dead Sea.

Tanner's stay yielded a number of successful efforts, such as *Flight into Egypt* (1899; Detroit Institute of Arts) and *A View in Palestine* (pl. 27). He recalled Palestine as a place of "great barren hills that can blossom like a rose,...a natural setting to a great tragedy."[216] The symbolic import Tanner attached to *A View in Palestine* further distinguished the artist as a religious painter rather than a biblical one. Whereas a biblical painter is deft at illustrating Bible stories, chapter and verse, the religious painter expands beyond the literal to infer related subjects. Tanner had already revealed himself as a religious painter in the 1897 *The Wailing Wall*.

Tanner's best-known work from the Holy Land sojourn is *Nicodemus* (pl. 28). The subject touches on the artist's favored theme of rebirth, although here he reverses his age-instructing-youth motif. According to the book of John, Nicodemus, a ruler of the Jews, came to Jesus by night to ask him questions. Jesus said to him "except a man be born again, he cannot see the Kingdom of God" (see John 3:1-5). The artist's father considered Nicodemus's visit to be one of three notable incidents of the second stage of Jesus's public ministry.[217]

The image of the rabbi coming to Jesus by night provided a biblical precedent for the worship habits of African-American slaves, as well as for post-emancipation practices. Slaves were not allowed either to have formal church services or to read the Bible, and their clandestine religious activities were perforce conducted at night.[218] Today many African-American denominations continue to hold full-fledged Sunday services at night.

The overall composition of *Nicodemus* was inspired by *Saint Jerome and Gerolamo Amadi*, by the Italian Renaissance master Piero della Francesca (c. 1420-1492). Tanner had seen the work in Venice at the Galleria dell'Accademia in 1897. Tanner interpreted his subject by having the two figures, local models, gaze at each other across an empty space. Light plays an extremely important role in the presentation of the narrative and it is as well thought-out as the arrangement of figures, architecture, and landscape. The result is a scene charged with kinetic energy. An overall pattern of essentially horizontal bands begins in the foreground and moves along the left side to a gentle glow on the horizon. The shadows cast by the figures on the balcony floor indicate moonlight coming from the upper right. To achieve the highlights on Jesus, Tanner brought an artificial light source up through the open stairwell. Despite these logical reasons for the play of light on Jesus, Tanner not only induces the viewer to accept all the illumination as deriving from the presence of Jesus, but also emphasizes his spirituality without resorting to the use of a halo. *Nicodemus* received favorable reviews and was believed to have prize-winning potential when it was shown at the Salon of 1899.[219] Although it did not win a medal at the Salon, the painting did win the Lippincott Prize at the Pennsylvania Academy of the Fine Arts annual exhibition in 1900.

Tanner's life changed drastically at the end of 1899. On December 14, at Saint Files-in-the-Fields, Bloomsbury, London, he married Jessie Macauley Olssen. She was a young white woman from San Francisco studying music in Europe whom Tanner had met the year before in Barbizon.[220] Their marriage was to be a singularly happy one.[221]

Marriage did not change Tanner's diligent work habits, but Jessie Tanner may have helped the artist accommodate his public. Helen Cole noted in 1900: "He is one of the hardest workers in the quarter, and has been very little known in student circles for the reason that with the roistering café habitués he has little sympathy. Now that he is so much sought, he is coming out of his shell a little more.... [F]or the first time, he will hold receptions twice a month in his studio in the Boulevard Saint Jacques."[222] Tanner rose early in the morning and worked through the afternoon. He set himself such a pace, in fact, that his patron Robert C. Ogden advised: "Allow me to caution you against overwork. Your art draws heavily upon your sympathies, and such work is always both mentally and physically exhausting. 'If you want to get there quick go slow.'"[223] This rigorous routine did not prevent Tanner from showing kindness to aspiring African Americans, such as the young sculptor Meta Vaux Warrick (1877-1968) and perhaps the painter Annie E. Anderson (1855-1929).[224] He also received Booker T. Washington in his studio in July 1899, and W. E. B. Du Bois the following year.[225] His pace of work resulted in a great deal of attention from the media and an impressive exhibition record.[226]

About this time, the artist began to move away from his customary method of finishing one painting before starting another. Along with *Christ Among the Doctors* (location unknown), he completed *Mary* (1900; Lasalle University Art Museum, Philadelphia) and another version of *Daniel in the Lions' Den* (location unknown). Tanner also worked on landscapes over a period of time. He wrote much later to his Atlanta patron J. J. Haverty about *Road to Emmaus* (location unknown): "As it is out of doors scene—it has been laid aside for the Winter, and other than by study and thought on it,—it has been put aside until I return to the country next spring."[227]

The intense work habits of the newlywed Tanner now included trying his hand again at illustration, a field he had essayed with some success in the 1880s. He worked on the story of Barabbas, the robber whom Pilate freed instead of Jesus (John 18:39-40), and for which *The Savior* (pl. 29) is probably an extant example. The painting represents Jesus waiting for his crown of thorns and purple robe in order to be mocked as King of the Jews (John 19:1-3). In this image Tanner did not render Jesus as an omnipotent and supernatural man.

However, the unnatural palette of chartreuse and brownish purples, with claylike tones in the face and green outline, removes the work beyond the realm of everyday encounters, and, in its methods, harks back to Tanner's Symbolist excursions in the circle of Gauguin at Pont-Aven during the summer of 1894. The artist submitted one or more pictures for publication to the Lippincott Company without success.[228] Harrison S. Morris attempted an explanation that certainly relates to *The Savior*: "I fear the Barabbas illustration is hardly what was required. Illustration requires a more definite treatment than you have given this. I hope that you can make another venture and succeed with the work as I should be rejoiced to find you take a front place in this growing American field."[229]

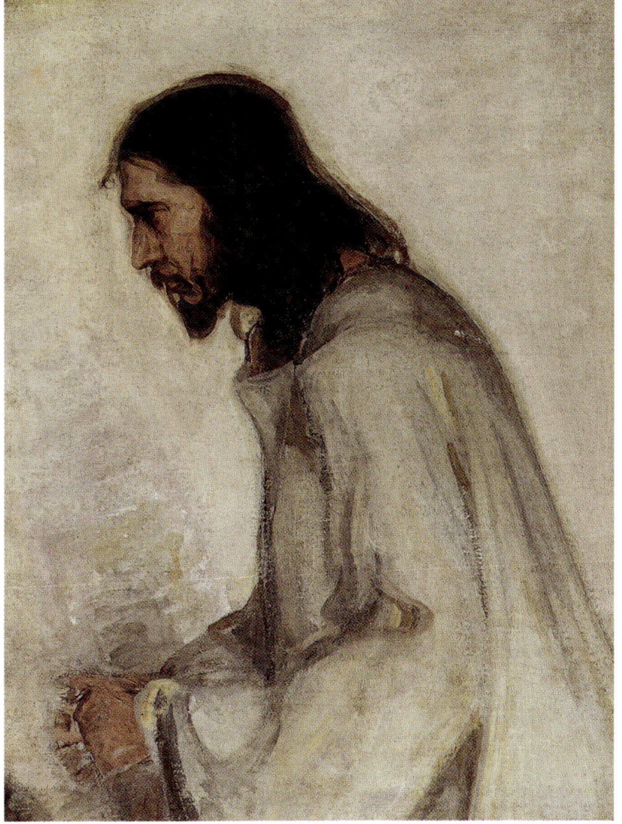

PLATE 29
The Savior, c. 1900-05
Oil on canvas
29 1/8 x 21 7/8 (74 x 55.6)
National Museum of American Art, Smithsonian Institution; gift of Mr. and Mrs. Norman B. Robbins

———— ♦ ————

During the summer of 1900 the Tanners resided in Trépied, north of Pont-Aven, near Etaples in Normandy. This region would remain important to them for the rest of their lives. Upon returning to Paris in November, Tanner continued his interest in illustration and proposed a group of six biblical subjects to Edward Bok, editor of the *Ladies Home Journal*.[230] This series intended to present revealing episodes in the lives of famous mothers of the Bible. Four were accepted: *Mary*, *Hagar*, *Sarah*, and *Rachel*; with these images Tanner's depictions of Old Testament events at least doubled, and his work became dominated by female figures. The illustrations appeared from September 1902 to January 1903. All of the final paintings are lost, but we can understand them through drawings, such as *Study for Rachel* (pl. 30) and *Study for Jesus* (pl. 31). For the former piece, the artist turned to Genesis (29:10-11). His choice surely had to do with his recent marriage because he wanted "to present the story in the picture [as] a love story of Biblical times with the fresh human interest of all times preserved."[231] The *Study for Jesus*, which incorporates Tanner's symbolic form of halo, relates to *Mary*. The scene depicts Mary pondering her son's assertion that he must be about his Father's business (Luke 2:46-49). The figure of Jesus is shown in the background engaged in carpentry chores learned from Joseph.

In September of 1901 the Tanners joined Bishop Tanner in London. During this trip they visited the Somerset home of Catherine Impey (1847-1923), a feminist and the founder of *Anti-Caste*, a publication that argued against racial discrimination.[232] Impey's views might have heightened Tanner's sensitivity to the status of women in society. The Tanner family was accompanied on this journey by Professor and Mrs. W. S. Scarborough. They attended a loan exhibition of Spanish paintings at the Guildhall Art Gallery and Tanner was most attracted to the work of Velásquez.[233] Regarded as a supreme realist and the father of modern art, Velásquez and his technique were frequently discussed and much admired at the end of the nineteenth century.[234] Indeed, earlier in his career Tanner was criticized for being overly imitative of Spanish artists.[235] Tanner might have had a special interest in Velásquez because in 1654 the Spanish artist allegedly freed his black slave, Juan de Pareja, who became an artist in his own right.[236]

The influence of the Guildhall exhibition was manifested in *Chamber Music* (1902; location unknown). Its models included Jessie Olssen Tanner playing the cello, her sister, Elna Olssen Charles, at the piano, and Tanner himself standing in the shadows.[237] When it was exhibited at the Salon, reviewers noted that Tanner

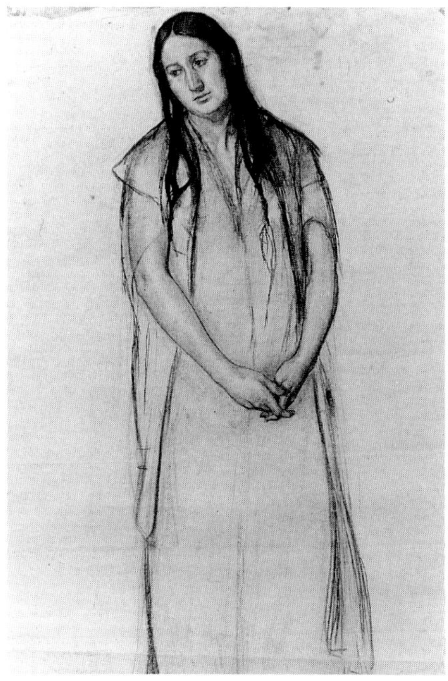

Plate 30
Study for Rachel, from the Mothers of the Bible, c. 1901
Charcoal on paper
23 x 13 5/8 (58.4 x 34.6)
National Museum of American Art, Smithsonian Institution; gift of Mr. and Mrs. Norman B. Robbins

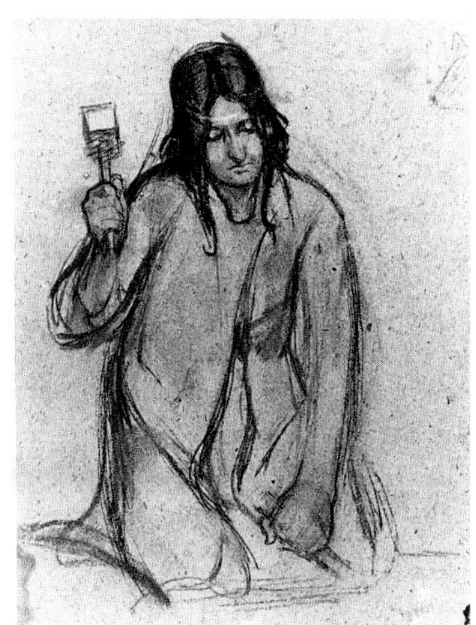

Plate 31
Study for Jesus, 1901
Charcoal on paper
11 3/4 x 9 1/4 (29.8 x 23.5)
Schomburg Center for Research in Black Culture, Art and Artifacts Division, The New York Public Library, Astor, Lenox and Tilden Foundation

seemed to have shed his personality and "now astonishes with amusing color."[238] The change in Tanner's palette and the canvas's elegant, linear composition reflected the artist's admiration for seventeenth-century Spanish painting.

In June 1902 the Tanners moved to Mt. Kisco, New York, to live with their friends and patrons Atherton and Louise Curtis.[239] While in the United States he painted a portrait of his first patron, Bishop Hartzell (1902; Hampton University Museum, Virginia), and sat for one by Thomas Eakins (1902; Hyde Collection, Glens Falls, New York).[240] The Tanners again traveled abroad. After a few months in Granada, Spain, in early 1903, and a trip to Paris, they returned to Mt. Kisco in August. Their only child was born in New York City on September 25, 1903, and named Jesse Ossawa Tanner, an indication that the artist continued to value his middle name and its tie with the abolitionist John Brown of Osawatomie. By early 1904 Tanner was having financial difficulties and engaged Booker T. Washington in a fund-raising scheme to sell a painting to the Metropolitan Museum of Art.[241] The plan failed and the Tanners abruptly returned to France on April 18, 1904.

The artist did not immediately return to painting fulltime, but when he did the influence of Spanish painting was apparent. The composition of *Return of the Holy Women* (pl. 32) calls to mind the low vantage point of several Spanish artists, as do the elongated figures pushing against the edges of the vertical format. The bright palette and John's daggerlike fingers—at once reaching out to comfort the Virgin Mary and calling attention to his own aching heart after the crucifixion—reflect the mannerisms of El Greco, but the headband worn by John is Tanner's own naturalistic shorthand for a halo, intended to signify the subject's religious nature.

During 1905 Tanner stepped up the pace of his artistic production and by early 1906 he had completed four major pictures. These new works included *Christ at the Home of Mary and Martha* (1905; Carnegie Museum of Art, Pittsburgh), *Christ Washing His Disciples Feet* (1906; location unknown), *Pilgrims at Emmaus* (pl. 33), and *Two Disciples at the Tomb* (pl. 34). Tanner returned to a dark brown palette, but with his own complex, Rembrandtesque treatment of light, as he used earlier in *The Resurrection of Lazarus.* He employed poses and gestures indebted to Velásquez and El Greco. In all of these works Tanner turned away from the bright colors and elongated figures of his El Greco-inspired paintings, such as *Return of the Holy Women.* It is fairly certain that this shift of palette had to do with the views of his patron Robert C. Ogden, who expressed them in a letter to Booker T. Washington in 1904:

> I fear that, in the development of his art, difficulties have arisen that will operate against the sale of his recent work. I have seen a half dozen of his pictures which are very mysterious in spirit, very abstruse in art, full of delicate sensitivity, and altogether too transcendental for popular appreciation.[242]

Ogden's view of what would be more popularly appreciated proved to be correct. One of the new dark pictures, *Pilgrims at Emmaus,* was shown in the 1906 Salon and purchased by the French government, joining *Lazarus* in the Musée du Luxembourg. This gave Tanner the rare distinction of having two works at that institution. As a result, he received the prestigious designation of *hors concours,* which meant he no longer had to submit his works to the scrutiny of the Salon jury. Across the Atlantic, a writer for the *North American* in Philadelphia called *Pilgrims at Emmaus* "one of Tanner's best paintings."[243] *Two Disciples at the Tomb* was described in New York's *Globe* as a "quite remarkable achievement of strength, dignity, and impressiveness."[244] At the Art Institute of Chicago's 1906 annual exhibition it was awarded the Harris Prize and entered the museum's permanent collection. With these successes Tanner became financially solvent and remained so over the next two decades.

Side by side these brownish canvases, Tanner painted some of what may be called his blue-sky, moonlight religious pictures. These include *Abraham's Oak* (pl. 35), depicting the dwelling place of the prophet at

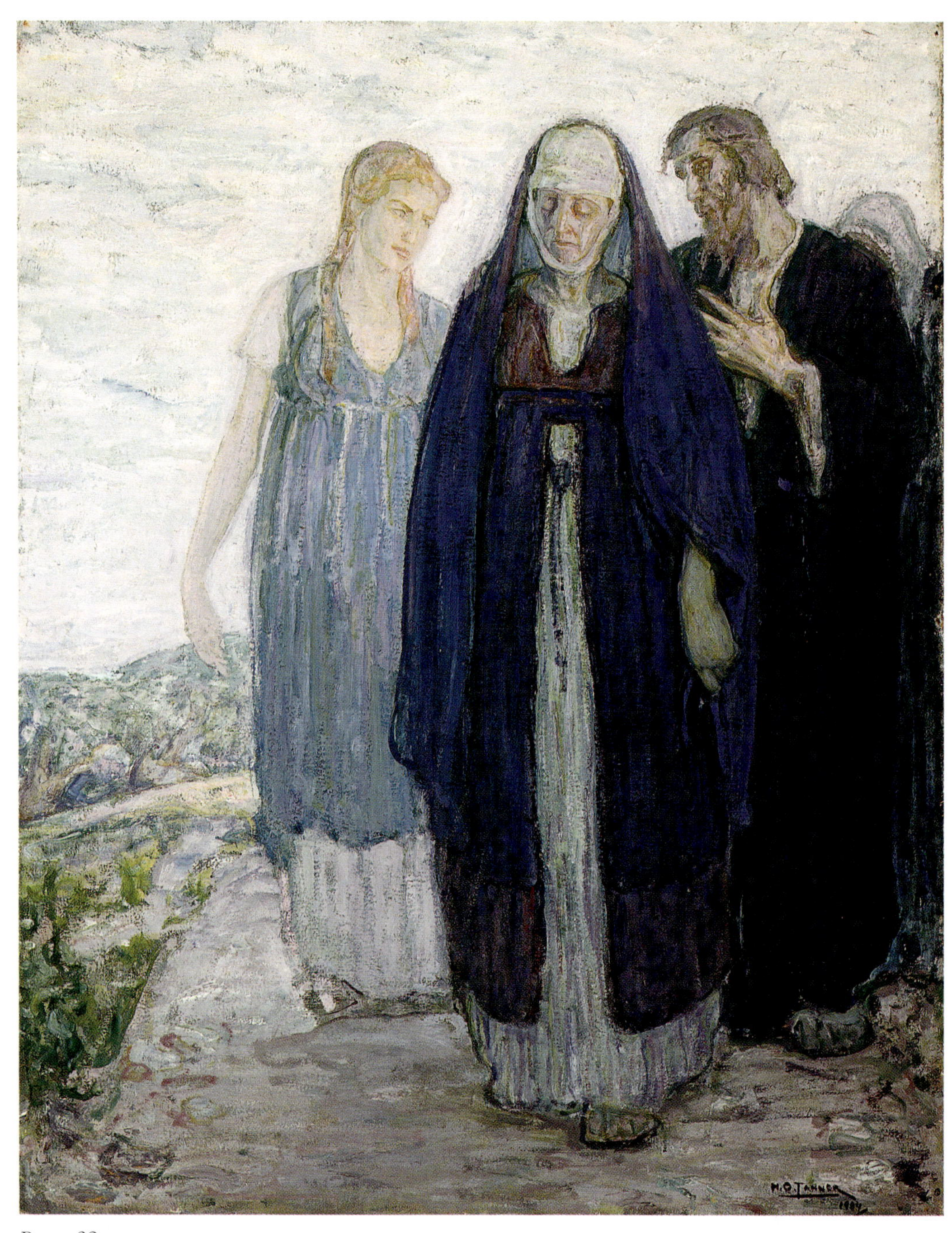

Plate 32
Return of the Holy Women, 1904
Oil on canvas
46 1/2 x 35 (118.1 x 88.9)
Cedar Rapids Museum of Art; Art Association Purchase, Club of Forty Fund

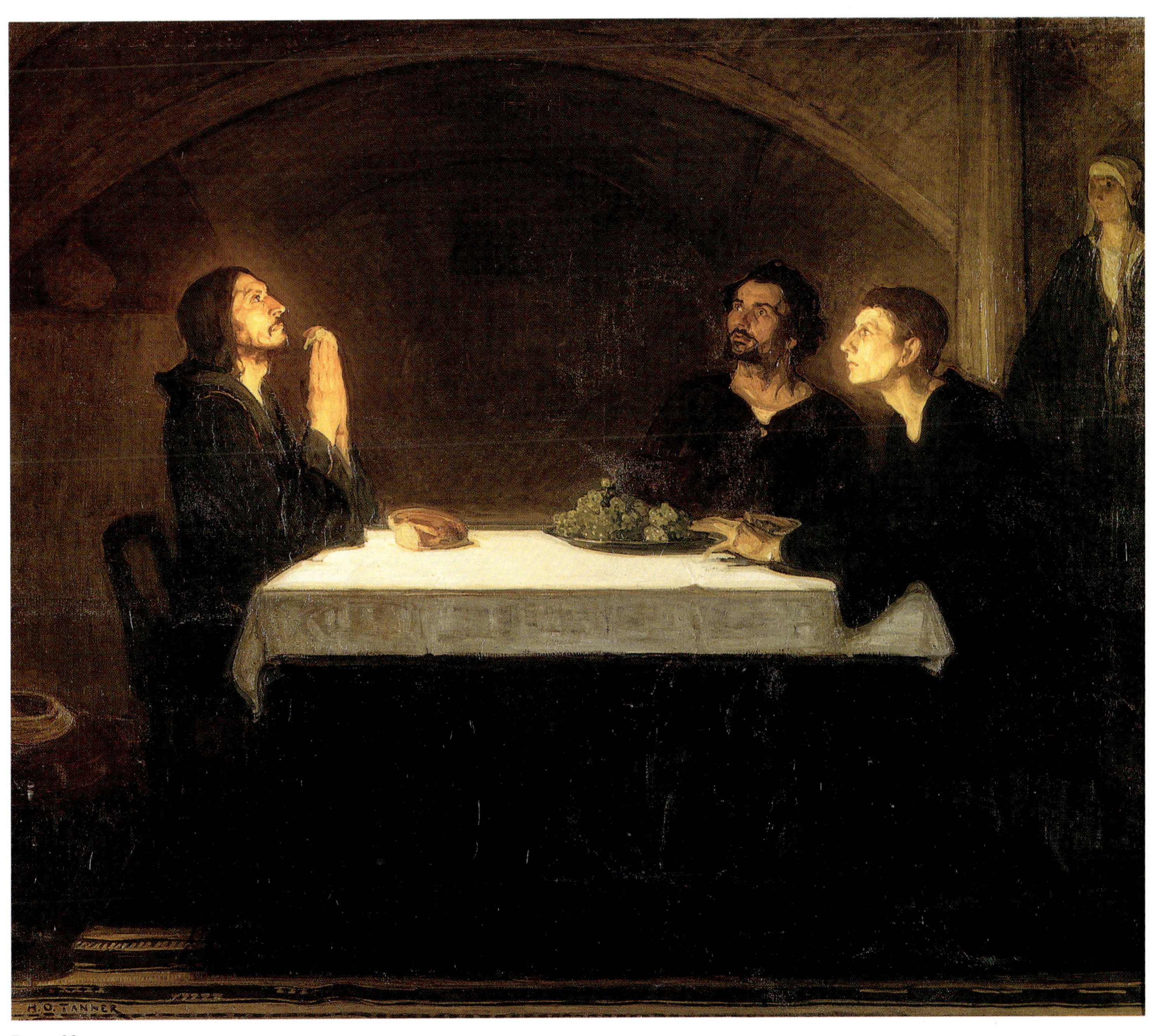

PLATE 33
Pilgrims at Emmaus, 1905
Oil on canvas
73 1/4 x 83 1/2 (186 x 212)
Musée d'Orsay, Paris

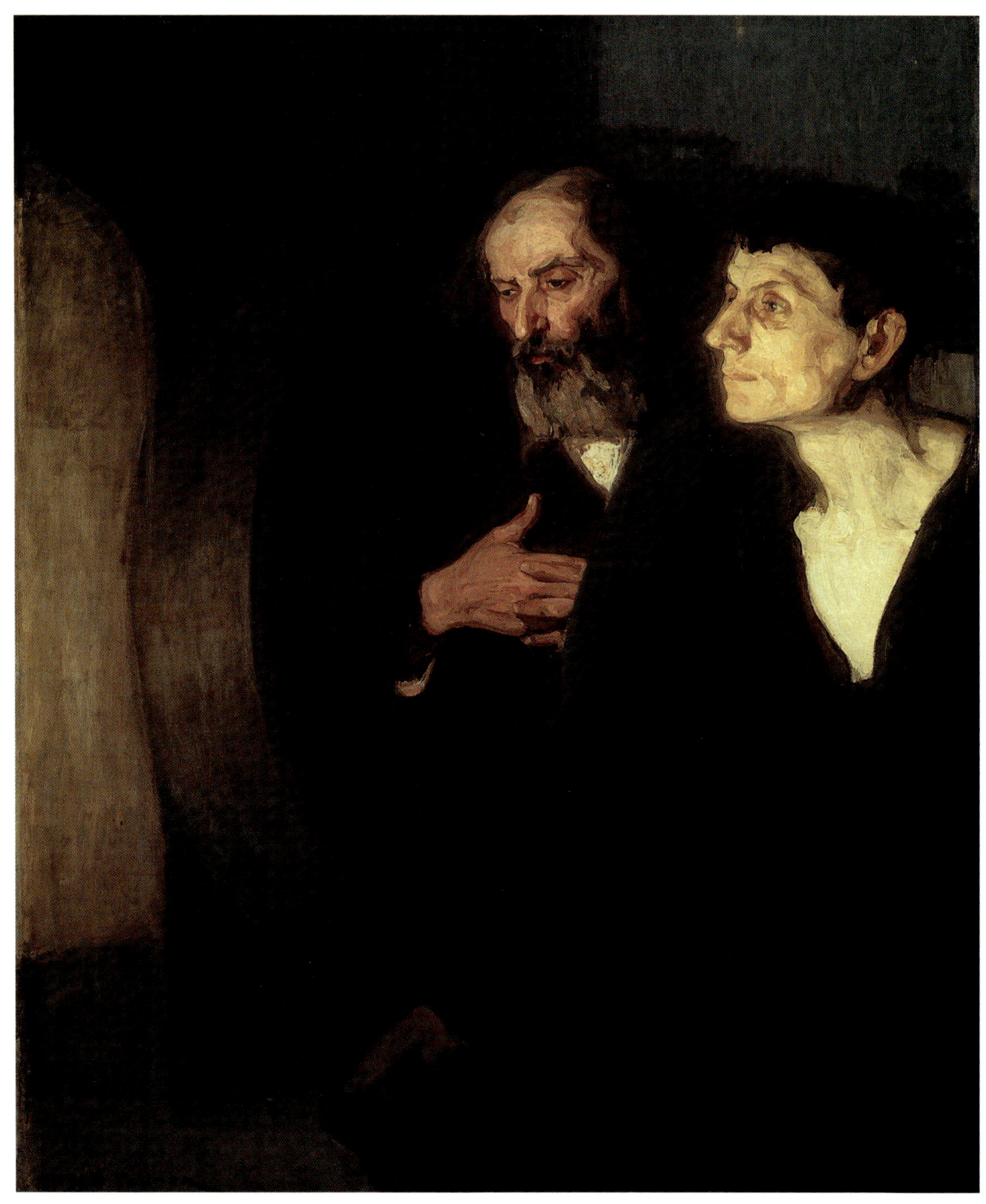

PLATE 34
Two Disciples at the Tomb, c. 1905-06
Oil on canvas
51 x 41 5/8 (129.5 x 105.7)
The Art Institute of Chicago; Robert A. Waller Fund, 1906.300

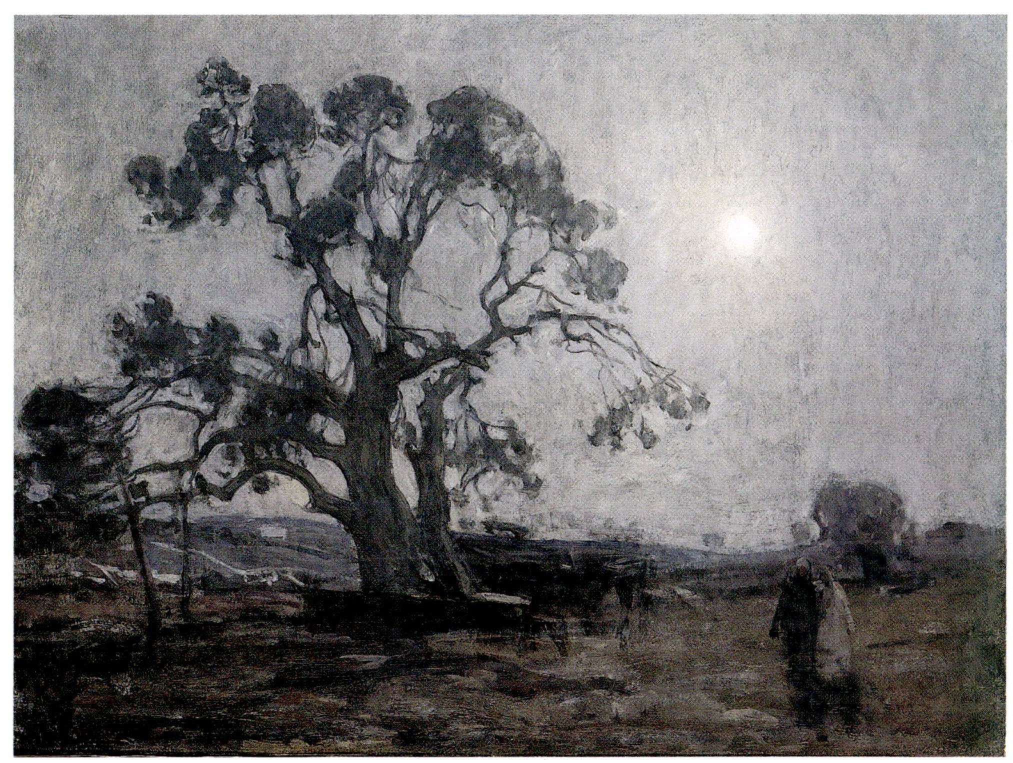

PLATE 35
Abraham's Oak, 1905
Oil on canvas
21 5/8 x 28 5/8 (54.9 x 72.7)
National Museum of American Art, Smithsonian Institution; gift of Mr. and Mrs. Norman B. Robbins

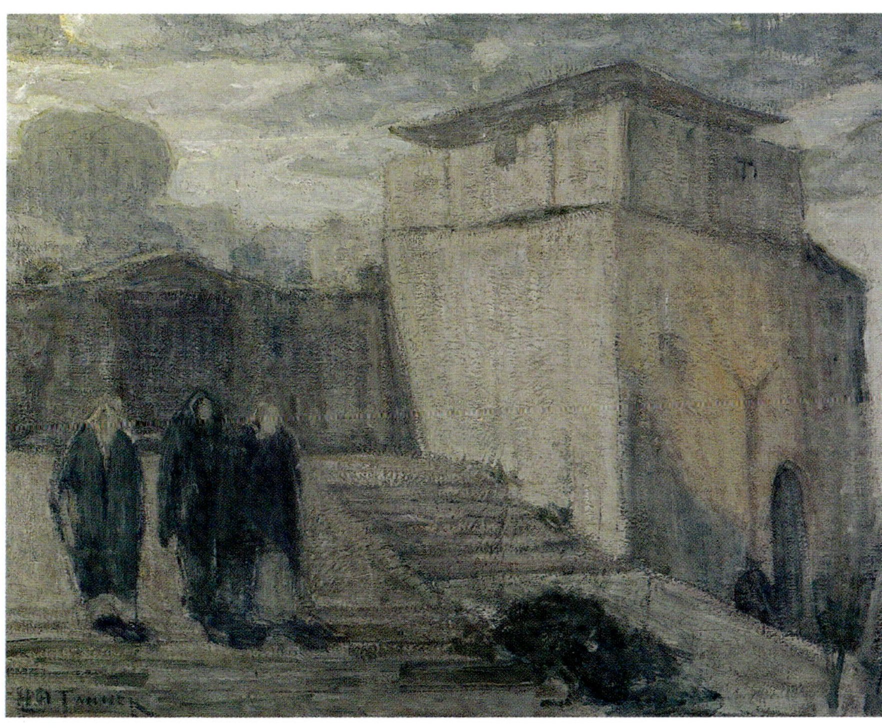

PLATE 36
Moonlight, Hebron, c. 1907
Oil on canvas
25 11/16 x 31 7/8 (65.3 x 81)
Milwaukee Art Museum; gift of Mr. and Mrs. Thomas Whipple Dunbar

Mamre in Hebron where God appeared to him (see Genesis 13:18, 18:1); *Moonlight, Hebron* (pl. 36), the region where Abraham and Sarah lived; *Flight into Egypt* (pl. 37); and *The Disciples See Christ Walking on the Water* (pl. 38). The latter work is representative of the group. The subject was taken from the Gospel of Matthew (14:24-27), where is related an account of the Apostles battling with a rough sea when Jesus came to them walking on the lake. Terrified, they cried out: "It is a ghost! But at once He spoke to them." The artist did not choose to depict the drama of a sudden storm, but captured the moment of awe through the poses of the Apostles. The phantomlike vertical shape in the upper left, recalling a similar figure in *The Annunciation*, is the symbol for Jesus; Peter stands tallest in the boat. To draw the image together Tanner rendered one of his most ambitious visual effects in this work. Although the composition is cropped on the top, we know that there is a cloudy sky because it is mirrored in the water, as are the mast and riggings of the boat. The moon, reflected in the water, is the actual source of light, fading as it recedes toward the right and glowing brighter as it reaches the ghostlike figure of Jesus. The miraculous and mystical nature of the painting is enhanced by Tanner's mature palette of violet, blues, and blue-greens, mixed to create a somewhat chalky surface.

In these paintings Tanner showed that he had clearly come into his own by around 1906. Influences of other artists are difficult to detect, and his particular brand of Symbolism was rarely compared to that of other artists in contemporary reviews. By the turn of the century Helen Cole noted that "the French critics invariably characterize his work as *personelle*, which is the highest praise it could receive."[245]

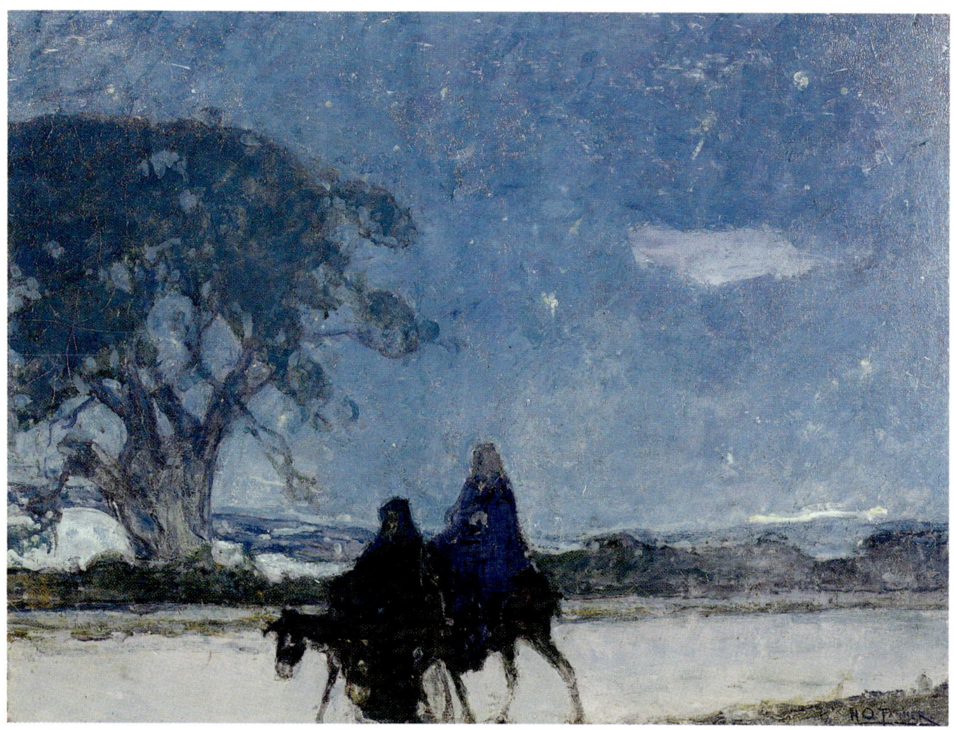

Plate 37
Flight Into Egypt, c. 1907-12
Oil on canvas
19 7/8 x 25 1/2 (50.5 x 64.8)
Willkie House, Inc., Des Moines, Iowa

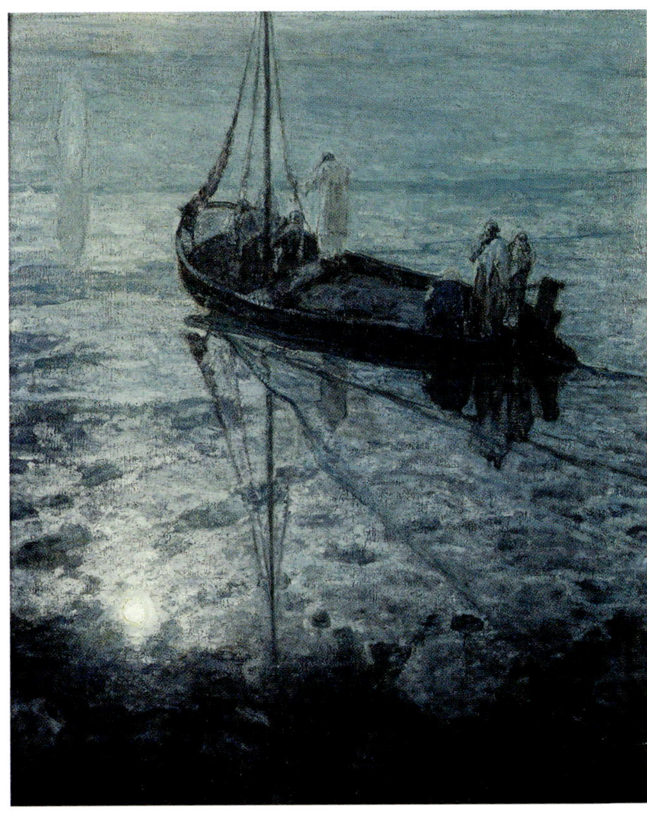

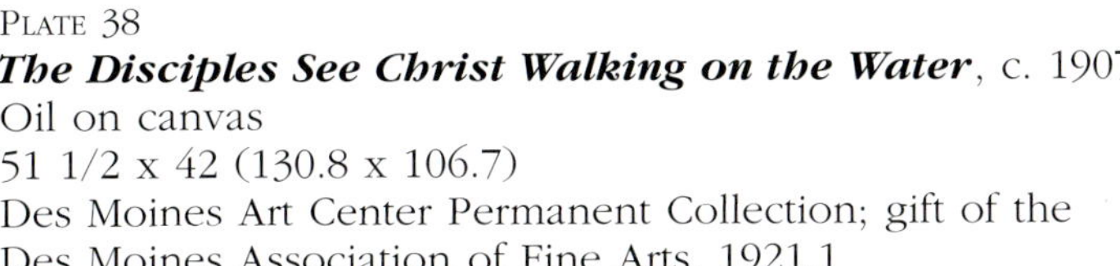

PLATE 38
The Disciples See Christ Walking on the Water, c. 1907
Oil on canvas
51 1/2 x 42 (130.8 x 106.7)
Des Moines Art Center Permanent Collection; gift of the Des Moines Association of Fine Arts, 1921.1

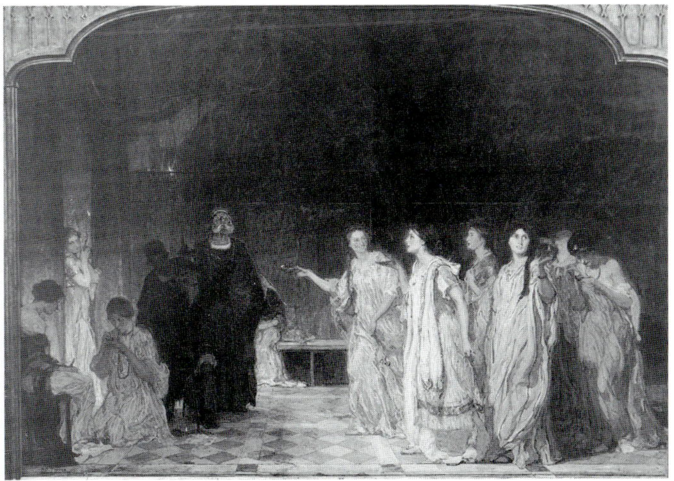

FIGURE 14
The Wise and Foolish Virgins (Behold! The Bridegroom Cometh), c. 1906-07
120 x 180 (304.8 x 457.2)
Location unknown; photograph courtesy of the Pennsylvania Academy of the Fine Arts Archives, Philadelphia

Tanner's ambition and self-confidence were fired by his successes in 1906. During part of that year and all of the next, he tackled the most ambitious undertaking of his career. On a canvas measuring ten by fifteen feet, he painted *The Wise and Foolish Virgins* (fig. 14), also known as *Behold! The Bridegroom Cometh*. The subject was based on a parable in which Jesus warns that the hour of the Second Coming cannot be foretold, thus everyone should be prepared (see Matthew 25:1-13). The five foolish virgins went to a marriage without taking oil for their lamps and missed the arrival of the bridegroom. Tanner described his approach in this work:

> In *Behold! the Bridegroom Cometh* I hoped to take off the hard edge too often given to that parable; how generally the wise virgins are made good but cold and unlovable; how I attempted to show that they were sympathetic for their sisters in distress...by the figure on the left on her knees...trying to bring to life the smoking lamp of her friend—in fact interpreting the whole parable in keeping with our knowledge of the goodness of God and what He considers goodness in us.[246]

Contemporary descriptions of this lost work indicate that it was a visual feast of color, light, and movement.[247] The art critics praised it even more than they had *Lazarus* a decade earlier.[248]

Orientalism, A Theory of Art, and a Flourishing Career, 1908-1914

Henry O. Tanner spent the winter of 1908 on yet another continent in another culture. He visited Algeria, where artists could be subsidized for a few months by the Algerian government at the Villa Abd el Tif.[249]

Several works that can be dated to this period, however, depict sites in Morocco rather than Algeria. Tanner did not travel to Morocco until 1912, but he often used photographs and postcards as sources and *aides-mémoires.* For example, *Palace of Justice, Tangier* (c. 1908; National Museum of American Art), where Moroccan architecture serves as a background for the biblical flight into Egypt, echoes the photographic reproductions in Jon Perdicaris's 1906 *National Geographic* article on his captivity in Morocco.[250] *Entrance to the Customs House, Tangier* (pl. 39) duplicates, with very little artistic license, the composition of the photographic reproduction of the site used in *Enciclopedia Universal Illustrada.*[251] The two conversing figures in the middle ground of the photograph are mirrored in the foreground of the painting. Tanner would certainly have recognized the interaction of this couple because the intensity of their conversation is parallel to the exchange between Nicodemus and Jesus that he depicted in 1899. Stylistically, the elongated figures, loose brushwork, and bright palette of *Customs House* recalls *Return of the Holy Women,* but it can also be considered a blue-sky, moonlight picture.

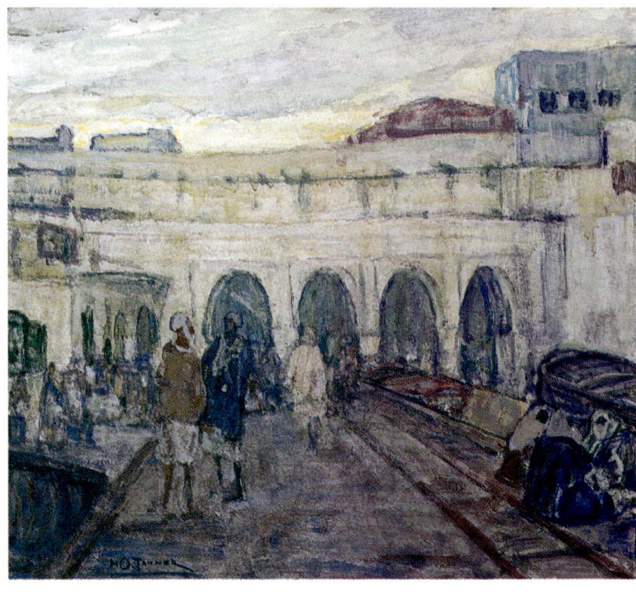

PLATE 39
Entrance to the Customs House, Tangier, c. 1908
Oil on panel
21 x 33 (53.3 x 58.4)
George and Joyce Wein; courtesy of Michael Rosenfeld Gallery, New York

Tanner was back in Paris by March 1908, where *The Wise and Foolish Virgins* was praised for its "color, opulence of artistic resources, profound reverential feeling and wonderful sympathetic effect of pictorial narrative."[252] Yet, as a result of racial insensitivity, Tanner could not bask completely in this glory. The *Baltimore Sun* proclaimed that the painting by an American Negro would win the Medal of Honor at the Salon.[253] The artist described the situation: "Now a paper in Baltimore wanted a photo of this 'Negro.' Of course they had none. So out they go and photograph the first dock hand they come across, and it looked like maybe some of my distant ancestors when they once came from Africa."[254] That the American press could not see past Tanner's race continued to plague the artist.

Henry and Jessie Tanner returned to the United States in November 1908 for the December opening of his first major solo exhibition. Held at the American Art Galleries in New York, it included thirty-three of his religious paintings. Although neither *The Resurrection of Lazarus* nor *Pilgrims at Emmaus* crossed the Atlantic from the Musée du Luxembourg, and the Wilstach Collection refused to send *The Annunciation* from Philadelphia, the exhibition received highly favorable reviews.[255]

The artist took a studio at 14 West 22nd Street, where he planned to remain until April 1909.[256] Apparently he did not produce a great deal of art because of a busy social life. The fiftieth wedding anniversary of Bishop Benjamin Tucker Tanner and Sarah Miller Tanner, as well as the bishop's retirement, were celebrated at a Tanner family reunion in Philadelphia.[257]

By early 1909, Tanner was unquestionably in the top echelon of his field. In April, he was one of twelve artists, along with Mary Cassatt, elected as associate members of the National Academy of Design. He began work on his autobiography for *World's Work*, which appeared during the summer. For this two-part article Tanner drew upon the characterizations of authors who had written about him, such as William J. Simmons in his 1887 *Men of Mark*, W. S. Scarborough in his *Southern Workman* article of 1902, and an anonymous author of a critique that appeared in the *New York Times* in 1908. Tanner's document articulated his artistic convictions and theories:

> It has very often seemed to me that many painters of religious subjects (in our time) seem to forget that their pictures should be as much works of art (regardless of the subject) as are other paintings with less holy subjects. To suppose that the fact of the religious painter having a more elevated subject than his brother artist makes it unnecessary for him to consider his picture as an artistic production, or that he can be less thoughtful about a color harmony, for instance, than he who selects any other subject, simply proves that he is less of an artist than he who gives the subject his best attention.... Religious art has come to mean an uninteresting, inartistic production.... The want of high ideals in religious art will, as in other things, be fatal.[258]

———— ♦ ————

Tanner returned to his adopted country in May 1909. During his mature years he made infrequent visits to the United States, although he continued to exhibit and make sales in America as well as in France.

During 1909 and 1910, Tanner was painting actively and he began to make variations on subjects and compositions from previous years, but with a predominantly blue palette. For example, *The Three Marys* (pl. 40) derives its composition and its focus on three women from *The Wise and Foolish Virgins*, its landscape recalls *The Good Shepherd* (c. 1902-03; Jane Voorhees Zimmerli Art Museum, Rutgers University, New Brunswick, New Jersey); and its architecture reflects Algeria. The subject is rare, however, because only the Gospel of Mark (16:1-4) mentions three women at Jesus's tomb. The three Marys were among the women and men credited with introducing Christianity to France at Les Saintes-Maries-De-La-Mer around 40 A.D. Another individual who was part of this group was Sarah, the black servant of one of the Marys. Tanner would have been especially attracted to the subject due to the inclusion of a black woman. His interest may have been furthered by the fact that Sarah was also the name of one of his sisters. Unfortunately, Tanner did not speak or write about such subtle issues. In fact, a black writer criticized him: "It may be interesting to note that our own great 'colored' artist, Tanner, though making a specialty of Biblical subjects, has not yet painted this one [*Adoration of*

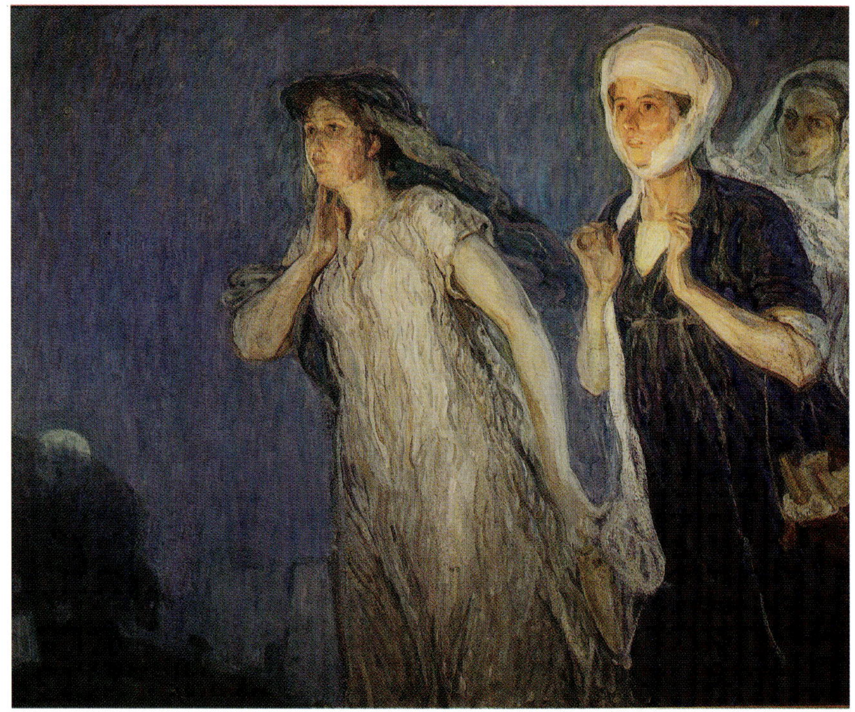

PLATE 40
The Three Marys, c. 1909
Oil on canvas
42 x 50 (106.7 x 127)
Fisk University, Nashville, Tennessee

the Magi] nor any other in which Ethiopians actually or presumably figured."[259] This writer seems to have ignored, or was unaware of, the dark-skinned figures in *The Resurrection of Lazarus.*

The artist also reused the motif of the arrival in Egypt in *The Holy Family* (pl. 41), in which the wood shavings on the floor suggest the interior of a crude shop. Tanner made a variation on his "brown method" by brightening certain areas, such as the green curtains. F. J. Campbell noted that Tanner used color "so variedly that we seem to find new combinations everywhere."[260] His characteristic complex light effects, too, are evident in the painting.

Tanner used a similar stylistic approach in *Christ and His Mother Studying the Scriptures* (pl. 42), an offshoot of his pedagogical motif. The artist's own wife and little son are the models in the picture.[261] Tanner's reflection on Jesus's youth could have been triggered by his own son learning to read and by a passage in the Gospel of Luke (4:16): "So he came to Nazareth, where he had been brought up, and went to synagogue on the Sabbath day as he regularly did. He stood up to read the lesson."

In addition to these religious subjects, Tanner portrayed his immediate environment in works like *Le Touquet* (pl. 43). It depicts an area near his summer home in Trépied on the Brittany coast. The faggot-carrier theme had been popular with French artists at Barbizon and Pont-Aven during the second half of the nineteenth century. Tanner concentrated on artistic effects for this canvas. Rather than his usual play of diagonal, horizontal, and vertical shapes to create a mood, the artist emphasized the surface through the dominant blue tonality with purple accents and directional brushstrokes.

These works, along with a number of other religious and Oriental scenes painted between 1907 and 1910, were shown in a solo exhibition at the Thurber Art Galleries in Chicago during February 1911. In a favorable review of the show in the *Chicago Daily Tribune*, Harriet Monroe called special attention to *The Holy Family, The Disciples See Christ Walking on the Water, Christ and His Mother Studying the Scriptures, Entrance to the Customs House, Tangier*, and *Moonlight, Hebron.*[262]

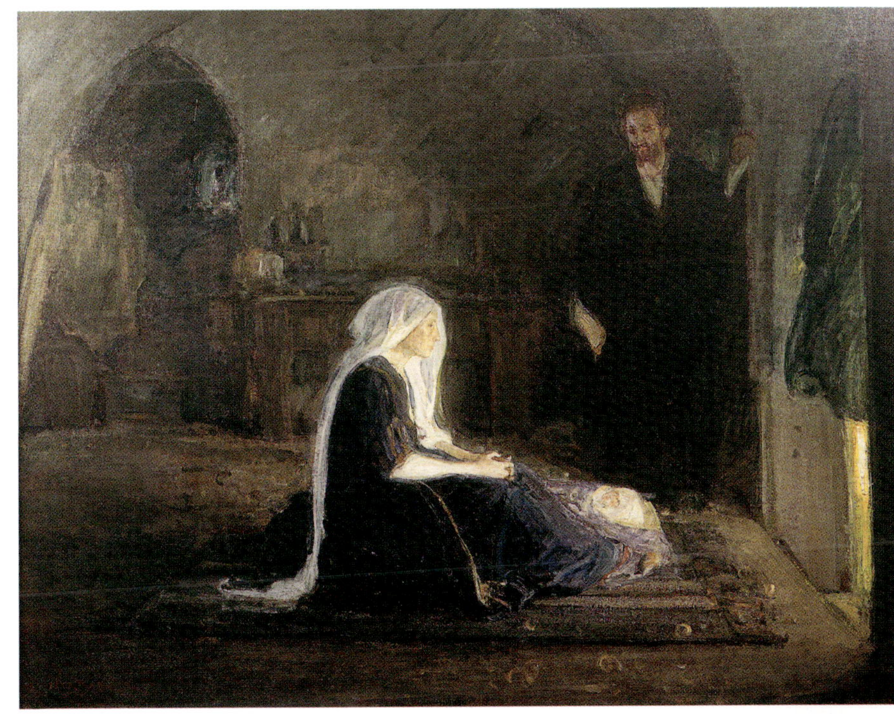

PLATE 41
The Holy Family, c. 1909-10
Oil on canvas
35 x 42 3/4 (88.9 x 108.6)
Muskegon Museum of Art, Michigan; Hackley Picture Fund

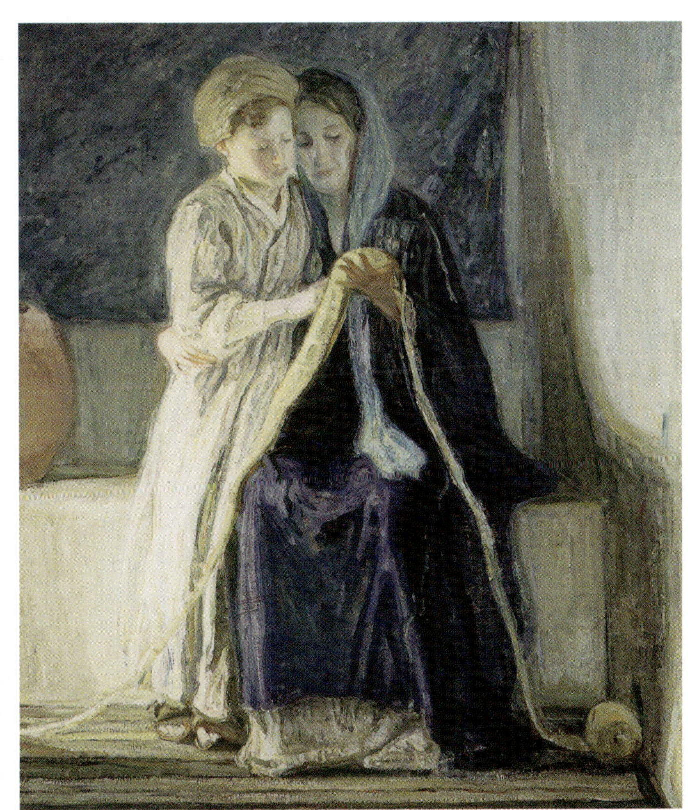

PLATE 42
Christ and His Mother Studying the Scriptures, c. 1909
Oil on canvas
48 3/4 x 40 (123.8 x 101.6)
Dallas Museum of Art; Deaccession Funds

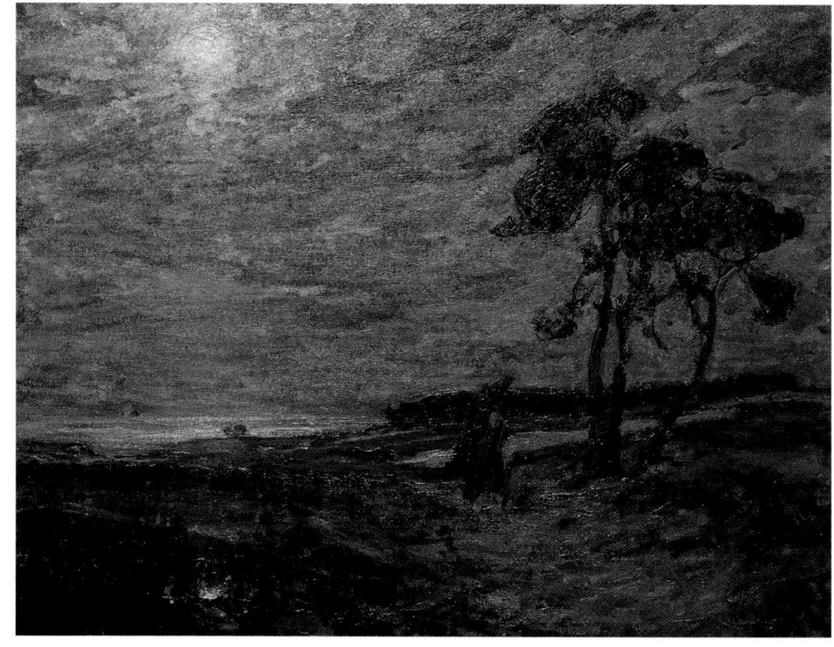

PLATE 43
Le Touquet, c. 1910
Oil on canvas
29 x 36 3/4 (73.7 x 93.3)
Des Moines Art Center Permanent Collection;
gift of Florence L. Carpenter, 1941.5

Tanner attended the opening and remained in the United States during the next month. At this time, academic painters in America were creating narrative scenes in modified versions of Impressionist technique, which by 1911 had become a relatively conventional mode.[263] Contemporary Europe was witnessing the further evolution of modern painting. The Fauvism of Henri Matisse (1869-1954), the Cubism of Pablo Picasso (1881-1973), and the Futurism of Gino Severini (1883-1966) were all leading gradually toward abstract painting.[264] Tanner was thinking about these issues during the summer of 1912. In keeping with his theory of art, Tanner believed that the ultimate effect of these new movements would be a good one: "It will lift up the color scheme, induce greater individuality and freedom, and afford a looser and more open and spontaneous handling of pigments."[265]

During the winter and spring of 1912, Tanner returned to the Near East, this time with notions of modernism in mind. He was based in Tangier, where sketching on site was not encouraged and where there was an outright taboo against portraiture of any kind.[266] However, North Africa offered him a variety of architectural motifs—arched doorways and windows, and interlacing borders of vegetation—and ample demonstrations of the principle of continuous decor, in which surfaces are diversely decorated in vertical and horizontal registers. From Tangier, Tanner went by mule to Tetuan to see an Islamic city uninfluenced by European civilization.[267] Visiting such an unspoiled area gave the artist the opportunity to concentrate on the formal qualities of the Oriental aesthetic, in the manner of such contemporary artists as Matisse, who was in Tangier from late January to mid-April 1912 and drew many of the same scenes as Tanner.

The paintings Tanner produced during this period moved away from his characteristic racial symbolism. Instead, the works reflect the contemporary focus on the ornamental elements of Oriental decoration while

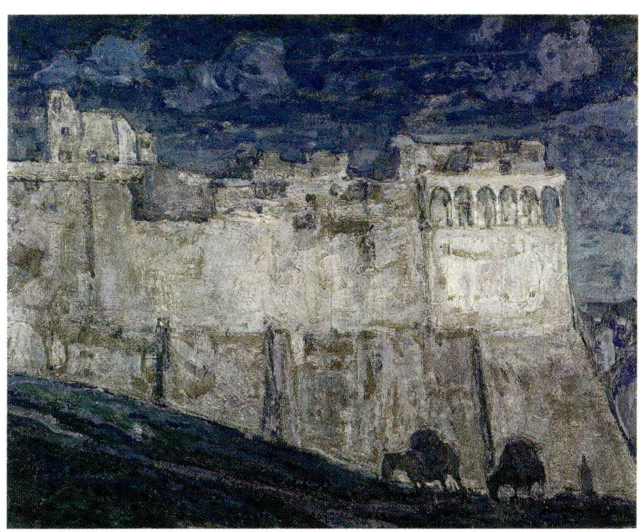

Plate 44
Moonrise, Tangier, c. 1912
Oil on panel
20 x 24 (50.8 x 61)
Hamilton College Collection; gift of Elihu Root

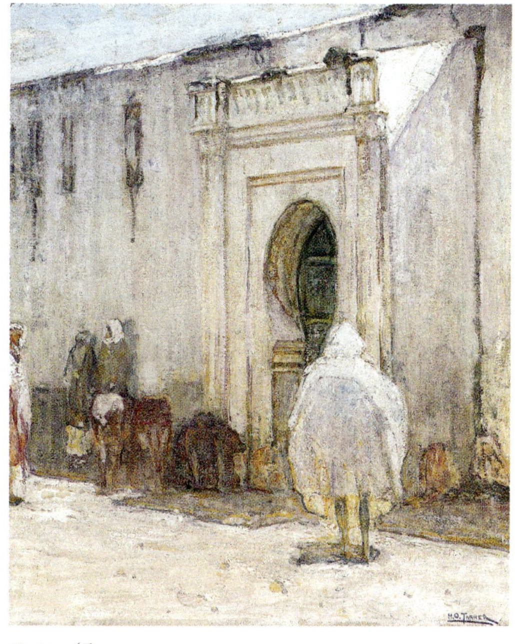

Plate 45
Near East Scene, 1912
Oil and casein on canvas
28 3/4 x 23 1/2 (73 x 59.7)
Des Moines Art Center Permanent Collection; bequest of Edith King Pearson, 1964.76

continuing his interest in moonlight effects. Unlike other American artists who absorbed the French Orientalist tradition, Tanner rendered the Near East with detail and based on firsthand observation, not imagination. In both *Moonrise, Tangier* (pl. 44) and *Near East Scene* (pl. 45) he treated the plunging views, the people, and their dress, as vehicles for exploring form and color. The flat decorative surfaces, achieved through the thick buildup of paint in *Moonrise* and high-keyed palette in *Near East Scene*, are completely modern. Tanner had begun to work out new methods by experimenting with pigments: "He finds that his results are more permanent, when working slowly, thus giving each glazed layer sufficient time to dry and harden."[268] This attention to process was in part a direct response to movements in contemporary art, which often forced attention to the surface of the canvas through the use of color, impasto, and collage.

The successful artist and art critic Clara T. MacChesney saw this body of Oriental work, which included some twenty-five canvases, and wrote: "His present style is much changed. Not only has he a great breadth of vision, but his effects are cooler, grayer in tone and higher in key, not as black and brown in the shadows, or hot in color, as formerly. Thus his new canvases have a more spiritual, dreamlike quality. They are more poetical and show a great advance from earlier efforts."[269]

Tanner showed these works in Chicago at the Thurber Art Galleries and at New York's Knoedler Galleries in early 1913. They received rave reviews in the New York press for the palette, method of application, and quality of emotional sentiment.[270] Tanner's exhibition came just after the International Exhibition of Modern Art, held at the Sixty-Ninth Regiment Armory in New York from February 17 to March 15, 1913, which introduced modern art to the United States. His new modernist pictures must have seemed sympathetic with the innovative European work seen in the Armory show.

Tanner's cooler palette carried over into 1914 in pictures such as *Miraculous Haul of Fishes* (pl. 46). After the resurrection, the apostles came home with empty nets after a night of fishing and they did not recognize the man who advised them, "Cast the nets on the right side of the ship and ye shall find. They cast therefore, and now they were not able to draw it for the multitude of fishes." Then John recognized Jesus (see John 21:3-7). Tanner concentrated on the moment in which the apostles pull in the heavy net, so full of fish that the boat tilts to the sea. The water roils and ripples with unseen fish, unlike the calm surface upon which another boat passes smoothly in the distance. A gleaming spot of light falls where the fish gather. The principal standing figure, who mans an oar and is without a cloak, can be identified as Simon Peter, who "was naked." The importance of this fisherman of men is illustrated further by the halolike glow around his head. All of the elements of the composition are held together by Tanner's characteristic blend of horizontals, verticals, and diagonals, and new high-keyed palette. He presented this work as his reception piece to the National Academy of Design when he was elected full academician in 1927.

During 1914 Tanner continued to exhibit in America at Pittsburgh and Chicago, and in Europe at London and Paris, and the critics continued to sing his praises. That year marked his last showing at the annual Paris Salon, the initial source of his artistic motivation and fame during the 1890s.

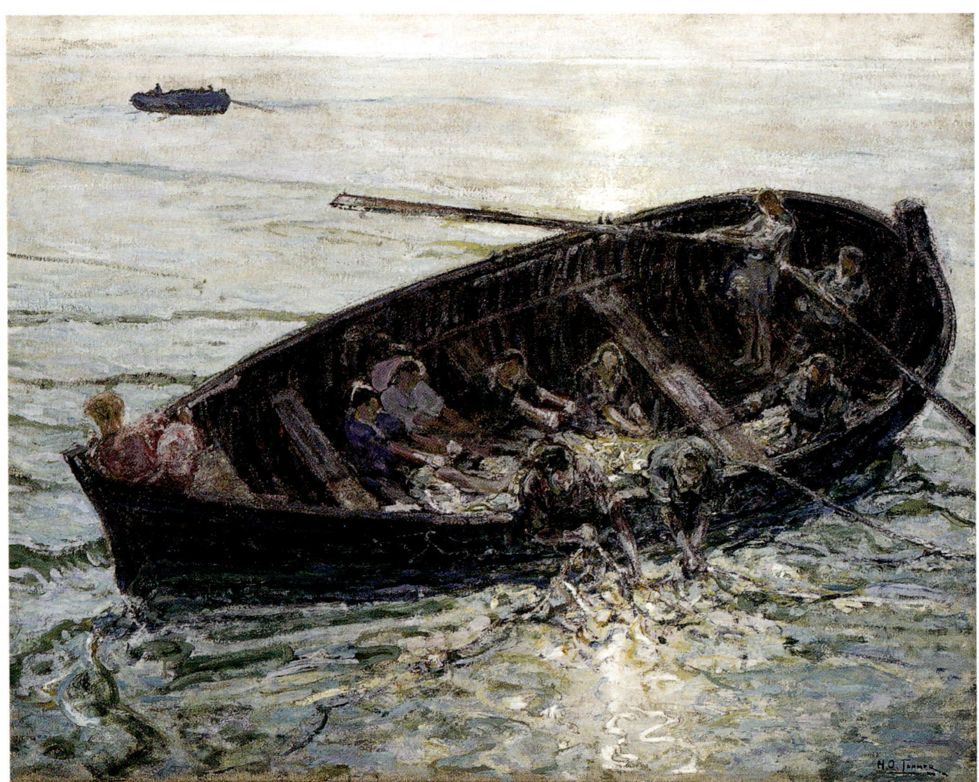

PLATE 46
Miraculous Haul of Fishes,
c. 1913-14
Oil on canvas
38 x 47 1/2 (96.5 x 120.7)
National Academy of Design

World War I, The Red Cross and Race, and Post-War Revival, 1914-1925

The energy, stylistic change, and exploration of new mediums that had characterized Tanner's career from 1908 came to an end late in the summer of 1914. Artistically, from this time on, he simply made pictures—when he was so inclined. In fact, Tanner produced very little between late 1914 and 1917. By early August 1914 the great powers of Europe were embroiled in the First World War. The Tanners were at their summer home on the Brittany coast, where Tanner was serving as president of the Société Artistique de Picardie, when President Woodrow Wilson proclaimed American neutrality in the European conflict. Americans in the region began evacuating; the Tanners went to England in late August and returned to France two weeks later.[271]

Tanner lost interest in making art as a result of world events. He wrote to Atherton Curtis on September 14:

> The Germans are on the retreat, Amiens evacuated, etc.—soon you can work say some of my friends—but how can I? What right have I to do, what right to be comfortable? In London I saw some of the Canadian contingent and many volunteers, fine, handsome, intelligent men going out to fight, to suffer and to die for principles which I believe in as strongly as they and sit down to paint a little picture, and thus make myself happy—No it cannot be done.[272]

The artist's outlook was certainly aggravated by the death of his mother exactly one month earlier.

Tanner did manage to record war activity during this period in *War Scene, Etaples, France* (pl. 47). Etaples, located near his summer home in Trépied, had from 75,000 to 100,000 British, Canadian, and Australian troops on a continual basis.[273] This work is far from ambitious and the palette does not reflect the high-keyed colors typical of the preceding years. In fact, the golden tan, green, and pink palette—along with controlled juicy brushstrokes—hark back to *The Young Sabot Maker*.

During the spring of 1915 Tanner returned to the United States to see his family and promote sales. He was not offering new works; in a letter to the collector Raymond Wyer, Tanner referred only to *Return of the Holy Women* and *Christ and His Mother Studying the Scriptures*, pictures painted years earlier.[274]

For a few months Tanner was away from the disasters in Europe, but the war encroached even at home: on March 28, 1915, an American went down on a British ship; on April 29 a German airplane attacked a U.S. merchant ship; and 128 Americans died on May 7 when the *Lusitania* was sunk.[275] Tanner set sail for Europe, despite the military troubles, and was in France on June 1, 1915.[276] Apparently, he felt uncomfortable in the United States as a result of the racial climate. When planning, with grave reservations, a return trip the next year, Tanner was advised by Atherton Curtis: "Spend your time quietly in Trépied and Paris and keep away from a country whose love of liberty and fair play is not so extraordinary as it tried to make the world believe."[277]

The artist continued to exhibit his work during the war years and reviews were favorable.[278] However, his general state of depression must have been deepened by the death of Thomas Eakins on June 25, 1916. Tanner's frame of mind is revealed in a letter to him from Atherton Curtis:

> In your special case today you must remember that you are living in times that are not conducive to artistic production.... You have been trying in these two years of awful anxiety and awful suffering to produce a work of art. It is not strange that at such a time, even more than ordinary times, your judgment should find itself at fault on your looking back on what you have done. It is naturally discouraging to be stopped suddenly this way. You will have to try to encourage yourself by thinking of the beautiful things done in the past by you and start again for the future.[279]

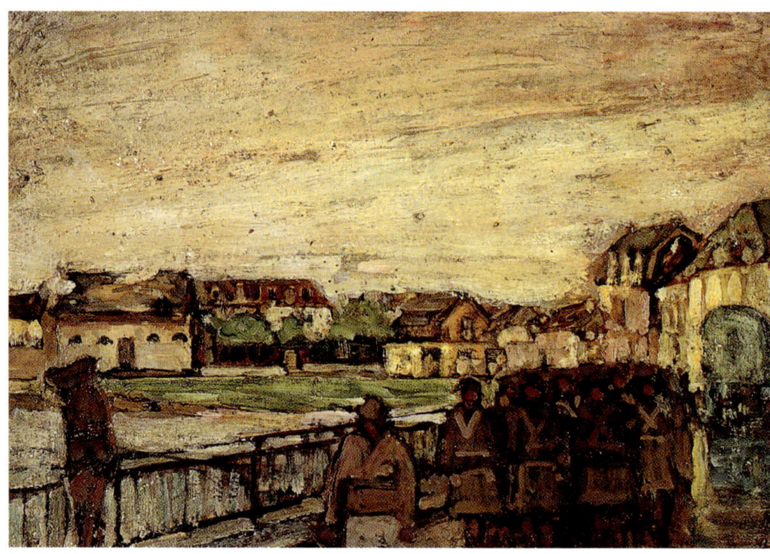

PLATE 47
War Scene, Etaples, France, c. 1914
Oil on cardboard
9 1/2 x 13 1/8 (24 x 33.3)
Clark Atlanta University Collection of African American Art

Tanner might very well have taken heart from Curtis's encouraging words and turned back to his earlier successful work. He made a third rendition of *Daniel in the Lions' Den* (c. 1917; Los Angeles County Museum of Art), which was the source of his first official Salon recognition some twenty years earlier. Pondering broad concerns of human suffering, the artist painted *The Good Shepherd* (pl. 48), which follows Jesus's allegory of himself as the good shepherd and his followers as his flock (see John 10:14-16). Tanner presented the subject in a panoramic landscape, which, with its squarish format, lower viewpoint, and mauve, blue, and lavender brushstrokes, interlaced with the primarily green palette, appears strikingly beautiful and modern. Also from this period is the posthumous *Portrait of Booker T. Washington* (pl. 49). Commissioned by the Iowa Federation of Colored Women's Clubs, Tanner rendered Washington frontally in a shallow space as he had done with his parents exactly twenty years earlier in Kansas City. The liquid and quickly-brushed paint forms puddles of lights and darks—an approach that he had used in *Christ Learning to Read* (c. 1917; Des Moines Art Center). In addition to the honor of depicting the great man, who had himself furthered the artist's career in the early 1900s, the Washington commission provided Tanner with much-needed income.

———— ♦ ————

Tanner's artistic production was again placed in abeyance when the United States entered the war in April of 1917. He was almost fifty-eight, which precluded his enlistment in the racially-segregated army, but he found his own way to aid the war effort. The artist devised a plan of growing produce and raising livestock on unused land around hospitals, using convalescing soldiers as a work force, in order to boost morale. This project may have been inspired by Booker T. Washington, who encouraged students to be self-reliant.[280] With the support of Walter Hines Page, then U.S. Ambassador to England and former editor of *World's Work*, Tanner's plan was accepted by the American Red Cross in France. In December, he enlisted in the Red Cross with the rank of lieutenant in the Department of Public Information; he was attached to the Farm Service Bureau and put his plan into effect.[281] By the summer of 1918, Tanner's scheme was an unqualified success and had spread from Vittel to Chaumont, Neufchateau, and other areas in the Military Advance Zone. He was promoted to assistant director of the Farm and Garden Services for the American Red Cross.[282]

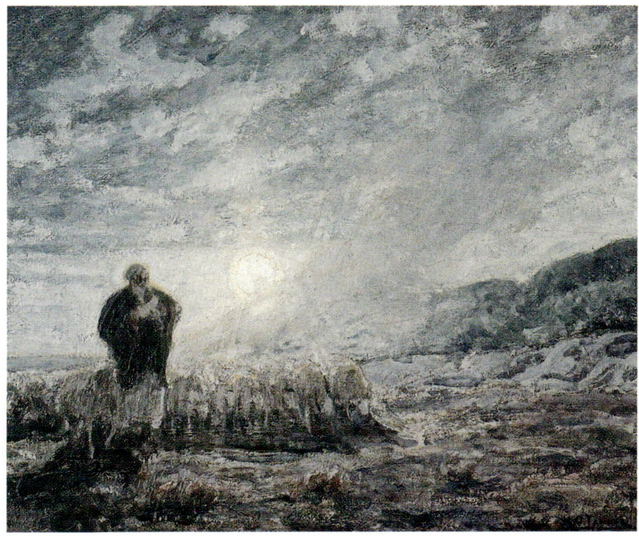

PLATE 48
The Good Shepherd, c. 1917
Oil on canvas
20 1/4 x 24 1/8 (51.4 x 61.3)
New Orleans Museum of Art; gift of Dr. I. M. Cline, New Orleans

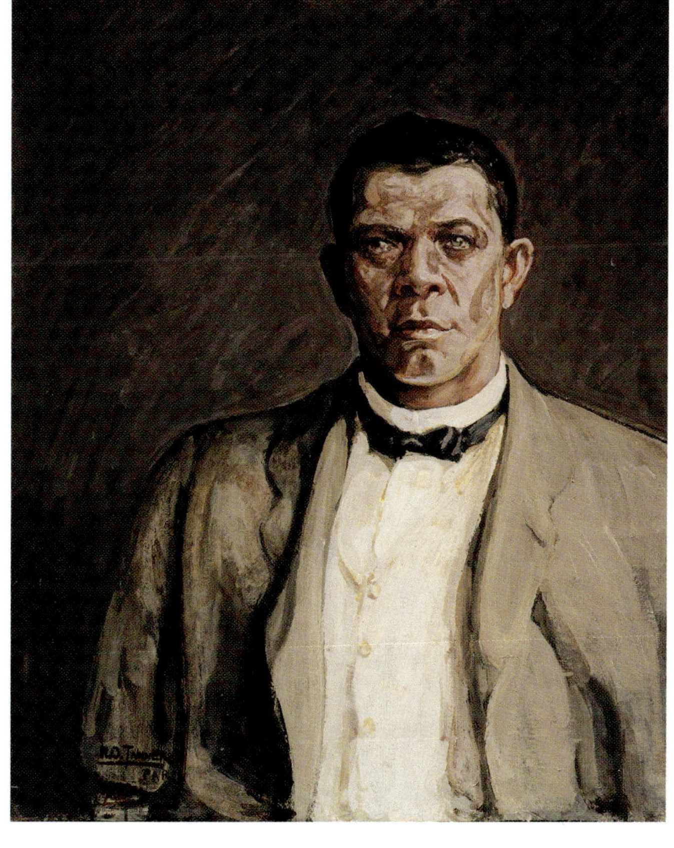

PLATE 49
Portrait of Booker T. Washington, 1917
Oil on canvas
31 3/4 x 25 5/8 (80.6 x 65.1)
State Historical Society of Iowa, Des Moines

In spite of Tanner's successful management of this innovative program, Red Cross histories of the era do not mention his practical contribution.[283] This oversight might be explained by an incident that Tanner recorded as "Some remembrances of the Red Cross." He noted:

> It had been a rather gay dinner when Capt. R— continuing his accounts of a trip to the front which had fired us all said "but we will have to kill several of those niggers down home before we will be able to get them back in their place."... Capt. R— and I had seen I to I [sic] on many subjects and had become quite friends which surprised me—as I knew the first time I met him that he was from the South...and like a good many people from the South he talked a great deal on religion. After the remark called forth by I have forgotten what he continued quite a tirade against the

> Negro. There was little said for or against his leading remark, as nearly all forgot to apply any of Christ's Spirit upon a subject in which their own prejudices and weaknesses were concerned.[284]

Racism and a callous disregard for his presence continued to haunt him.

By September 1918 Tanner's desire to produce art, rather than vegetables and livestock, had been rekindled. He was granted permission to sketch in the Military Advance Zone. His permit specifically limited him to depicting Red Cross activities, and all his work was subject to prevailing wartime censorship.[285]

The results of these art expeditions, and Tanner's subtle response to "the tirade against the Negro," can be seen in the drawing *A.R.C. Canteen, World War I* (pl. 50) and the painting *American Red Cross Canteen at the Front* (pl. 51). The subjects of both works are similar to postcards published by the Red Cross based on photographs by Paul Rainey (dates unknown), although it does not appear that Tanner based his works on these postcards. The similarity of the images may be due in part to wartime censorship, as both he and Rainey worked within the same restrictive guidelines. Unique to Tanner's work is their depiction of black soldiers. In the drawing, the artist emphasized this figure through having the viewer look over the waiter's shoulder into the black soldier's face. He further stands out through the contrast of his dark skin against the highlights around him, which, along with the slashing vertical charcoal lines, enliven the entire surface. In the painting, Tanner crowded several figures into a shallow interior space and suggested even more figures beyond the doorway. It is through the light in the background that we notice the black soldier. These two pictures may be the only official Red Cross images that acknowledge the presence of black people in the First World War.

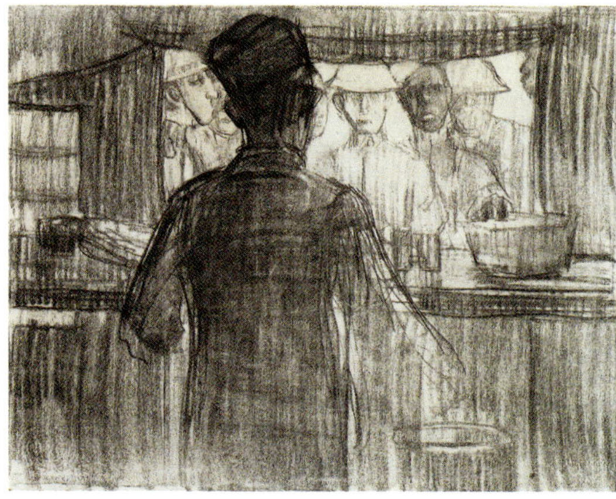

PLATE 50
A.R.C. Canteen, World War I, 1918
Charcoal on paper
17 1/2 x 22 (44.5 x 55.9)
National Museum of American Art, Smithsonian Institution; gift of Mr. and Mrs. Norman B. Robbins

Tanner mustered out of military service in June 1919 and, despite ill health, continued to be active as an artist. He painted *The Arch* (pl. 52), also called *Les Fêtes de Morts*, "a souvenir of the solemn festival of 13 July 1919, in honor of the dead."[286] France's war losses were some 1,385,000. Tanner depicted the event with his characteristic blue and green palette, but with a liquid quality. In order to create the throng, he drew the figures in a cursory manner and used the subdued light to accent some of them.

In September 1919, Robert C. Vose offered Tanner an exhibition in his Boston gallery. This show provided an impetus for his production over the next year. It opened in January 1921 and included ten old and new works of familiar subjects. The show did not generate much response in the art press, but George W. Forbes of the *A.M.E. Church Review* covered it. He wrote: "His mode of expressing his feeling has been refined to the most exquisite simplicity, directness and freedom from exaggeration or barbaric crudeness. A scion of the

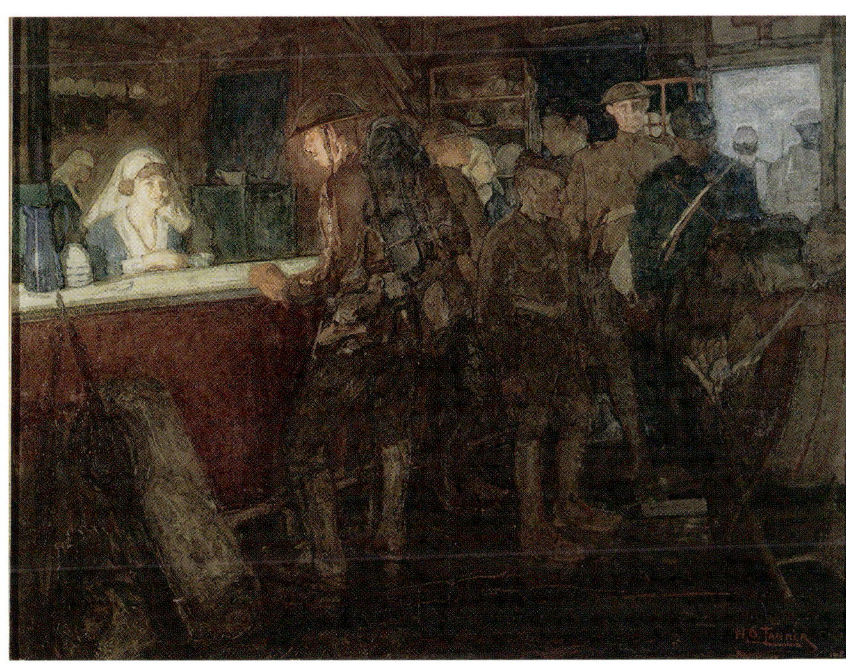

PLATE 51
American Red Cross Canteen at the Front, 1918
Oil on canvas
48 x 61 (121.9 x 154.9)
American Red Cross

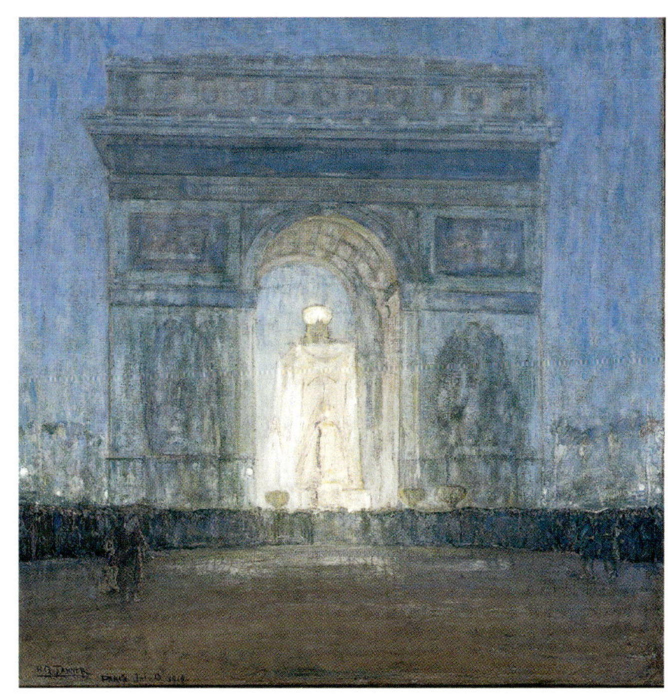

PLATE 52
The Arch, 1919
Oil on canvas
39 1/4 x 38 3/8 (99.7 x 97.5)
The Brooklyn Museum; gift of Alfred W. Jenkins 32.10

race that is supposed to revel in jazz, he belongs in artistry with Cesar Franck."[287] However, Forbes chided Tanner: "It impresses that this representation of one of the 'silent, sullen races' has depicted his Son of God and his Holy Women as Nordic blondes."[288]

Toward the end of the year, Tanner painted one of his rare Old Testament scenes, *Moses in the Bullrushes* (pl. 53). It includes elongated figures, showing the influence of El Greco and Velásquez, similar to those of an earlier *Hiding of Moses* (location unknown).[289] The technique of painting with a nearly dry brush is like that seen in the *Good Shepherd* of 1917. The artist completely reversed himself in *Etaples Fisher Folk* (pl. 54) by returning to his brownish palette of *Two Disciples at the Tomb*. The use of a lantern as a light source, which appears in several paintings of this period, harks back to the *Night (Return of the Fisherman)* (1905; Herbert F. Johnson Museum of Art, Cornell University, Ithaca, New York). However, the mixture of oil and tempera shows his continued experiment with pigments to activate the surface.

On December 26, 1921, Tanner was proposed for the prestigious Cross of the Legion of Honor, the highest honor the French government bestowed upon nonmilitary personnel.[290] In April 1923 the award was confirmed, in recognition of the fact that Tanner had "exhibited his works and received numerous awards in the French Salons since 1894."[291] Tanner produced his last illustration in 1922. *Head of a Bethlehem Woman* appeared on the cover of the *Crisis* in the December issue that year.

Tanner's major undertaking of the early 1920s was *Two Disciples at the Tomb* (pl. 55), a revision of the 1905 painting of the same subject. He executed numerous studies for this painting culled from the Gospel of John (20:4-6). The youthful John kneels at the door to the sepulcher of Jesus, and Peter is seen only as a dim figure approaching in the background. The large figure of John dominates the composition. His posture and the verticality of the fluted folds of his garment further underscore the importance of this figure, which is illuminated by the supernatural light from within the sepulcher. The thickly textured paint, blue-green palette, and striated brushstrokes, which emphasize the canvas surface, are characteristic of Tanner's style during the mid-1920s and of his continued experimentation with pigments. Also typical is the manner in which color and background light define the time of day—in this scene, night, as dawn approaches.

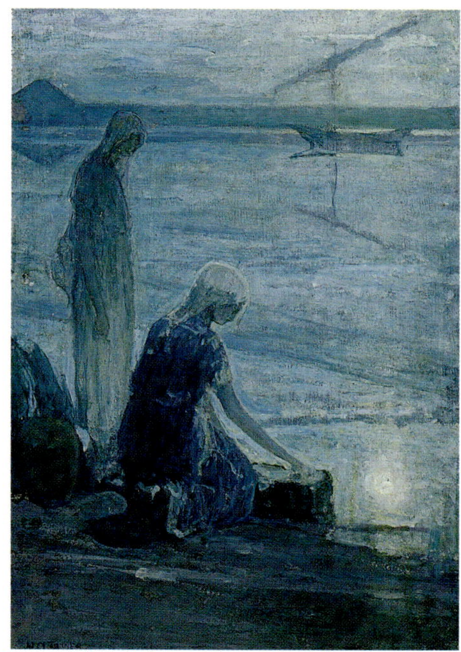

PLATE 53
Moses in the Bullrushes, 1921
Oil on wood
22 3/8 x 15 1/4 (56.8 x 38.7)
National Museum of American Art,
Smithsonian Institution; gift of
Mr. and Mrs. Norman B. Robbins

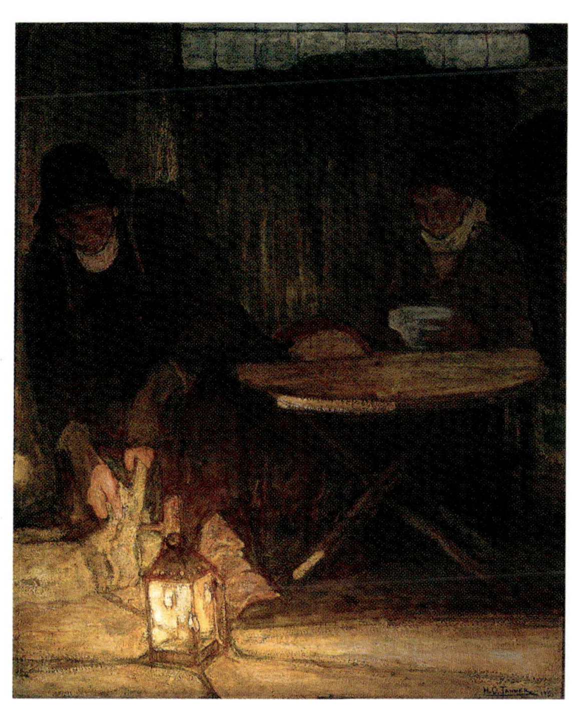

PLATE 54
Etaples Fisher Folk, 1923
Tempera and oil on canvas
47 5/16 x 38 5/16 (120.2 x 97.3)
High Museum of Art, Atlanta, Georgia;
J. J. Haverty Collection, 36.16

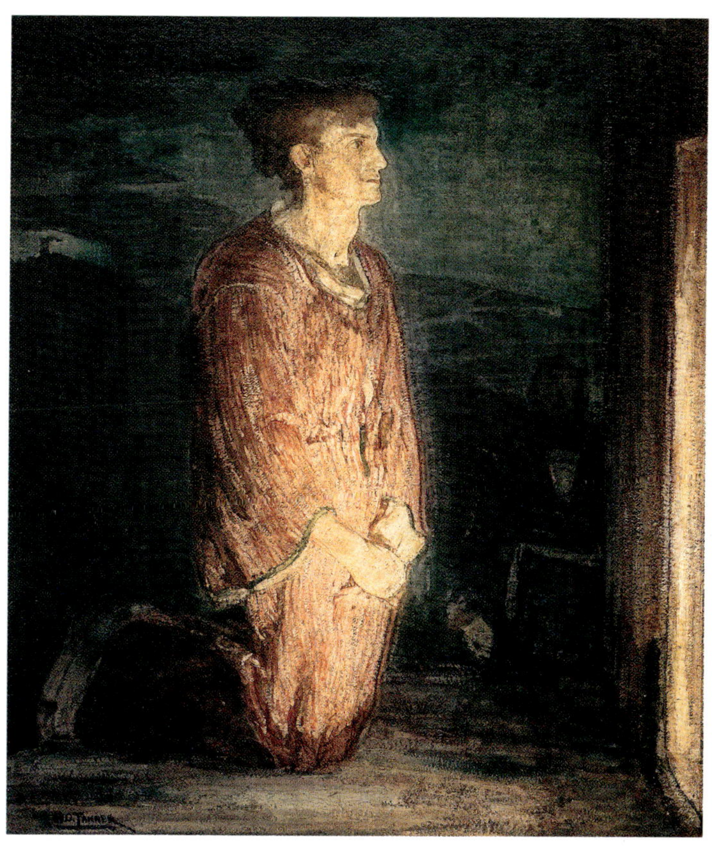

PLATE 55
Two Disciples at the Tomb, c. 1923
Oil on board
51 1/2 x 43 1/4 (130.8 x 109.9)
Merton D. Simpson

In November 1923 Tanner boarded a ship for New York to participate in his third solo exhibition there and the last major show of his lifetime. It opened at Grand Central Art Galleries on January 21, 1924, and included nineteen familiar religious and genre titles. The show received two mostly favorable reviews in the *New York Times*.[292] Harrison Morris, Tanner's good friend and the retired director of the Pennsylvania Academy, appealed to the president of the Metropolitan Museum of Art for the purchase of a work out of the Grand Central exhibition. Morris's efforts were not successful.[293]

For Tanner, the mid-1920s were a time of professional success and personal tragedy. Bishop Benjamin Tucker Tanner died on January 15, 1923, and two old friends from the Société Artistique de Picardie—Henry Boddington (dates unknown) and Paul Bartlett (1865-1925)—both died two years later. But the most damaging blow was the fatal illness that had afflicted his wife since 1924. Jessie Tanner died on September 25, 1925, leaving a tremendous void in the artist's life. Married for nearly twenty-six years, their happiness had defied the stern advice against mixed marriages given in the Book of Daniel (2:43): "And whereas thou sawest iron mixed with miry clay, they shall mingle themselves with the seed of men, but they shall not cleave one to another, even as iron is not mixed with clay." When Tanner lost his "iron" his active career as an artist was essentially over.

Semi-Retirement and the Final Years, 1926-1937

Henry Ossawa Tanner was sixty-seven years old on June 21, 1926, in failing health, and faced with a series of personal crises. He had lost his motivation to make art with the death of his wife the preceding year. He was also preoccupied with a drawn-out lawsuit against the Bethel A.M.E. Church in Philadelphia regarding the commission of a bronze commemorative plaque of Bishop Richard Allen.[294] Tanner certainly must have been hurt by the appearance in Joseph Pennell's 1925 autobiography of the section entitled "The Coming of the Nigger," a thinly veiled discussion of Tanner as a student at the Pennsylvania Academy in 1880-81.[295] The artist was also, for the most part, neglected by the mainstream art world. A critic of the 1926 annual exhibition in Chicago was an exception and called attention to "the reverence, the mystery, the faith which breathes in all of Mr. Tanner's works."[296] The lofty perch that he had occupied during the first decade and a half of the twentieth century was eclipsed by artists like Henri Matisse and Pablo Picasso and their new renditions of color and forms of construction.[297] Finally, Tanner's son, Jesse, was hospitalized in London with a nervous breakdown in 1927.

That Tanner's late works display little interest in current artistic developments is not surprising given the artist's age. This can be seen in *At the Gates* (pl. 56). It is a variation on the flight-into-Egypt theme. In spite of its beauty, the surface of the painting is not as painterly or layered with color as *Two Disciples at the Tomb*. The fact that Tanner did not embrace new modes was recognized by a critic for the *New York World*: "The artist's work seems to have changed hardly at all since his last appearance here [in 1913]. He still sticks to the cool color arrangements, in which blue predominates, and within its limited range plays slight variations in closely related tone and color."[298]

The artist had a few bright moments in 1927. He completed *Nicodemus Coming to Christ*, which had been commissioned by the Cheyney Training School for Teachers in Pennsylvania. (This painting does not count among his most successful efforts.) *At the Gates* was awarded a bronze medal and a $250 cash prize at the National Arts Club in New York; it was purchased by the Atlanta collector J. J. Haverty, who became one of Tanner's keenest supporters during the late 1920s. The National Academy of Design in New York elected him an academician.[299] He became good friends with his niece Sadie Tanner Mossell Alexander and her husband,

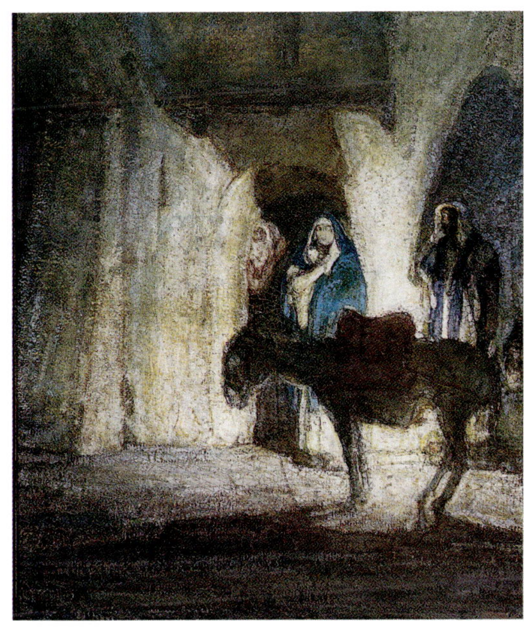

PLATE 56
At the Gates, c. 1926
Oil on panel
24 x 19 (61 x 48.3)
Private collection

Raymond Pace Alexander. Their faithful correspondence over the last decade of the artist's life was a source of intellectual stimulation and comfort.

Tanner's energy seems to have increased around 1930, but by no means to its previous level. He wrote to J. S. Carpenter, his supporter and representative in Des Moines:

> I have 5 or 6 pictures underway—all unfinished—but I hope soon to remedy this state of affairs. I have not changed my principal at this date—unless I believe in a canvas I do not send it out—However, things are beginning to change and I have two which I hope to finish within the month.... I have been working on a tempera mixture for the last 5 or 6 years and have finally a wonderful binder. I am now using it exclusively and I am sure you will find no loss of quality in my painting.[300]

The results of Tanner's complicated medium during the last phase of his career can be seen in *The Lost Sheep* (pl. 57) and *Disciples Healing the Sick* (pl. 58). The subject of the former painting was familiar, but the latter was new. *Disciples Healing the Sick* continues Tanner's practice of rendering specific Bible scriptures. While the painting has previously been interpreted as representing a generic miracle, it seems to relate specifically to the Acts of the Apostles (5:15-16): "Insomuch that they brought forth the sick into the streets, and laid them on beds and couches, that at the least the shadow of Peter passing by might overshadow some of them. There came also a multitude out of the cities round about into Jerusalem, bringing sick folks, and them who were vexed with unclean spirits; and they were healed every one."

Both of these paintings are characterized by a crusty build-up of pigments that echo the use of collage in the early phases of the Cubist movement. They share the patterned brushstrokes of Tanner's *Two Disciples at the Tomb* and enamellike surfaces that call to mind thirteenth-century French Limoges enamels. Atherton Curtis, Tanner's dearest friend and long-time financial supporter, compared the artist's mixing methods to that of the fourteenth-century Flemish artists Jan and Hubert Van Eyck (c. 1390-1441 and 1366-1426, respectively). Unfortunately, Tanner never commented on Curtis's suggestion.[301]

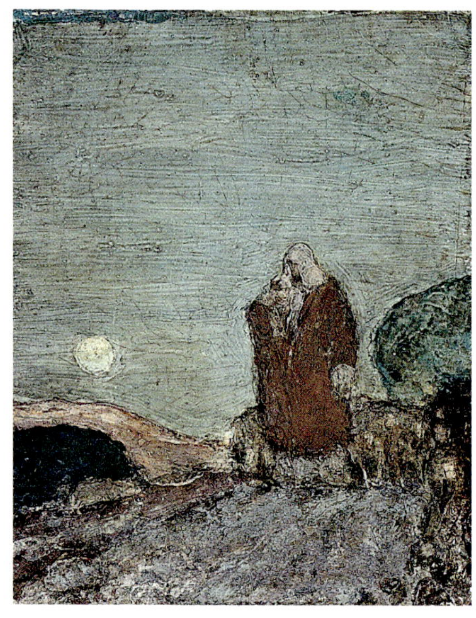

PLATE 57
The Lost Sheep, c. 1930
Oil and tempera on paperboard
10 5/8 x 8 1/8 (27 x 20.7)
The Menil Collection

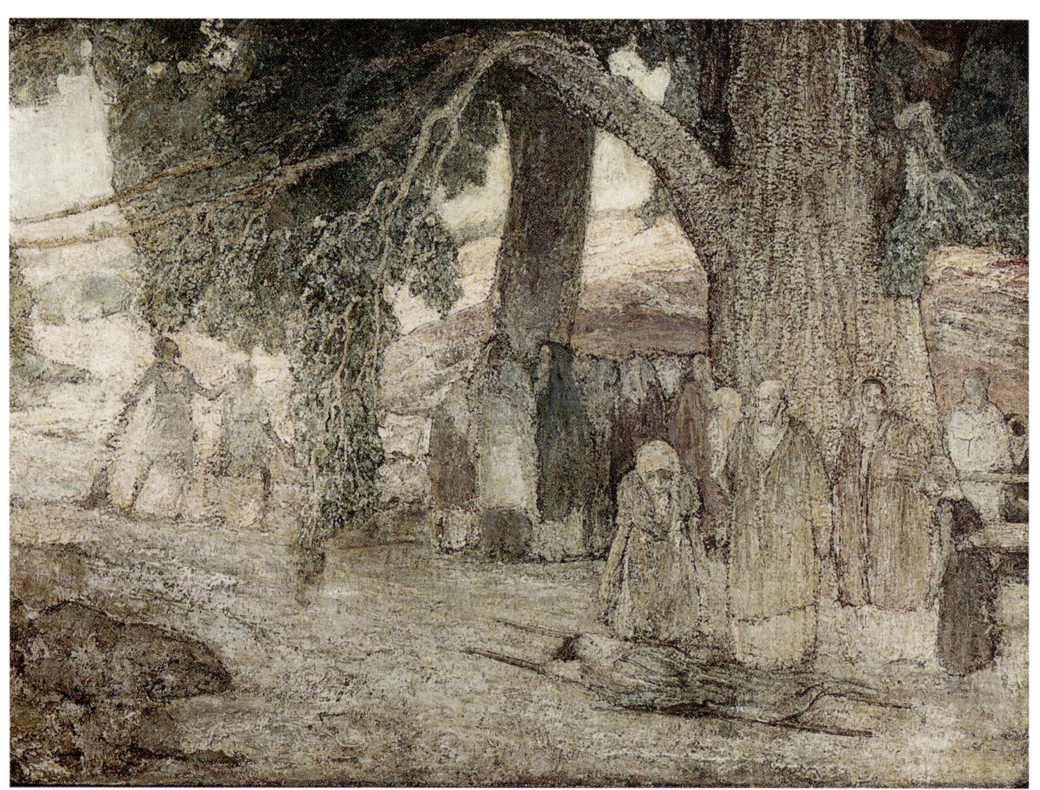

PLATE 58
Disciples Healing the Sick,
c. 1930
Oil on cardboard
36 x 48 (91.4 x 121.9)
Clark Atlanta University Collection
of African American Art

The size and handling of *The Lost Sheep* suggests that Tanner took an earlier, existing study for a painting and imposed his complicated tempera medium on it. The same approach of reworking is recognizable in a small version of *Gateway in Tangier* (c. 1924; private collection).

The final years of Henry Ossawa Tanner's life and career coincided with the Great Depression. When the stock market crashed in 1929, Tanner had orders on hand worth eighty thousand francs, nearly all of which were lost to him. His agent J. S. Carpenter outlined the bleakness of the economy in September 1931:

> The times in this country are very strenuous.... In fact, we are in the worst depression this country has known for many years, and it has almost reached the stage of a panic.... Our Art Association has suspended activities for the year. This is, we are not going to ask our members for any membership dues, and will simply fill our gallery with a loan collection of pictures and let it hang through the year.[302]

As the Depression wore on, unemployment reached staggering levels and blacks learned the cruel truth of the saying "last to be hired, first to be fired."[303] In 1933 Tanner was unhappy to learn that one of his African-American patrons, John Nail, had been adversely affected: "I was so very sorry to hear that Nail was the only man of 'our group' who ever bought one of my pictures to be forced to sell. It is too bad but I do not suppose if he had not bought them he would have had the $1200—(or more) stored away when he could have called upon it."[304] Despite the hard times, Tanner found time to encourage younger black artists, such as Hale Woodruff (1900-1980) and Palmer Hayden (1890-1973), and the poet Countee Cullen (1903-1946).[305]

During these troubled days, Tanner found himself in increasingly poor health. He wrote to his favorite sibling, Mary Tanner Mossell: "I have been having some trouble with my eyes, and I am only within the last weeks or so been using them. So it is small doses of writing and reading.... Have orders ahead for two or three pictures of good size, but the trouble is to get them done."[306] He did not sell a single work in 1933, probably because he did not finish any.[307] However, he retained his prowess as a draughtsman. In *Study for Mary, Return from the Crucifixion* (pl. 59), Tanner used the flowing lines of the model's headdress and arm as things of beauty in themselves. The darks and lights, achieved with the edge of the crayon and using a minimum of rubbing, emphasize details and animate the composition. The face, with its portraitlike quality, is one of the most expressive in Tanner's oeuvre. The mature artist understood sadness and presented it here as if it were palpable.

During the mid-1930s, Tanner was again distracted by a lawsuit to recover a cash loan he had made to Clarence Cameron White, an African-American composer and professor of music at Hampton University. Further bad news came early in 1934: J. J. Haverty canceled his option on *Supper at Emmaus* (c. 1934; Merton Simpson) because "it was now three years since this picture was ordered...and the depression has made us all poor."[308] Haverty also complained about the condition of *Road to Emmaus*, already in his collection, asking Tanner to repair it or exchange it for a work painted in his earlier, nonexperimental style. The artist ended up exchanging the award-winning *Etaples Fisher Folk* (pl. 53) for *Emmaus*, a transaction that again left him less well off.[309] Yet, Tanner's financial plight was not desperate; he continued to receive a monthly stipend from Atherton Curtis.[310]

Tanner's public career fell into relative obscurity. In the mid-1930s, the black printmaker Albert Smith (1896-1940), who had lived in France since 1933, wrote to the African-American bibliophile Arthur Schomburg: "Sometime ago, you remember, you asked me to see about a Tanner,—well he is a mystery painter to me—his works are not on display in Paris dealers, and there are but one or two in the museums, where they go to I don't know."[311]

The artist's situation improved slightly early in 1935 when he sold a painting, *Flight into Egypt* (1935; private collection), to his cousin Maudelle B. Bousfield in Chicago. This is a familiar subject and the composition

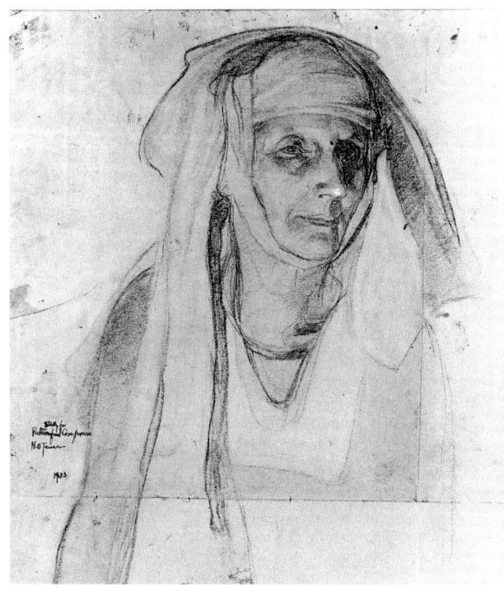

PLATE 59
Study for Mary, Return from the Crucifixion, c. 1933
Pencil and conte crayon on paper mounted on paperboard
15 1/16 x 14 3/16 (39.6 x 37.6)
National Museum of American Art, Smithsonian Institution; gift of Mr. and Mrs. Norman B. Robbins

echoes his previous renditions. The attenuated trees are abstractions of the type found in *Le Touquet.* Tanner himself pointed out that "in fact it had on a small scale the same light problem as *The Disciples at the Tomb* in Chicago."[312] On the other hand, the beautiful enamellike surface belongs to the best creations of the African-American artist's final years.

In spite of this success and inclusion in juried exhibitions during the period, the artist's intimate correspondence to his niece Sadie T. M. Alexander and her husband, Raymond, was spiked with the fatalistic *D.V.*, the French equivalent of "God willing."[313] Moreover, in November 1935, the artist had a fall while walking the streets of Paris and was admitted to the American hospital. His one-day stay there and the attitude of the staff led him to initiate yet another law suit, further distracting him from his art.[314]

Tanner described his work habits and way of life to Erwin S. Barrie, his dealer and the director of the Grand Central Art Galleries in the spring of 1936:

> My health is quite a little better so that nearly everyday I work on small pictures and with some success but I am not able yet to commence new pictures of any importance, and do not see myself doing so this summer. I have given up my studio in Paris [to Jean Hélion (1904-1987)] which I have had for 30 years and it is only in the summer I could work on a [large] picture.... I am then in the country and have more rooms. This does not mean that the quality of the work has lost but that I am not so energetic and can do less—and also that I have financial worries along with it. The exchange value of the $ being only 60 cents has very much upset me financially. The money I had been able to save I had put into property and now my property is mostly rented to work people who cannot find work and those houses which formerly made a good income now bring only enough to pay taxes and not always enough.... Please excuse this wandering letter, what I mean to say is that though I am better than last summer I still have to avoid any strain that would overdo myself.[315]

Tanner spent the summer of 1936 at the estate of Atherton Curtis in Bourron Seine-et-Marne. He produced at least two new paintings—*Landscape: Early Frost* and *Landscape With Four Poplars*—both lost.[316] In

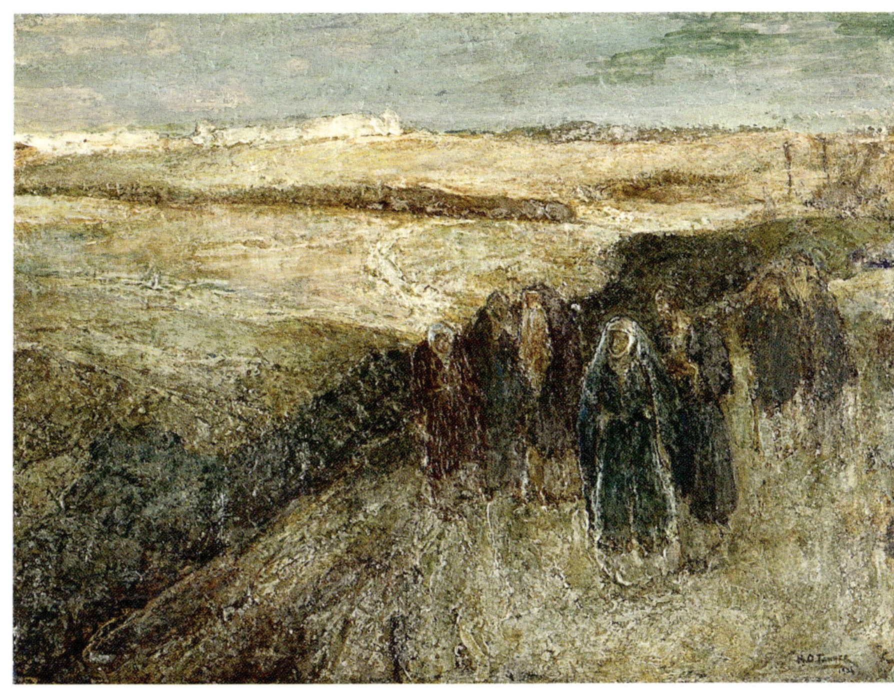

PLATE 60
Return from the Crucifixion, 1936
Oil and tempera on plywood
17 x 22 (43 x 55.8)
Howard University Gallery of Art,
Washington, D.C.

November he was visited in Paris by the black artist and art historian James A. Porter (1905-1971), who arranged for the purchase of a picture still on Tanner's easel, *Return from the Crucifixion* (pl. 60).[317] The subject is familiar—John accompanies Mary in compliance with the edict of Jesus (John 19:26-27): "When Jesus therefore saw his mother, and the disciple standing by...he saith unto his mother, Woman, behold thy son! Then saith he to the disciple, Behold thy mother! And from that hour the disciple took her unto his own home." The composition was drawn from an earlier *Return of the Holy Woman* (c. 1905; location unknown), however the blend of oil and tempera gives an overall luminosity to the picture, even in its shadows. Porter noted: "The old sincerity persisted, as did his ability to suggest infinite meaning with a reduced palette—a certain indication of the mastery of his art."[318]

Return from the Crucifixion, Tanner's last signed and dated work, was purchased through public subscription by the Howard University Gallery of Art in March of 1937. It was altogether fitting that Tanner should be so honored during his lifetime and that this last work should be acquired by an African-American institution on whose board his father had served. Two months later, he wrote to Mrs. Alexander: "I hope you are all including Mary Elizabeth are very well. I am beginning to feel some older. Sorry."[319] Tanner died in his sleep two days later, on May 24, 1937.[320]

Epilogue: Henry Ossawa Tanner's Legacy

The legacy of Henry Ossawa Tanner can be seen in the exhibition histories of his works, his influence on other artists, and the wide range of his audience. After Tanner's death, there was a lull in public exhibitions of his art until a memorial show was held at the Philadelphia Art Alliance in 1945.[321] From then until the late

1960s, Tanner and his art were largely forgotten by exhibition organizers. Between 1967 and 1972, a flurry of shows devoted to him appeared on the scene.[322] Again, between 1970 and 1990, Tanner's work did not often appear in exhibitions. With the 1990s, Henry Tanner is once again being considered on his own and in the context of his generation. In 1991, the Philadelphia Museum's exhibition surveyed the artist's entire career, bringing it back into focus. That work accomplished, it set the stage for exhibitions such as this one.

Artists, black and white, have been affected by Tanner's work over the course of a century. His influence on other artists deserves to be the subject of a future study. Even in a cursory glance we can detect the impact of his work on the paintings of Harry Roseland (1868-1950), whose *Odd Couple Looking at a Portrait of Lincoln* (c. 1892; National Museum of American Art) was attributed to Tanner until recently. The successful Salon artist Robert MacCameron (1866-1912) wrote to Tanner in 1908: "Let me thank you for your kind note of congratulation on my second medal. There is no painter living whose judgement I value more and the influence of your superb color in every canvas you paint has had a good influence on my work."[323] The famous Tanner palette of blues and blue-greens seems also to be at work in *Christmas* (c. 1939; private collection) by Palmer Hayden, who met the older artist around 1930. In 1992, the award-winning painter Howardena Pindell (b. 1942) noted: "I was determined to be an artist and was inspired by the presence of work by Henry Ossawa Tanner in the home of my friend who was one of his relatives."[324]

Another aspect of Tanner's legacy is his audience. The great nineteenth-century poet and critic Charles Baudelaire remarked: "A simple method of learning an artist's range is to examine his public."[325] It is possible to understand Tanner's public through an idea articulated by a biographer of the poet Paul Laurence Dunbar: "The black writer must not merely live in two worlds; he inevitably writes for two worlds. Whatever he writes is affected by what Ralph Ellison called 'the complex relationship between the Negro-American subculture and North American culture as a whole.'"[326] Indeed, Tanner's career reached across continents and cultures and he can be said to have painted for three worlds: for African Americans, for America, and for France.

Perhaps Tanner's greatest legacy was his career as a whole, his great success against bad odds. The generation of African-American artists who contributed to the Harlem Renaissance, born some forty years after the Emancipation Proclamation, would be difficult to imagine without the example of Tanner's single-minded pursuit of artistic success and his subsequent international recognition.[327]

On Tanner's first birthday, his father wrote in his daybook: "Whether the preservation of Henry's life and health will prove a blessing the Lord only knows. For how can I, a mortal man, look into the future and see his life, see whether he will love God and man, or whether he will be an enemy of both."[328] He would have been pleased to know that the life of Henry Ossawa Tanner was an inspiration and a challenge to aspiring artists, and that his work remains a monument of sturdy endeavor and exalted achievement.

Notes

In the notes, citations are given in full the first time, and in a shortened form each subsequent use.

1. In his own day, Tanner and his career were most cogently studied by Helen Cole, F. J. Campbell, and Charles Wesley. Wesley's consideration of the artist is particularly helpful in its outlining the conflicting feelings Tanner caused among black people of his era. From the 1920s until 1960, Tanner and his art eluded serious scholars. The first book-length study, a 1960 doctoral dissertation by Walter Augustus Simon, attempted to place Tanner's life in the ethnographic and sociological context of his time, but discussion of his art is limited. In 1969, Marcia Mathews wrote a biography of the artist that drew upon the following: selected letters and other documentation among the Tanner papers deposited at the Archives of American Art, Smithsonian Institution; contemporary discussions of the artist; and the reminiscences of his son, Jesse Ossawa Tanner. The Philadelphia Museum of Art embarked on a major study of the artist's life and art in 1991. See Helen Cole, "American Artists in Paris," *Brush and Pencil*, 4 (July 1899), pp. 201-202, and "Henry O. Tanner, Painter," *Brush and Pencil*, 6 (June 1900), pp. 97-107; F. J. Campbell, "Henry O. Tanner's Biblical Pictures," *Fine Arts Journal*, 25 (March 1911), pp. 163-166; Charles H. Wesley, "Henry O. Tanner, the Artist: An Appreciation," *Howard University Record*, 15 (April 1920), pp. 299-306; Walter Augustus Simon, "Henry O. Tanner: A Study of the Development of an American Negro Artist, 1859-1937," Ph.D. dissertation, New York University, 1960; and Marcia M. Mathews, *Henry Ossawa Tanner, American Artist* (Chicago: University of Chicago Press, 1969).

2. The noted scholar Henry Louis Gates, Jr., cogently outlined the challenges of thinking about racial identity and individual works of art in "On the African-American in American Art and Literature," in *Harvard University Art Museums Review*, 2 (Fall 1992), pp. 1-2. Columnist Les Payne took up the issue in "Is It Black Art, American Art, or Just Art," *The Post Standard* (Syracuse, N.Y.), March 2, 1993, p. A-6.

3. The Editor [Benjamin T. Tanner], "The Paris Exposition in 1900," *A.M.E. Church Review*, 14 (October 1897), p. 278.

4. W. E. B. Du Bois, *The Souls of Black Folk* (New York: Dodd, Mead, 1961; originally published 1903), p. 54.

5. "Afro-American Painter Who Has Become Famous in Paris," *Current Literature*, 45 (October 1908), p. 406.

6. Booker T. Washington, *Up From Slavery* (New York: Penguin Books, 1986; originally published 1901), p. 202.

7. Quoted in "Afro-American Painter Who Has Become Famous in Paris," p. 407.

8. E. Azalia Hackley, "How the Color Question Looks to an American in France," *A.M.E. Church Review*, 23 (January 1907), p. 211.

9. William E. Barton, "An American Painter of the Resurrection," *Advance* (March 20, 1913), p. 2011.

10. Ann J. Lane, *The Brownsville Affair: National Crisis and Black Reaction* (Port Washington, N.Y.: Kennikat Press, 1971), pp. 70, 111, 138-139.

11. Quoted in Mathews, *Tanner*, pp. 142-143.

12. See, for example, Cedric Dover, *American Negro Art* (Greenwich, Conn.: New York Graphic Society, 1960), p. 29.

13. Hans Bhalla and Edmund B. Gaither, *Henry O. Tanner: An Afro-American Romantic Realist (1859-1937)*, exh. cat. (Atlanta: Spelman College, 1969), n.p.

14. C. E. Allen, "American Finds Roots in Rural France," *International Herald Tribune*, October 2, 1987, p. 8.

15. Jane Dillenberger and Joshua C. Taylor, "Henry Ossawa Tanner" in *The Hand and the Spirit: Religious Art in America, 1700-1900*, exh. cat. (Berkeley, Calif.: University Art Museum, 1972), n.p.

16. Quoted in Mathews, *Tanner*, pp. 142-143.

17. Mathews, *Tanner*, pp. 142-143.

18. Benjamin T. Tanner, *The Negro's Origins and Is the Negro Cursed* (Philadelphia, 1869), p. 22.

19. John Brown was much on the minds of those favoring abolition during 1859; he was hung for treason on December 2 of that year.

20. Henry O. Tanner to Mrs. Eunice Tietjens, May 25, 1914, Henry Ossawa Tanner Papers, 1850-1978, Archives of American Art, Smithsonian Institution, Washington, D.C., roll D308, frame 119. Albert Boime also noticed this important omission. See Albert Boime, "Henry Ossawa Tanner's Subversion of Genre," *Art Bulletin*, 75 (September 1993), p. 418.

21. Du Bois, *Black Folk*, p. 85.

22. William H. Ferris, *The African Abroad or His Evolution in Western Civilization, Tracing His Development Under Caucasian Milieu* (New Haven, Conn.: Tuttle, Morehouse & Taylor, 1913), vol. 1, p. 296.

23. Henry O. Tanner to Sadie T. M. Alexander, March 23, 1936, Alexander Papers, Archives, University of Pennsylvania, Philadelphia. Kathe Sandler's excellent documentary *The Question of Color* (1993) illuminates the issues surrounding Tanner's reference to dark skin color.

24. Quoted in Mathews, *Tanner*, pp. 196-197.

25. W. E. B. Du Bois to Henry O. Tanner, October 24, 1932; confirmation of receipt of donation, H. Branch to Henry O. Tanner, March 24, 1933, Tanner Papers, Archives of American Art, roll D306, frame 747.

26. Henry O. Tanner to Sadie T. M. Alexander, January 22, 1937, Alexander Papers, University of Pennsylvania.

27. For a discussion of this act see W. E. B. Du Bois, *The Philadelphia Negro; A Social Study* (New York: Schocken Books, 1967; originally published 1899), p. 45.

28. For a discussion of his career see Rae Alexander-Minter, "The Tanner Family: A Grandniece's Chronicle" in *Tanner*, 1991, pp. 23-29.

29. B. T. Tanner, *The Negro's Origin and Is the Negro Cursed*, n.p.

30. For a concise history of the family, see "The Tanner Family," *Negro History Bulletin* (April 1947), pp. 147-152, 167.

31. L. R. Harlan, ed., *The Booker T. Washington Papers* (Urbana: University of Illinois Press, 1972-1989), vol. 3, p. 192.

32. Du Bois, *Philadelphia Negro*, pp. 112, 178, 209.

33. Unless otherwise noted, all factual information on Tanner's life is taken from Henry O. Tanner, "The Story of an Artist's Life," *World's Work*, 18 (June and July 1909), pp. 11661-66, 11769-75.

34. Ibid., p. 11662.

35. As editor of the *Christian Recorder*, Rev. Tanner urged young blacks to study the *Magazine of Art* during the 1880s; this periodical began only in 1878. Thus Tanner's early readings on art probably were in the *Penn Monthly*, *Scribner's Monthly*, and *Atlantic Monthly: A Magazine of Literature, Art, and Politics.*

36. Tanner, "The Story," p. 11663.

37. Ibid.

38. Ibid. Edward Moran (1829-1901) was the teacher of several of the marine artists that Tanner admired in Earle's Gallery and the window of Bailey's Jewelry Store. It would have been logical for Tanner to approach him, considering their shared interest in marine painting.

39. Ibid. On average household budgets, see Du Bois, *Philadelphia Negro*, p. 174.

40. Henry O. Tanner, "An Artist's Autobiography," *The Advance* (March 20, 1913), p. 2012. Sir Edwin Landseer (1802-1873) was an English painter who gained immense popularity from his animal pictures.

41. William R. Lester, "Henry O. Tanner, Exile for Art's Sake," *Alexander's Magazine*, 7 (December 15, 1908), p. 70.

42. See Darrel Sewell in *Tanner*, 1991, p. 71.

43. Maria Teski et al., *A City Revitalized: The Elderly Lose at Monopoly* (Lanham, Md.: University Press of America, 1983), pp. 66-67.

44. Henry O. Tanner, "Compulsory Education and Valedictory Address," *Christian Recorder*, 15 (July 12, 1877), p. 3.

45. Tanner, "The Story," p. 11664.

46. See Linda R. Hartigan, *Sharing Traditions: Five Black Artists in Nineteenth-Century America*, exh. cat. (Washington, D.C.: National Museum of American Art, 1985), p. 69.

47. See Harlan, *Washington Papers*, vol. 4, p. 44.

48. Roger Lane, *William Dorsey's Philadelphia and Ours: On the Past and the Future of the Black City in America* (New York: Oxford University Press, 1991), p. 123; and Juanita Marie Holland, *Edward Mitchell Bannister (1828-1901)*, exh. cat. (New York: Kenkeleba House, 1992), p. 34.

49. Lane, *Dorsey's Philadelphia*, p. 120.

50. Ibid., pp. 122-123.

51. For a list of jobs, with salaries, known to have been held by African Americans, see Du Bois, *Philadelphia Negro*, p. 101.

52. Benjamin T. Tanner, *Hints to Ministers, Especially Those of the African Methodist Episcopal Church* (Philadelphia, 1902), p. 10.

53. See Geraldine Collins, *The Brighton Story: Being the History of Paul Smiths, Gabriels and Rainbow Lake* (Lakemont, N.Y.: North Country Books, 1977), pp. 21, 90-93.

54. W. E. B. Du Bois, *John Brown* (New York: International Publishers, 1962; originally published 1909), p. 110.

55. For a good discussion, although tinged by racism, see Robert Penn Warren, *John Brown: The Making of a Martyr* (New York: Payson and Clarke, 1929), pp. 57-86.

56. Benjamin Quarles, *Blacks on John Brown* (Urbana: University of Illinois Press, 1972), pp. 23-24.

57. Collins, *Brighton Story*, p. 21.

58. The inscription on the lower left of this canvas—*Paris/Tanner/Apres Shryer* [sic]—cannot be taken seriously to mean that the picture was painted in Paris by Tanner after a composition by Adolphe Shreyer (1828-1899), who executed winter

scenes. The handling of *Ewe With Dead Lamb and Crows* is far removed from the sophistication of any of Tanner's Paris period. Thus, the authenticity of the inscription is suspect.

59. Holland, *Bannister*, p. 45.

60. Tanner, "The Story," p. 11664.

61. Tanner, "Autobiography," p. 2013.

62. William Crary Brownell, "The Art Schools of Philadelphia," *Scribner's Monthly*, 28 (1879), pp. 737-750.

63. Fairman Rogers to George Henry Corliss, September 30, 1878, Archives, Pennsylvania Academy of the Fine Arts, Philadelphia.

64. Joseph Pennell, *The Adventures of an Illustrator, Mostly in Following his Authors in America & Europe* (Boston: Little, Brown and Co., 1925), pp. 49-50.

65. Ibid., p. 54.

66. Ibid., p. 50.

67. Tanner, "Autobiography," p. 2013.

68. For Eakins's teaching method, see Lloyd Goodrich, *Thomas Eakins* (Cambridge, Mass.: Harvard University Press, 1982), vol. 1, p. 175.

69. "The Century's American Artists Series: Henry O. Tanner," *Century Illustrated Monthly Magazine*, n.s. 37 (November 1899-April 1900), p. 962.

70. William Scarborough, "Henry Ossian [sic] Tanner," *Southern Workman*, 31 (December 1902), p. 662.

71. Goodrich, *Eakins*, vol. 1, p. 186.

72. Hale Woodruff, "My Meeting With Henry O. Tanner," *Crisis* (January 1970), p. 9.

73. Pennell, *Adventures*, pp. 53-54.

74. Ibid., p. 54.

75. Tanner, "The Story," pp. 11664-65.

76. "Personal," *Christian Recorder*, 19 (Nov. 24, 1881), p. 3.

77. "Local News," *Christian Recorder*, 20 (March 30, 1882), p. 2.

78. Tanner, "Autobiography," p. 2013.

79. *Pursuing Cavalry* could very well be the picture called *Fauna* (1878-79; Hampton University Museum, Virginia). When Tanner was at Rainbow Lake, it was legal to hunt deer with dogs, but was made illegal around 1880 in favor of sitting on a watch spot (see Collins, *Brighton Story*, pp. 31-32). Tanner's perk-eared doe in *Fauna* could very well be aware of dogs and hunters in pursuit.

80. Workers of the Federal Writers' Project of the Works Progress Administration, *Rhode Island, a Guide to the Smallest State* (Boston: Houghton Mifflin Co., 1937), p. 338.

81. This work could be *Harbor Scene* (1876; John Quincy Johnson). Measuring fourteen by twenty inches, it is one of the largest of Tanner's early works and has descended in the family.

82. F. A. L., "Our Art Exhibition," *People's Advocate*, 5 (October 30, 1880), n.p.

83. See Collins, *Brighton Story*, p. 31.

84. Ibid., pp. 24-25.

85. Tanner, "The Story," p. 11665.

86. Ibid.

87. Sewell in *Tanner*, 1991, p. 79.

88. "Personal," *Christian Recorder*, 22 (March 20, 1884), p. 2.

89. Quoted in Ibid.

90. Quoted in William J. Simmons, *Men of Mark: Eminent, Progressive and Rising* (Cleveland: G. M. Rewell & Co., 1887), p. 1129.

91. Ibid., p. 184.

92. Charles A. Wardner, whose family owned the Rainbow Lake Inn, noted in his memoirs: "I value a...painting made for me by H. O. Tanner in 1886." Charles A. Wardner, "Sunset on Adirondack Trails," unpublished manuscript, Adirondack Museum, Blue Mountain Lake, New York, manuscript MS 67-24, roll 4.31.

93. Tanner, "The Story," p. 11665.

94. Simmons, *Men of Mark*, p. 181.

95. Leofranc Holford-Strevens, *Aulus Gellius* (Chapel Hill: University of North Carolina Press, 1989), pp. 11-12.

96. Tanner, "The Story," p. 11665.

97. For a full discussion of the sources of this work, see Mosby in *Tanner*, 1991, pp. 80-82.

98. See Ibid., p. 80 and p. 293, note 1.

99. Tanner, "The Story," p. 11665.

100. Simmons's *Men of Mark*, which was prepared for publication in May 1887, mentioned this sheet, p. 182.

101. Simmons, *Men of Mark*, p. 182.

102. Kate U. Clark, "Old Win-ne-Wan's Star," *Harper's Young People*, 9 (January 10, 1888), pp. 185-187.

103. Naurice Frank Woods, Jr., "The Life and Work of Henry O. Tanner," Ph.D. dissertation, Columbia Pacific University, 1987, p. 68.

104. Scarborough, "Tanner," p. 664.

105. See Virginia B. Geyer, "Further Notes on Henry Wynkoop," *Bucks County Historical Society Journal*, 1 (Fall 1976), pp. 1, 8.

106. "Personal," *Christian Recorder*, 25 (October 13, 1887), p. 5.

107. Du Bois, *Black Folk*, p. 110.

108. Tanner, "The Story," p. 11666.

109. Mathews, *Tanner*, p. 36.

110. One of the other rare oils surviving from this time is *Ram's Head Study*, signed and dated 1889, suggesting Tanner's interest in animal studies continued. See Parke-Bernet (New York), sale, January 26, 1974, lot 623.

111. Mementos of this friendship are housed in the "Henry Ossawa Tanner Collection (1907-1937)," Trevor Arnett Library, Atlanta University.

112. Carlyn G. C. Romeyn, "Henry O. Tanner: Atlanta Interlude," *Atlanta Historical Society Journal*, 27 (Winter 1983-84), p. 37. (Tanner added to this confusion when he mentioned at the 1893 Columbian Exposition that he was a professor at Clark University.)

113. Barnitz is identified by Carlyn G. Crannel [Romeyn], "In Pursuit of Culture: A History of Art Activity in Atlanta, 1847-1926," Ph.D. dissertation, Emory University, 1981, p. 196; Simon, "Tanner," p. 99.

114. Romeyn, "Atlanta Interlude," p. 37.

115. Mathews, *Tanner*, p. 40.

116. Woods, "Life and Work," pp. 74-75.

117. See Goodrich, *Eakins*, vol. 1, p. 296.

118. Tanner, "The Story," p. 11770.

119. John Milner, *The Studios of Paris: The Capital of Art in the Late Nineteenth Century* (New Haven, Conn.: Yale University Press, 1988), pp. 11-12.

120. Ibid., p. 12.

121. Ibid.

122. Catherine Fehrer, "New Light on the Académie Julian and its Founder (Rodolphe Julian)," *Gazette des Beaux-Arts*, 103 (May-June, 1984), p. 208.

123. For a discussion of Tanner's personal relationships with his teachers, see Simon, "Tanner," pp. 127-130, 134-135, 137; see also Jane Munro in *The Orientalists: Delacroix to Matisse: The Allure of North Africa and the Near East*, exh. cat. (Washington, D.C.: National Gallery of Art, 1984), pp. 116-117.

124. For an unrelated discussion of Tanner and the nude figure, see Ibid., pp. 83-84.

125. Ibid., pp. 147-148.

126. Tanner's name is not listed on the registration for copying at the Louvre, Archive, Musée du Louvre, Paris, LL 23-24, 27, 31.

127. See Julie Manet, *Journal (1893-1899): Sa jeunesse parmi les peintres impressionists et les hommes de lettres* (Paris: C. Klincksleck, 1979), pp. 140-141.

128. For more on this topic, see David Sellin and James K. Ballinger, *Americans in Brittany and Normandy, 1860-1910*, exh. cat. (Phoenix: Phoenix Art Museum, 1982).

129. *L'Ecole de Pont-Aven dans les Collections Publiques et Privées de Bretagne*, exh. cat. (Quimper, France: Musée des Beaux-Arts, 1978), n.p.

130. Tanner's autobiography muddles his chronology at this point. The fact that *Apple Orchard* (location unknown), painted partly in Concarneau in the summer of 1892, was rejected by the Salon in 1893, indicates Tanner's awareness of the Salon at that date. For more on this see Mosby in *Tanner*, pp. 110-113.

131. See Henry Bataille, *Théâtre Complet* (Paris: Ernest Flammarion, 1922), vol. 1, pp. 11, 15.

132. Mathews, *Tanner*, p. 62.

133. Tanner, "The Story," p. 11772.

134. James A. Porter, *Modern Negro Art* (New York: The Dryden Press, 1943), p. 68.

135. F. P. Noble, "The Chicago Congress on Africa," *Our Day*, 12 (October 1983), p. 299.

136. Ibid., p. 285.

137. Statement in Tanner's hand, undated, Files, Pennsylvania School for the Deaf, Philadelphia.

138. Peter Revell, *Paul Laurence Dunbar* (Boston: Twayne Publishers, 1979), chronology.

139. It is interesting to note that Tanner's first teacher, Thomas Eakins, was also working in sculpture at this time. See Moussa M. Domit, *The Sculpture of Thomas Eakins*, exh. cat. (Washington, D.C.: Corcoran Gallery of Art, 1969).

140. "A Bust of Bishop Payne," *Christian Recorder*, 31 (December 14, 1893), p. 2.

141. Simmons, *Men of Mark*, p. 1083.

142. "Bust of Bishop Payne," p. 2.

143. B. T. Tanner, *Theological Lectures*, p. 65.

144. Ibid.

145. See Hugh Honour, *The Image of the Black in Western Art* (Cambridge, Mass.: Menil Foundation, 1989), vol. 4, pp. 187-204.

146. Tanner, "The Story," p. 11772.

147. See Sewell in *Tanner*, 1991, p. 126.

148. See Harlan, *Washington Papers*, vol. 8, p. 43, note 13.

149. "Art Notes," *Daily Evening Telegraph* (Philadelphia), April 28, 1894, p. 11.

150. Sewell in *Tanner*, 1991, p. 119.

151. See Ibid.

152. Milner, *Studios*, p. 52.

153. Tanner, "The Story," p. 11771.

154. Ibid., p. 11772.

155. See Lane, *Dorsey's Philadelphia*, pp. 121-122.

156. Ibid., p. 122.

157. Ibid.

158. Ibid.

159. Judy Le Paul, *Gauguin and the Impressionists at Pont-Aven* (New York: Abbeville Press, 1987), p. 98.

160. W. Jaworska, "Armand Séguin: Peintre ou Graveur 1869-1903," *Gazette des Beaux-Arts*, 77 (Mar. 1971), pp. 145-146.

161. Le Paul, *Gauguin*, p. 99, note 33.

162. Denys Sutton and Catherine Puget, *Une vie de Bohème: Lettres du Peintre Armand Séguin à Roderic O'Conor 1895-1903* (Pont-Aven, France: Musée de Pont-Aven, 1989), p. 61.

163. *L'Ecole de Pont-Aven*, "Chronologie."

164. Ibid., passim.

165. John Rewald, *The History of Impressionism* (New York: Museum of Modern Art, 1961), p. 554.

166. Henry O. Tanner to John S. Durham, May 23, 1895, Tanner File, Library, Philadelphia Museum of Art.

167. Le Paul, *Gauguin*, p. 99.

168. See Mathews, *Tanner*, p. 71.

169. "Personal," *Christian Recorder*, 33 (April 4, 1895), p. 2.

170. See Guy Chapman, *The Dreyfus Case: A Reassessment* (London: Rupert Hart-Davis, 1955), passim; also, Boime, "Tanner's Subversion," p. 437.

171. See B. T. Tanner, *Theological Lectures*, pp. 60-61.

172. Scarborough, "Tanner," p. 666.

173. Salons de 1894-1897, Archives Nationales, Paris, F21 4090B (Dossier 1).

174. See Gerald Ackerman in *French Salon Paintings from Southern Collections*, exh. cat. (Atlanta: High Museum of Art, 1982), p. 17.

175. Tanner, "The Story," p. 11772.

176. Mathews, *Tanner*, p. 74.

177. Harlan, *Washington Papers*, vol. 4, p. 3.

178. Romeyn, "Atlanta Interlude," p. 38.

179. Ibid.

180. Harlan, *Washington Papers*, vol. 4, p. 58.

181. Tanner, "The Story," pp. 11772-11773.

182. Du Bois, *Black Folk*, p. 220.

183. Henry H. Mitchell, *Black Preaching* (Philadelphia: Lippincott, 1970), pp. 70-72.

184. Scarborough, "Tanner," p. 666.

185. See Albert Maignon, "Le Salon de 1897," *Gazette des Beaux-Arts*, 17 (May 1897), p. 353; and "Mr. H. O. Tanner's Picture *The Raising of Lazarus*," *Harper's Weekly*, 41 (August 7, 1897), p. 780.

186. Quoted in Mathews, *Tanner*, p. 80.

187. See Mary Anne Stevens, "Western Art and its Encounter with the Islamic World, 1798-1914," in *The Orientalists*, p. 22.

188. Tanner, "The Story," p. 11774.

189. Quoted and discussed further in Boime, "Tanner's Subversion," pp. 436-437.

190. Letter of June 14, 1897, Henry O. Tanner File, Archives Nationales, Paris, F21 2151; and Henry O. Tanner to Harrison S. Morris, June 23, 1897, Henry Ossawa Tanner File, Archives, Pennsylvania Academy of the Fine Arts.

191. Susan Greenbaum, *The African-American Community in Kansas City, Kansas: A History* (Kansas City: City of Kansas City, Kansas, 1982), passim.

192. Conversations between Margaret Conrads, Samuel Sosland Curator of American Art, The Nelson-Atkins Museum of Art, and Suzanne Knowles, Pierian Club member, Spring 1994.

193. Henry O. Tanner to Sadie T. M. Alexander, June 19, 1932, Alexander Papers, University of Pennsylvania.

194. Tanner painted the portrait of his mother on a canvas purchased in Kansas City; Henry O. Tanner to Sadie T. M. Alexander, June 19, 1932, Alexander Papers, University of Pennsylvania.

195. See *Philadelphia African Americans: Color, Class and Style, 1840-1940*, exh. cat. (Philadelphia: Balch Institute for Ethnic Studies, 1988), p. 50.

196. See Mary D. Sheriff, "Invention, Resemblance, and Fragonard's Portraits de Fantaisie," *Art Bulletin*, 69 (March 1987), p. 83.

197. Quoted in Noble, "Chicago Congress," p. 285.

198. Henry O. Tanner to Harrison S. Morris, May 22, 1898, Tanner File, Pennsylvania Academy of the Fine Arts.

199. See Dewey F. Mosby, *Alexandre-Gabriel Decamps* (New York: Garland Publishers, 1977), vol. 1, pp. 59-62.

200. Maignon, "Le Salon," p. 53.

201. Atherton Curtis, entry of December 1899, Journal Sommaire 1894-1943, Bibliothéque Nationale, Paris.

202. Ibid., December 6, 1897.

203. H. F. Kletzing and W. H. Crogman, *Progress of a Race, or The Remarkable Advancement of the Afro-American* (Atlanta: J. L. Nichols & Co., 1901), p. 573.

204. See Mosby in *Tanner*, 1991, p. 146; and Boime, "Tanner's Subversion," p. 433.

205. Tanner, "Autobiography," p. 2014.

206. See N. C. Cooper-Lewter and Henry H. Mitchell, *Soul Theology: The Heart of American Black Culture* (San Francisco: Harper & Row, 1986), p. 96.

207. Campbell, "Henry O. Tanner's Biblical Pictures," p. 165.

208. Henry O. Tanner to Ingeborg Curtis, c. 1909, Tanner Papers, Archives of American Art, roll D306, frame 1170.

209. Cole, "Tanner," p. 101.

210. See Michael Wentworth, *James Tissot* (Oxford: Clarendon Press; Oxford University Press, 1984), pp. 175, 181-182; and Annette Blaugrund, *Paris 1889: American Artists at the Universal Exposition*, exh. cat. (Philadelphia: Pennsylvania Academy of the Fine Arts, 1989), p. 159.

211. In addition to Cole, "Tanner," p. 101, see, for example, Elbert F. Baldwin, "A Negro Artist of Unique Power," *Outlook, A Weekly Newspaper*, 44 (January-April 1900), p. 793; and F. J. Ziegler, "Sixty-Eighth Annual Exhibition of the Pennsylvania Academy of the Fine Arts," *Brush and Pencil*, 3 (February 1899), p. 294.

212. Harrison S. Morris to Henry O. Tanner, May 16, 1898, Morris Letter Book, Archives, Pennsylvania Academy of the Fine Arts.

213. Henry O. Tanner to Ingeborg Curtis, c. 1909, Tanner Papers, Archives of American Art, roll D306, frame 1170.

214. See Stanley Shaw, *William of Germany* (London: Methuen, 1913), p. 176.

215. Tanner, "The Story," p. 11773.

216. Ibid., p. 11774.

217. The other two events were the Passover at Jerusalem and Jesus leaving the city, but remaining in Judea to preach. B. T. Tanner, *Theological Lectures*, p. 126.

218. Cooper-Lewter and Mitchell, *Soul Theology*, p. 99.

219. See Cole, "American Artists," p. 201; and Cole, "Tanner," p. 102.

220. Mathews, *Tanner*, p. 94.

221. Ibid., p. 97.

222. Cole, "Tanner," pp. 103-104.

223. Quoted in Mathews, *Tanner*, p. 100.

224. "Miss Meta V. Warrick and Henry O. Tanner—Recognized Among the Most Noted Americans in Paris," *Philadelphia Tribune*, c. 1901, in Tanner Papers, Archives of American Art; and see Ferris, *African Abroad*, vol. 2, p. 857.

225. Washington first wrote about his visit in the *Washington Colored American*, and retold of that experience in *Up From Slavery* (New York: Penguin Books, 1986; originally published in 1901), pp. 280-281. On Du Bois's visit, see Jack B. Moore, *W. E. B. Du Bois* (Boston: Twayne Publishers, 1981), chronology.

226. Among the most important of these events was his exhibition of three canvases in the Pennsylvania Academy's 1900 annual exhibition, as well as the appearance of Elbert F. Baldwin's, "A Negro Artist of Unique Power," *Outlook*, 44 (January-April 1900), pp. 793-796.

227. Henry Tanner to J. J. Haverty, January 5, 1930, Tanner Papers, Archives of American Art, roll D306, frame 570.

228. Henry O. Tanner to Harrison S. Morris, May 1, 1899, Tanner File, Pennsylvania Academy of the Fine Arts.

229. Harrison S. Morris to Henry O. Tanner, June 12, 1899, Morris Letter Book, Pennsylvania Academy of the Fine Arts.

230. See Mosby in *Tanner*, 1991, p. 295, note 42.

231. Harrison S. Morris to Henry O. Tanner, April 14, 1902, Morris Letter Book, Pennsylvania Academy of the Fine Arts.

232. See Harlan, *Washington Papers*, vol. 3, pp. 33-34.

233. Scarborough, "Tanner," p. 669.

234. Jonathan Brown, *Velásquez: Painter and Courtier* (New Haven, Conn.: Yale University Press, 1986), p. 307.

235. Cole, "Tanner," pp. 98-99.

236. See Edward J. Sullivan and Nina A. Mallory, *Painting in Spain, 1650-1700, from North American Collections*, exh. cat. (Princeton, N.J.: University Art Museum; Princeton University Press, 1982), p. 99. Velásquez's *Portrait of Juan de Pareja* is in the Metropolitan Museum of Art, New York.

237. Mathews, *Tanner*, p. 128.

238. Ibid.

239. Curtis, Journal, June 23, 1902.

240. Eakins rendered Tanner in a cravat that prefigures the colors of the Black Liberation flag, with black representing the people, green for the motherland, Africa, and red for the blood lost in the struggle for freedom.

241. Harlan, *Washington Papers*, vol. 7, p. 458.

242. Ibid., p. 450. See also an interpretation of this situation in Boime, "Tanner's Subversion," pp. 440-441.

243. "The American Negro Who Leads France in Art," *North American* (Philadelphia), June 10, 1906, n.p.

244. "Pennsylvania Academy," *Globe* (New York), Jan. 21, 1907, Tanner Papers, Archives of American Art.

245. Cole, "Tanner," p. 105.

246. Tanner, "The Story," p. 1174.

247. See Mosby in *Tanner*, 1991, pp. 156-157.

248. Ibid.

249. See Stevens, *Orientalists*, p. 23, note 84.

250. Jon Perdicaris, "Morocco, 'The Land of the Extreme West' and the Story of My Captivity," *National Geographic*, 273 (March 1906), pp. 117-157, passim.

251. *Enciclopedia Universal Illustrada Europeo-Americana* (Madrid: Espasa-Calpe, c. 1930; originally published 1907?).

252. W. R. Lester, "104th Annual Exhibition," unidentified clipping, Tanner Papers, Archives of American Art.

253. Sterling Heilig, "Henry Tanner, An American Negro, May Win This Year's Medal of Honor at the Great Paris Salon," *Baltimore Sun*, June 14, 1908, p. 14.

254. Quoted in Boime, "Tanner's Subversion," p. 418. Tanner confused this incident as occurring in 1897 with *The Resurrection of Lazarus*. In fact it occurred with *The Wise and Foolish Virgins*. Neither the *Baltimore Sun* nor the *Baltimore American* for 1897 have such a photograph. The artist also exaggerated the appearance of the gentleman pictured in his stead in the *Baltimore Sun* article (see note 253).

255. "Religious Works in Tanner Exhibit: Emotional Picturesqueness Manifest in Paintings at American Galleries," *New York Times*, December 19, 1908, p. 7.

256. "New York American Art News," unidentified clipping, Tanner Papers, Archives of American Art.

257. Mathews, *Tanner*, p. 133.

258. Tanner, "The Story," p. 11775.

259. F. H. M. Murray, "'The Adoration of the Magi,' With Special Reference to Mabuse's Painting," *A.M.E. Church Review*, 29 (October 1912), p. 95.

260. Campbell, "Henry O. Tanner's Biblical Pictures," p. 166.

261. Barton, "American Painter," p. 2012.

262. Harriet Monroe, "Artist Shows His Pictures," *Chicago Daily Tribune*, February 2, 1911, p. 3.

263. H. H. Arnason, *History of Modern Art: Painting, Sculpture, Architecture* (Englewood Cliffs, N.J.: Prentice-Hall, 1968), p. 84.

264. For an excellent synopsis of these events, see Sam Hunter, *Modern French Painting, 1855-1956* (New York: Dell Publishing Co., 1956), pp. 237-239.

265. Quoted in Clara T. MacChesney, "A Poet-Painter of Palestine," *International Studio*, 50 (July 1913), p. xii.

266. Ibid.; see also Barton, "American Painter," p. 2012.

267. MacChesney, "Poet-Painter," p. xiv.

268. Ibid., p. xi.

269. Ibid., p. xiv.

270. See Mathews, *Tanner*, p. 147; also "Paintings by Henry O. Tanner," *New York Times*, April 12, 1913, p. 14.

271. Mathews, *Tanner*, pp. 153-154.

272. Quoted in Ibid., pp. 156-157.

273. Henry O. Tanner to John W. Beatty, May 17, 1919, Archives, Carnegie Institute, Pittsburgh.

274. Henry O. Tanner to Raymond Wyer, April 18, 1915, Muskegon Museum of Art, Michigan.

275. Samuel E. Morrison et al., *A Concise History of the American Republic* (New York: Oxford University Press, 1977), vol. 2, p. 545.

276. Mathews, *Tanner*, p. 160.

277. Tanner Papers, Archives of American Art, roll D306, frames 136-137.

278. See, for example, Michael Williams, "A Pageant of American Art," *Art and Progress*, 6 (August 1915), p. 347; and Raymond Wyer, "Art Collecting and Psychology," *International Studio*, 58 (June 1916), p. cxxvi.

279. Quoted in Mathews, *Tanner*, p. 159.

280. See Booker T. Washington, *Working with the Hands; Being a Sequel to 'Up from Slavery,' Covering the Author's Experiences in Industrial Training at Tuskegee* (New York: Doubleday, Page, & Co., 1904), passim.

281. Mathews, *Tanner*, p. 161.

282. See Tanner's American Red Cross correspondence, Tanner Papers, Archives of American Art, roll D306, frames 1405-1406, 1425, 1430.

283. See, for example, Carter H. Harrison, *With the American Red Cross in France, 1918-1919* (Chicago: R. F. Seymour, 1947). It is interesting to note that Harrison knew Tanner and wanted to buy one of his works (see Mathews, *Tanner*, p. 174).

284. Quoted in Mathews, *Tanner*, pp. 176-177.

285. See Ibid., p. 173 for a general chronology of events. For specifics, which do not affect the dates of paintings, see Permis de Séjour dans la Zone des Armées, May 21, 1916, Tanner Papers, Archives of American Art, roll D307, frames 0200-0202.

286. George W. Forbes, "Within the Sphere of Letters: Tanner's 'First in Boston,'" *A.M.E. Church Review*, 37 (April 1921), p. 252.

287. Ibid.

288. Ibid.

289. Inventory list, Tanner Papers, Archives of American Art, roll D307, frame 0906.

290. Minister of Foreign Affairs to Minister of Fine Arts, February 20, 1922, Tanner File, Archives Nationale, Paris, F21 4342.

291. Ibid.

292. See "Art Exhibitions of the Week—The Grand Central Galleries are Exhibiting Religious Paintings by H. O. Tanner," *New York Times*, January 27, 1924, p. 12; and "Tanner Exhibits Paintings: Negro Artist Shows Pictures at Grand Central Art Galleries," *New York Times*, January 29, 1924, p. 9.

293. Harrison Morris to Robert DeForest, February 8, 1924, Tanner Papers, Archives of American Art, roll D306, frame 296.

294. See correspondence between Henry O. Tanner and Raymond Pace Alexander, Alexander Papers, University of Pennsylvania.

295. Pennell, *Adventures*, pp. 53-54.

296. Karen Fish, "The Annual American Exhibition at the Art Institute of Chicago," *American Magazine of Art*, 17 (December 1926), pp. 622, 624.

297. See Hunter, *French Painting*, pp. 206-207.

298. Quoted in Mathews, *Tanner*, p. 201.

299. See Henry O. Tanner to Sadie and Raymond Alexander, May 30, 1927, Alexander Papers, University of Pennsylvania.

300. Quoted in Mathews, *Tanner*, p. 219.

301. Ibid., pp. 236-237.

302. Quoted in Ibid., p. 220.

303. Morrison et al., *American Republic*, vol. 2, p. 595.

304. Henry O. Tanner to Sadie T. M. Alexander, August 30, 1933, Alexander Papers, University of Pennsylvania.

305. Henry O. Tanner to Sadie T. M. Alexander, December 29, 1936, Alexander Papers, University of Pennsylvania; Countee Cullen to Tanner, September 23, 1928, Tanner Papers, Archives of American Art, roll D306, frame 502; and Palmer Hayden to Tanner, September 25, 1930, Tanner Papers, Archives of American Art, roll D306, frame 620.

306. Henry O. Tanner to Mary Tanner Mossell, December 16, 1931, Alexander Papers, University of Pennsylvania.

307. See Henry O. Tanner to Sadie and Raymond Alexander, November 16, 1933, Alexander Papers, University of Pennsylvania.

308. Mathews, *Tanner*, p. 226.

309. Ibid, pp. 240-241.

310. Ibid, pp. 227-228.

311. Albert Smith to Arthur Schomburg, February 15, [1935?], Albert Smith Letters, Schomberg Center for Research in Black Culture, New York Public Library.

312. Henry O. Tanner to Maudelle B. Bousfield, March 24, 1935, Tanner Papers, Archives of American Art.

313. See Henry O. Tanner to Sadie and Raymond Alexander, Alexander Papers, University of Pennsylvania, passim.

314. Draft of letter by Henry O. Tanner to the Director of the American Hospital, c. November, 1936, Tanner Papers, Archives of American Art, roll D306, frame 1190.

315. Quoted in Mathews, *Tanner*, pp. 247-248.

316. Inventory, Tanner Papers, Archives of American Art, roll D307.

317. James A. Porter to Henry O. Tanner, November 29, 1936, Tanner Papers, Archives of American Art, roll D306, frame 1107.

318. Porter, *Modern Negro Art*, pp. 75-76.

319. Henry O. Tanner to Sadie T. M. Alexander, May 22, 1937, Alexander Papers, University of Pennsylvania.

320. Atherton Curtis, Journal, gave Tanner's death as May 24 and burial as May 26. Newspaper accounts corroborate this. See "Henry Tanner, 77, Dies in Paris; Was American Negro Painter," *New York Herald Tribune*, May 26, 1937, p. 16.

321. *Memorial Exhibition of Paintings by Henry O. Tanner*, exh. cat. (Philadelphia: Philadelphia Art Alliance, 1945).

322. See, for example, *Henry O. Tanner: An Afro-American Romantic Realist (1859-1937)*, exh. cat. (Atlanta: Spelman College, 1969); *The Art of Henry O. Tanner (1859-1937)*, exh. cat. (Washington, D.C.: Frederick Douglass Institute and National Collection of Fine Arts, 1969); and *The Art of Henry Ossawa Tanner (1859-1937): From the Collection of the Museum of African Art/Frederick Douglass Institute*, exh. cat. (Glens Falls, N.Y.: Hyde Collection, 1972).

323. Robert MacCameron to Henry O. Tanner, June 25, 1908, Tanner Papers, Archives of American Art, roll D306, frame 89.

324. *Howardena Pindell, Paintings and Drawings* (Potsdam: Roland Gibson Gallery at Potsdam College of the State University of New York, 1992), p. 20.

325. Charles Baudelaire, *Art in Paris, 1845-1862*, translated and edited by Jonathan Mayne (London: Phaidon, 1965), p. 99.

326. Revell, *Paul Laurence Dunbar*, p. 17.

327. See Bhalla and Gaither in Spelman College, *Tanner*, 1969, n.p.; and *Harlem Renaissance: Art of Black America*, exh. cat. (New York: Studio Museum in Harlem; Abrams, 1987), passim.

328. Quoted in Mathews, *Tanner*, p. 3.

EXHIBITION CHECKLIST

All works in the exhibition are illustrated as plates. Measurements are given in inches followed by centimeters; height precedes width.
*denotes Kansas City venue only
**denotes Kansas City and Dallas venues only

Burnt Pines: Adirondacks (Flora), c. 1880
Oil on canvas
39 3/4 x 31 1/2 (101 x 80)
Signed lower right: HOTanner [monogram]
Hampton University Museum, Virginia

Point Judith, c. 1880
Oil on canvas board
8 x 12 (20.3 x 30.5)
Signed lower right: HOTanner [monogram]
Private collection

Seascape: Three Men in a Boat, c. 1880
(possible original title *Hazy Morning at Narragansett*)
Oil on canvas
17 1/2 x 28 (44.5 x 71.1)
Unsigned
Dr. Rae Alexander-Minter

Camping Scene: Adirondack Reminiscence, 1880
Oil on canvas
18 1/4 x 14 1/4 (46.4 x 36.2)
Signed and dated lower right: HOTanner [monogram]/1880
Dr. and Mrs. Dwight L. McKenna, New Orleans, Louisiana

Sister Sarah, c. 1881-82
Oil on canvas
16 x 13 (40.6 x 33)
Signed and inscribed lower right: To my Sister Sarah/Henry O. Tanner
Private collection

Sand Dunes at Sunset, Atlantic City, c. 1885
(possible original title *Back from the Beach*)
Oil on canvas
29 1/4 x 58 3/4 (74.3 x 149.2)
Signed lower left: HOTanner [monogram]
Dr. Rae Alexander-Minter

Study for Androcles, c. 1885-86
Oil on canvas
31 x 18 (78.7 x 45.7)
Signed upper right: Tanner
Private collection

Adirondack Landscape, 1886
(formerly *Georgia Landscape*)
Oil on canvas
16 x 25 (40.6 x 63.5)
Scratched into paint lower right: H. O. Tanner/1886
The Springfield Museum of Art, Ohio

Lion Licking Its Paw, 1886
Oil on canvas
30 x 36 (76.2 x 91.4)
Signed and dated lower right: HOTanner [monogram]/1886
Allentown Art Museum, Pennsylvania; gift of Mr. and Mrs. Philip Berman, 1962 (62.05)

Wynkoop House, Old Haarlem, 1888
Oil on canvas
18 1/2 x 13 1/2 (47 x 34.3)
Signed and dated lower left: H. O. Tanner/1888
New Britain Museum of American Art; John Butler Talcott Fund

Mountain Landscape, Highlands, North Carolina, c. 1889
Watercolor, pencil and colored pencil on paper
10 13/16 x 15 (27.5 x 38.1)
Unsigned
National Museum of American Art, Smithsonian Institution; gift of Mr. and Mrs. Norman B. Robbins

Mountain Landscape, Highlands, North Carolina, c. 1889
Oil on canvas
24 x 36 (61 x 91.4)
Signed lower left: HOTanner [monogram]
Berea College Art Department, Kentucky

Concarneau, 1891
Oil on canvas
10 x 17 (25.4 x 43.2)
Signed, inscribed, and dated lower left: H. O. Tanner/
Concarneau/91
Mr. William R. Dorsey

Bust-Length Study of a Bearded Man with Short Hair, c. 1891-93
Charcoal on paper
12 x 9 1/2 (30.5 x 24.1)
Unsigned
Schomburg Center for Research in Black Culture, Art and Artifacts Division, The New York Public Library, Astor, Lenox and Tilden Foundation

Still Life With Fruit, c. 1894
Oil on canvas
19 x 25 (48.3 x 63.5)
Signed lower left: H. O. Tanner
Schomburg Center for Research in Black Culture, Art and Artifacts Division, The New York Public Library, Astor, Lenox and Tilden Foundation

Study for The Thankful Poor, c. 1894
Oil on canvas
12 3/4 x 16 1/4 (32.4 x 41.3)
Unsigned
Du Sable Museum of African American History, Inc., Chicago, Illinois

****Pont-Aven Landscape***, 1894
Oil on canvas
18 1/2 x 14 3/4 (47 x 37.5)
Signed and dated lower right: H. O. Tanner 94
Du Sable Museum of African American History, Inc., Chicago, Illinois

Bagpipe Player, 1895
Oil on canvas
21 1/2 x 18 (54.6 x 45.7)
Signed, inscribed and dated lower left: H. O. Tanner/
Paris 95
Private collection

The Young Sabot Maker, 1895
Oil on canvas
41 x 35 (104.1 x 88.9)
Signed and dated lower left: H. O. Tanner/1895
Private collection; courtesy of Michael Rosenfeld Gallery, New York

The Wailing Wall, c. 1897
Oil on canvas
25 1/2 x 19 1/4 (64.8 x 48.9)
Signed lower right: H. O. Tanner
Museum of Art, Rhode Island School of Design; gift of Mr. and Mrs. Leonard Granoff

Bishop Benjamin Tucker Tanner, 1897
Oil on canvas
13 x 9 1/4 (33 x 23.5)
Inscribed, signed, and dated lower right: a hurried study of my dear/Father/H. O. Tanner/Kan. City/Sep. 1897
Dr. Rae Alexander-Minter

****Kansas City, Kansas***, 1897
Watercolor and pencil on paper
9 7/8 x 13 7/8 (25.1 x 35.3)
Unsigned
National Museum of American Art, Smithsonian Institution; gift of Mr. and Mrs. Norman B. Robbins, 1983.95.29

Kansas City, Kansas, 1897
Watercolor and pencil on paper
9 3/16 x 13 7/8 (24.9 x 35.3)
Inscribed lower left: Kansas City, Kansas
National Museum of American Art, Smithsonian Institution; gift of Mr. and Mrs. Norman B. Robbins, 1983.95.30

Mother of Henry O. Tanner, 1897
Oil on wood
13 x 9 1/4 (30 x 23.5)
Unsigned
National Museum of American Art, Smithsonian Institution; gift of Dr. Nicholas Zervas

Portrait of the Artist's Mother, 1897
Oil on canvas
29 1/4 x 39 1/2 (74.3 x 100.3)
Inscribed, signed, and dated lower right: To my dear Mother/H. O. Tanner/1897
Philadelphia Museum of Art; partial gift of Dr. Rae Alexander-Minter and purchased with the W. P. Wilstach Fund, the George W. Elkins Fund, and funds contributed by the Dietrich Foundation and a private donor

The Annunciation, 1898
Oil on canvas
57 x 71 1/2 (144.8 x 181.6)
Signed and dated lower left: H. O. Tanner/1898
Philadelphia Museum of Art; purchased with the W. P. Wilstach Fund

A View in Palestine, c. 1898-99
Oil on canvas
22 1/2 x 37 (57.2 x 94)
Signed lower left: H. O. Tanner
The Frances Lehman Loeb Art Center, Vassar College, Poughkeepsie, New York; gift of Mrs. Walter Driscoll (Margaret L. Weyerhaeuser, class of 1923), Mrs. F. Rodman Titcomb (Elizabeth L. Weyerhaeuser, class of 1915) and Mrs. Robert J. Sivertsen (Sarah Weyerhaeuser, ex class of 1930)

*****Nicodemus***, 1899
Oil on canvas
33 11/16 x 39 1/2 (85.6 x 100.3)
Signed and dated lower left: H. O. Tanner/ Jerusalem 1899
Pennsylvania Academy of the Fine Arts, Philadelphia; Joseph E. Temple Fund, 1900.1

The Savior, c. 1900-05
Oil on canvas
29 1/8 x 21 7/8 (74 x 55.6)
Unsigned
National Museum of American Art, Smithsonian Institution; gift of Mr. and Mrs. Norman B. Robbins

Study for Rachel, from the Mothers of the Bible, c. 1901
Charcoal on paper
23 x 13 5/8 (58.4 x 34.6)
Unsigned
National Museum of American Art, Smithsonian Institution; gift of Mr. and Mrs. Norman B. Robbins

Study for Jesus, 1901
Charcoal on paper
11 3/4 x 9 1/4 (29.8 x 23.5)
Unsigned
Schomburg Center for Research in Black Culture, Art and Artifacts Division, The New York Public Library, Astor, Lenox and Tilden Foundation

Return of the Holy Women, 1904
Oil on canvas
46 1/2 x 35 (118.1 x 88.9)
Signed and dated lower right: H. O. Tanner/1904
Verso painting: *Study for Two Disciples at the Tomb*
Cedar Rapids Museum of Art; Art Association Purchase, Club of Forty Fund

Abraham's Oak, 1905
Oil on canvas
21 5/8 x 28 5/8 (54.9 x 72.7)
Signed lower left: H. O. Tanner
National Museum of American Art, Smithsonian Institution; gift of Mr. and Mrs. Norman B. Robbins

Pilgrims at Emmaus, 1905
Oil on canvas
73 1/4 x 83 1/2 (186 x 212)
Signed and dated lower left: H. O. Tanner/-MCM.V-
Musée d'Orsay, Paris

Two Disciples at the Tomb, c. 1905-06
Oil on canvas
51 x 41 5/8 (129.5 x 105.7)
Signed lower left: H. O. Tanner
The Art Institute of Chicago; Robert A. Waller Fund, 1906.300

The Disciples See Christ Walking on the Water, c. 1907
Oil on canvas
51 1/2 x 42 (130.8 x 106.7)
Signed lower right: H. O. Tanner
Des Moines Art Center Permanent Collection; gift of the Des Moines Association of Fine Arts, 1921.1

Moonlight, Hebron, c. 1907
Oil on canvas
25 11/16 x 31 7/8 (65.3 x 81)
Signed lower left: H. O. Tanner
Milwaukee Art Museum; gift of Mr. and Mrs. Thomas Whipple Dunbar

Flight Into Egypt, c. 1907-12
Oil on canvas
19 7/8 x 25 1/2 (50.5 x 64.8)
Signed lower right: H. O. Tanner
Willkie House, Inc., Des Moines, Iowa

*****Entrance to the Customs House, Tangier***, c. 1908
Oil on panel
21 x 23 (53.3 x 58.4)
Signed lower left: H. O. Tanner
Verso: Sketch in charcoal, *Arrival of the Three Wisemen*
George and Joyce Wein; courtesy of Michael Rosenfeld Gallery, New York

Christ and His Mother Studying the Scriptures, c. 1909
Oil on canvas
48 3/4 x 40 (123.8 x 101.6)
Signed lower left: H. O. Tanner
Dallas Museum of Art; Deaccession Funds

The Three Marys, c. 1909
Oil on canvas
42 x 50 (106.7 x 127)
Signed lower right: H. O. Tanner
Fisk University, Nashville, Tennessee

The Holy Family, c. 1909-10
Oil on canvas
35 x 42 3/4 (88.9 x 108.6)
Signed lower left: H. O. Tanner
Muskegon Museum of Art, Michigan; Hackley Picture Fund

Le Touquet, c. 1910
Oil on canvas
29 x 36 3/4 (73.7 x 93.3)
Signed and inscribed lower right: H. O. Tanner
Des Moines Art Center Permanent Collection; gift of Florence L. Carpenter, 1941.5

Moonrise, Tangier, c. 1912
Oil on panel
20 x 24 (50.8 x 61)
Unsigned
Hamilton College Collection, New York; gift of Elihu Root

Near East Scene, 1912
Oil and casein on canvas
28 3/4 x 23 1/2 (73 x 59.7)
Signed lower right: H. O. Tanner
Des Moines Art Center Permanent Collection; bequest of Edith King Pearson, 1964.76

*****Miraculous Haul of Fishes***, c. 1913-14
Oil on canvas
38 x 47 1/2 (96.5 x 120.7)
Signed lower right: H. O. Tanner
National Academy of Design, New York

War Scene, Etaples, France, c. 1914
Oil on cardboard
9 1/2 x 13 1/8 (24 x 33.3)
Unsigned; inscribed on the verso by Jesse Ossawa Tanner: War Scene 1914-1918/Etaples, France JT
Clark Atlanta University Collection of African American Art, Atlanta, Georgia

The Good Shepherd, c. 1917
Oil on canvas
20 1/4 x 24 1/8 (51.4 x 61.3)
Signed lower left: H. O. Tanner
New Orleans Museum of Art; gift of Dr. I. M. Cline, New Orleans

Portrait of Booker T. Washington, 1917
Oil on canvas
31 3/4 x 25 5/8 (80.6 x 65.1)
Signed, inscribed, and dated lower left: H. O. Tanner/Paris/1917
State Historical Society of Iowa, Des Moines

A.R.C. Canteen, World War I, 1918
Charcoal on paper
17 1/2 x 22 (44.5 x 55.9)
Unsigned
National Museum of American Art, Smithsonian Institution; gift of Mr. and Mrs. Norman B. Robbins

American Red Cross Canteen at the Front, 1918
Oil on canvas
48 x 61 (121.9 x 154.9)
Signed, inscribed, and dated lower right: H. O. Tanner/Neufchateau, France 1918
American Red Cross

The Arch, 1919
Oil on canvas
39 1/4 x 38 3/8 (99.7 x 97.5)
Signed lower left: H. O. Tanner; additional signature and reworked inscription lower left: H. O. Tanner/Paris July 13, 1914
The Brooklyn Museum; gift of Alfred W. Jenkins 32.10

Moses in the Bullrushes, 1921
(originally titled *Hiding of Moses*)
Oil on wood
22 3/8 x 15 1/4 (56.8 x 38.7)
Signed and dated lower left: H. O. Tanner/1921
National Museum of American Art, Smithsonian Institution; gift of Mr. and Mrs. Norman B. Robbins

Two Disciples at the Tomb, c. 1923
Oil on board
51 1/2 x 43 1/4 (130.8 x 109.9)
Signed lower left: H. O. Tanner
Merton D. Simpson

*****Etaples Fisher Folk***, 1923
Tempera and oil on canvas
47 5/16 x 38 5/16 (120.2 x 97.3)
Signed and dated lower right: H. O. Tanner/1923
High Museum of Art, Atlanta, Georgia; J. J. Haverty Collection, 36.16

At the Gates, c. 1926
Oil on panel
24 x 19 (61 x 48.3)
Unsigned
Private collection

Disciples Healing the Sick, c. 1930
Oil on cardboard
36 x 48 (91.4 x 121.9)
Unsigned
Clark Atlanta University Collection of African American Art, Atlanta, Georgia

The Lost Sheep, c. 1930
(The Good Shepherd)
Oil and tempera on paperboard
10 5/8 x 8 1/8 (27 x 20.7)
Inscribed on verso: partially illegible notes on technique for application of paint
The Menil Collection

Study for Mary, Return from the Crucifixion, c. 1933
Pencil and conte crayon on paper mounted on paperboard
15 1/16 x 14 3/16 (39.6 x 37.6)
Inscribed, signed, and dated lower left: Study for/Return from the Crucifixion/H. O. Tanner/1933
National Museum of American Art, Smithsonian Institution; gift of Mr. and Mrs. Norman B. Robbins

Return from the Crucifixion, 1936
Oil and tempera on plywood
17 x 22 (43 x 55.8)
Signed and dated lower right: H. O. Tanner/1936
Howard University Gallery of Art, Washington, D.C.

SELECTED BIBLIOGRAPHY

Monographic Sources

Archives and Manuscript Collections

Archives Nationales. Paris, France. Henry O. Tanner (1859-1937) Files.

Archives of American Art. Smithsonian Institution. Washington, D.C. Henry Ossawa Tanner Papers, 1850-1978.

Archives of the Carnegie Institute. Pittsburgh, Pennsylvania. John W. Beatty (1851-1924) Papers.

Pennsylvania Academy of the Fine Arts Archives. Philadelphia, Pennsylvania. Henry Ossawa Tanner File, 1885-1904.

Trevor Arnett Library. Atlanta University. Atlanta, Georgia. Henry Ossawa Tanner Collection (1907-1937).

University of Pennsylvania Archives. Philadelphia, Pennsylvania. Alexander Papers: Papers of or Relating to Henry Ossawa Tanner (1859-1937).

Books, Dissertations, and Exhibition Catalogues

The Art of Henry O. Tanner (1859-1937), exh. cat. (Washington, D.C.: Frederick Douglass Institute and National Collection of Fine Arts, 1969).

The Art of Henry Ossawa Tanner (1859-1937) from the Collection of The Museum of African Art/Frederick Douglass Institute, exh. cat. (Glens Falls, N.Y.: Hyde Collection, 1972).

Catalogue of Recent Paintings by Henry O. Tanner, exh. cat. (New York: M. Knoedler and Co., 1913).

Drawings, Lithographs, Etchings and Watercolors by Henry O. Tanner, N.A. (1859-1937), exh. cat. (New York: Grand Central Art Galleries, 1968).

Exhibition of Paintings by Henry O. Tanner, exh. cat. (Chicago: Thurber Art Galleries, 1911).

Exhibition of Paintings by Henry O. Tanner, exh. cat. (Chicago: Thurber Art Galleries, 1913).

Henry O. Tanner: An Afro-American Romantic Realist (1859-1937), exh. cat. (Atlanta: Spelman College and the Coordinated Art Program of the Atlanta University Center, 1969).

Henry Ossawa Tanner, exh. cat. (Philadelphia: Philadelphia Museum of Art, 1991).

Illustrated Catalogue of Religious Paintings by the Distinguished American Artist Mr. Henry O. Tanner, exh. cat. (New York: American Art Galleries, 1908).

Mathews, Marcia M., *Henry Ossawa Tanner, American Artist* (Chicago: University of Chicago Press, 1969).

Memorial Exhibition of Paintings by Henry O. Tanner, exh. cat. (Philadelphia: Philadelphia Art Alliance, 1945).

Paintings by H. O. Tanner, exh. cat. (Boston: Vose Galleries, 1921).

Paintings by Henry O. Tanner, exh. cat. (New York: Grand Central Art Galleries, 1924).

Simon, Walter A., "Henry O. Tanner: A Study of the Development of an American Negro Artist, 1859-1937," Ph.D. dissertation, New York University, 1960.

Woods, Naurice Frank, Jr., "The Life and Work of Henry O. Tanner," Ph.D. dissertation, Columbia Pacific University, 1987.

Periodicals

"Academy Elects Members, Twelve Painters and Six Sculptors Win the Honor," *New York Times*, April 15, 1909, p. 18.

"Afro-American Painter Who Has Become Famous in Paris," *Current Literature*, 45 (October 1908), pp. 404-408.

Allen, Charles E., "American [Dr. Rae Alexander-Minter] Finds Roots in Rural France," *International Herald Tribune*, October 2, 1987, p. 8.

"American Artists Rank High Abroad: Exhibits at Old Salon Now Compete With World," *New York Journal of Commerce*, April 30, 1914, p. 6.

"American Negro Who Leads France in Art," *North American* (Philadelphia), June 10, 1906, n.p.

"Art Exhibitions of the Week," *New York Times*, January 27, 1924, p. 12.

"Art News of the Week," *New York Sun*, April 13, 1913, p. 3.

"Art Notes," *Daily Evening Telegraph* (Philadelphia), April 28, 1894, p. 11.

"Art Prize Won by Negro: Henry O. Tanner Awarded Harris Gift at the Institute," *Chronicle* (Chicago), October 30, 1910.

"Artist Tanner in America," *A.M.E. Church Review*, 14 (October 1897), pp. 278-280.

Bal, George, "M. Tanner a Terminé son Envoi au Salon," *New York Herald* (Paris), March 28, 1908, p. 6.

Baldwin, Elbert T., "A Negro Artist of Unique Power," *Outlook*, 44 (January-April 1900), pp. 793-796.

Barton, William E., "An American Painter of the Resurrection," *The Advance* (March 20, 1913), pp. 2011-2014.

Bently, Florence L., "Henry O. Tanner," *Voice of the Negro* (November 1906), pp. 480-482.

Boime, Albert, "Henry Ossawa Tanner's Subversion of Genre," *Art Bulletin*, 75 (September 1993), pp. 415-442.

Burke, Daniel, "Henry Ossawa Tanner's *La Sainte-Marie*," *Smithsonian Studies in American Art*, 2 (Spring 1988), pp. 64-73.

"A Bust of Bishop Payne," *Christian Recorder*, 31 (December 14, 1893), p. 2.

Campbell, F. J., "Henry O. Tanner's Biblical Pictures," *Fine Arts Journal*, 25 (March 1911), pp. 163-166.

"The 'Century's' American Artists Series: Henry O. Tanner," *Century Illustrated Monthly Magazine*, 59 (November 1899-April 1900), p. 962.

Clark, Kate U., "Old Win-ne-Wan's Star," *Harper's Young People*, 9 (January 10, 1888), pp. 185-187.

Cole, Helen, "Henry O. Tanner, Painter," *Brush and Pencil*, 6 (June 1900), pp. 97-107.

Du Bois, W. E. B., "Tanner," *Crisis*, 28 (May 1924), p. 12.

_______ , "Tanner," *Crisis*, 31 (January 1926), p. 146.

"Editor's Notes," *Christian Recorder*, 32 (April 19, 1894), p. 8.

Fauset, Jessie, "Henry Ossawa Tanner," *Crisis*, 27 (April 1924), pp. 255-258.

"Fine Pictures Are Shown by Negro Artist: Views in Morocco Are Feature of Mr. Henry O. Tanner's Work," *New York Herald*, April 19, 1913.

Forbes, George W., "Within the Sphere of Letters: Tanner's 'First in Boston,'" *A.M.E. Church Review*, 37 (April 1921), p. 252.

Forman, Nessa, "Lost Painting by Black Artist Found in Basement of School," *Philadelphia Bulletin*, December 20, 1970, sect. G.

Harper, Jennifer J., "The Early Religious Paintings of Henry Ossawa Tanner: A Study of the Influences of Church, Family, and Era," *American Art*, 6 (Fall 1992), pp. 69-86.

Heilig, Sterling, "Henry Tanner, An American Negro, May Win This Year's Medal of Honor at the Great Paris Salon," *Baltimore Sun*, June 14, 1908, p. 14.

"Henry Tanner, 77, Dies in Paris; Was American Negro Painter," *New York Herald-Tribune*, May 26, 1937, p. 16.

James, Milton M., "Henry O. Tanner," *Negro History Bulletin*, 20 (February 1957), pp. 98, 115-117.

Joseph, Oscar L., "Henry O. Tanner's Religious Paintings," *Epworth Herald*, March 6, 1909, pp. 1042-1043.

Lester, William R., "Henry O. Tanner, Exile for Art's Sake," *Alexander's Magazine*, 7 (December 15, 1908), pp. 69-73.

"Local News," *Christian Recorder*, 20 (March 30, 1882), p. 2.

MacChesney, Clara T., "A Poet-Painter of Palestine," *International Studio*, 50 (July 1913), pp. xi-xv.

Mitchell, Charles B., "An American Religious Painter," *Westminster* (January 30, 1909), p. 10.

Monroe, Harriet, "Artist Shows His Pictures," *Chicago Daily Tribune*, February 2, 1911, p. 3.

[Morris, Harrison S.], "Mr. H. O. Tanner's Great Religious Paintings," *Ladies Home Journal* (September 1902), p. 1.

"Mr. H. O. Tanner's Picture *The Raising of Lazarus*," *Harper's Weekly*, 41 (August 7, 1897), p. 780.

"The Negro in Art: H. O. Tanner's Latest Triumph," *A.M.E. Church Review*, 14 (July 1897), pp. 165-167.

"Negro's Painting a Paris Sensation: Place of Honor in Salon for Brother-in-Law of Pastor of Howard Place Church," *Scranton Times* (Pennsylvania), May 22, 1908.

"Notes and Comments," *Christian Recorder*, 32 (January 11, 1894), p. 2.

"Paintings by Henry O. Tanner," *New York Times*, April 13, 1913, p. 14.

"Pays Tribute to Henry O. Tanner: *Current Literature* Praises Former Local Artist," *Kansas City Journal* (Missouri), October 18, 1908, p. 5.

"Personal," *Christian Recorder*, 18 (April 8, 1880), p. 4.

_______ , 19 (November 24, 1881), p. 3.

_______ , 20 (August 17, 1882), p. 2.

_______ , 23 (April 16, 1885), p. 2.

_______ , 23 (May 21, 1885), p. 2.

_______ , 24 (September 16, 1886), p. 2.

_______ , 25 (October 13, 1887), p. 5.

_______ , 26 (January 26, 1888), p. 5.

Pyne, Kathleen, "Henry Ossawa Tanner (1859-1937)," *Bulletin of the Detroit Institute of Arts*, 55 (1977), pp. 106-109.

"Religious Works in Tanner Exhibit: Emotional Picturesquesness Manifest in Paintings at American Galleries," *New York Times*, December 19, 1908, p. 7.

Richard, Paul, "About the Henry Tanner Hangup," *Washington Post*, August 3, 1969, p. G4.

Romeyn, Carlyn G. C., "Henry O. Tanner: Atlanta Interlude," *Atlanta Historical Society Journal*, 27 (Winter 1983-84), pp. 27-40.

St. Laurent, Philip, "The Negro in World History: Part 51, Henry Ossawa Tanner," *Tuesday Magazine*, 6 (January 1971), pp. 10-11, 14, 16, 20.

Scarborough, W. S., "Henry Ossian [sic] Tanner," *Southern Workman*, 31 (December 1902), pp. 661-670.

Secrest, Meryle, "Paintings by Black Expatriate," *Washington Post*, July 22, 1969, p. C7.

"Tanner Exhibits Paintings: Negro Artist Shows Pictures at Grand Central Art Galleries," *New York Times*, January 29, 1924, p. 9.

"The Tanner Family," *Negro History Bulletin* (April 1947), pp. 147-152, 167.

Tanner, Henry O., "An Artist's Autobiography," *The Advance* (March 20, 1913), pp. 2012-2014.

_______ , "Compulsory Education and Valedictory Address," *Christian Recorder*, 15 (July 12, 1877), p. 3.

_______ , "A Series of Four Great Biblical Paintings. I: Sarah," *Ladies Home Journal* (September 1902), p. 9.

_______ , "A Series of Four Great Biblical Paintings. II: Hagar," *Ladies Home Journal* (October 1902), p. 13.

_______ , "This is the Third of a Series of Four Great Biblical Paintings. III: Rachel," *Ladies Home Journal* (November 1902), p. 13.

_______ , "The Last of a Series of Four Great Biblical Paintings. IV: Mary," *Ladies Home Journal* (January 1903), p. 13.

_______ , "The Story of an Artist's Life," *World's Work*, 18 (June and July 1909), pp. 11661-66, 11769-75.

_______ , "A Visit to the Tomb of Lazarus," *A.M.E. Church Review*, 15 (January 1908), pp. 359-361.

"Tanner Jubilee: Hampton Institute Shows Off its Henry Ossawa Turner [sic] Collection," *American Visions*, 1 (July/August 1986), pp. 20-23.

"Tanner's Art Full of Religious Spirit," *Public Ledger* (Philadelphia), December 20, 1908, sect. 1, p. 14.

Thompson, Vance, "American Artists in Paris: H. O. Tanner; the Brother in Black," *Cosmopolitan*, 29 (May 1900), pp. 17-20.

Wesley, Charles H., "Henry O. Tanner," *Negro History Bulletin*, 31 (January 1968), p. 6.

_______ , "Henry O. Tanner, the Artist: An Appreciation," *Howard University Record*, 15 (April 1920), pp. 299-306.

Wilson, Judith, "Lifting 'The Veil': Henry O. Tanner's *The Banjo Lesson* and *The Thankful Poor*," *Contributions in Black Studies*, 9-10 (1990-1992), pp. 31-54.

Woodruff, Hale, "My Meeting with Henry O. Tanner," *Crisis* (January 1970), pp. 7-12.

General Sources on Art

Books, Dissertations, and Exhibition Catalogues

American Expatriate Painters of the Late Nineteenth Century, exh. cat. (Dayton, Ohio: Dayton Art Institute, 1976).

American Imagination and Symbolist Painting, exh. cat. (New York: Grey Art Gallery and Study Center, New York University, 1979).

Americans in Brittany and Normandy, 1860-1910, exh. cat. (Phoenix: Phoenix Art Museum, 1982).

Art and Artists of the South: The Robert P. Coggins Collection, exh. cat. (Columbia: University of South Carolina Press, 1984).

Bearden, Romare, and Harry Henderson, *Six Black Masters of American Art* (New York: Zenith Books, 1972).

Boime, Albert, *The Academy and French Painting in the Nineteenth Century* (London: Phaidon, 1971).

Cain, Jules, Jean Vallery-Radot, and Jean Prinet, *La Collection Curtis: estampes et dessins de maitres* (Paris: Bibliotheque Nationale, 1951).

Crannell [Romeyn], Carol G., "In Pursuit of Culture: A History of Art Activity in Atlanta 1847-1926," Ph.D. dissertation, Emory University, 1981.

Dover, Cedric, *American Negro Art* (Greenwich, Conn.: New York Graphic Society, 1960).

L'Ecole de Pont-Aven dans les Collections Publiques et Privées de Bretagne, exh. cat. (Quimper, France: Musée des Beaux-Arts, 1978).

Edward Mitchell Bannister, exh. cat. (New York: Kenkeleba House, 1992).

Fine, Elsa Honig, *The Afro-American Artist: A Search for Identity* (New York: Holt, Rinehart and Winston, 1973).

Fink, Lois Marie, *American Art at the Nineteenth-Century Paris Salons* (Cambridge: Cambridge University Press, 1990).

Free Within Ourselves: African-American Artists in the Collection of the National Museum of American Art, exh. cat. (Washington, D.C.: National Museum of American Art, 1992).

French Salon Paintings from Southern Collections, exh. cat. (Atlanta: High Museum of Art, 1982).

Hall, James, *Dictionary of Subjects and Symbols in Art* (New York: Harper & Row, 1979).

The Hand and The Spirit: Religious Art in America 1700-1900, exh. cat. (Berkeley, Calif.: University Art Museum, 1972).

Harlem Renaissance: Art of Black America, exh. cat. (New York: Studio Museum in Harlem, 1987).

Honour, Hugh, *The Image of the Black in Western Art*, 4 vols. (Cambridge, Mass.: Menil Foundation, 1989).

Hunter, Sam, *Modern French Painting, 1855-1956* (New York: Dell Publishing, 1956).

Igoe, Lynn, *250 Years of Afro-American Art: An Annotated Bibliography* (New York: Bowker, 1981).

J. J. Haverty: The Taste of a Southern Collector, exh. cat. (Atlanta: High Museum of Art, 1981).

Jackman, Rilla Evelyn, *American Arts* (Chicago: Rand, McNally & Co., 1928).

Le Paul, Judy, *Gauguin and the Impressionists at Pont-Aven* (New York: Abbeville Press, 1987).

Matisse in Morocco: The Paintings and Drawings, 1912-1913, exh. cat. (Washington, D.C.: National Gallery of Art, 1990).

Milner, John, *The Studios of Paris: The Capital of Art in the Late Nineteenth Century* (New Haven, Conn.: Yale University Press, 1988).

Modern Meets the Masses: 1910-1920, exh. cat. (Southampton, N.Y.: Parrish Art Museum, 1994).

Mosby, Dewey F., *Alexandre-Gabriel Decamps (1803-1860),* 2 vols. (New York: Garland Publishing, 1977).

The Orientalists: Delacroix to Matisse: The Allure of North Africa and the Near East, exh. cat. (Washington, D.C.: National Gallery of Art, 1984).

Paris 1889: American Artists at the Universal Exposition, exh. cat. (Philadelphia: Pennsylvania Academy of the Fine Arts, 1989).

Pennell, Joseph, *The Adventures of an Illustrator Mostly in Following His Authors in America and Europe* (Boston: Little, Brown, & Co., 1925).

Pennsylvania Academy of the Fine Arts, *The Annual Exhibition Record of the Pennsylvania Academy of the Fine Arts 1876-1913,* edited by Peter Hastings Falk (Madison, Conn.: Sound View Press, 1989).

Porter, James, *Modern Negro Art* (New York: The Dryden Press, 1943).

The Realist Tradition: French Paintings and Drawings 1830-1900, exh. cat. (Cleveland: Cleveland Museum of Art, 1980).

The Remarkable Morgan State Collection (Baltimore: Baltimore Life Insurance Company, n.d.).

Rewald, John, *The History of Impressionism* (New York: Museum of Modern Art, 1961).

The Romantics to Rodin, exh. cat. (Los Angeles: Los Angeles County Museum of Art, 1980).

Sharing Traditions: Five Black Artists in Nineteenth-Century America from the Collections of the National Museum of American Art, exh. cat. (Washington, D.C.: National Museum of American Art, 1985).

A Special Exhibition of Paintings and Sculpture by Six American Artists Resident in Paris, exh. cat. (St. Louis: Museum of Fine Arts, 1907).

Sullivan, Edward J., and Nina A. Mallory, *Painting in Spain 1650-1700 from North American Collections,* exh. cat. (Princeton, N.J.: Princeton University Museum of Art, 1982).

Sutton, Denys, and Catherine Puget, *Une Vie de Bohème: Lettres du Peintre Armand Séguin à Roderic O'Conor 1895-1903* (Pont-Aven, France: Musée de Pont-Aven, 1989).

Le Symbolisme en Europe, exh. cat. (Rotterdam: Museum Boymans-Van Beuningen, 1976).

Ten Afro-American Artists in the Nineteenth Century, exh. cat. (Washington, D.C.: Howard University Gallery of Art, 1967).

Three Nineteenth-Century Afro-American Artists: Joshua Johnston (c. 1765-1830), Robert S. Duncanson (1821-1872) and Henry O. Tanner (1859-1937), exh. cat. (Cedar Rapids, Iowa: Cedar Rapids Arts Center, 1980).

Ward, Meredith, *Adventure and Inspiration: American Artists in Other Lands* (New York: Hirschl & Adler Galleries, 1988).

Winslow Homer's Images of Blacks: The Civil War and Reconstruction Years, exh. cat. (Austin: University of Texas Press, 1989).

Periodicals

Alexandre, Arsène, "Artistes Français," *Le Figaro,* April 30, 1910, pp. 3-5.

"L'Amerique au Temps de la Statue de la Liberté," *Le Petit Journal des Grandes Expositions*, 163 (1986).

"American Art is Represented at Paris Salon: Authority at 132nd Exhibition of Society of French Artists Declares 'Americans Who Came to Learn are Staying to Teach,'" *Buffalo News*, April 29, 1914.

Borgmeyer, Charles-Louis, "The Luxembourg Museum and its Treasures," *Fine Arts Journal* (May 1912), pp. 303-304.

Brownell, W. C., "The Art Schools of Philadelphia," *Scribner's Monthly*, 28 (1879), pp. 737-750.

Caffin, Charles H., "Exhibition of the Society of American Artists," *International Studio*, 22 (March 1904), pp. cclxvi, cclxxii.

_______ , "The Picture Exhibition at the Pan-American Exposition," *International Studio*, 13-14 (1901), p. xxxi.

Clement-Jamin, J., "Le Salon," *L'Action*, April 30, 1910.

Cole, Helen, "American Artists in Paris," *Brush and Pencil*, 4 (July 1899), pp. 201-202.

Conroy, Sarah Booth, "Paris Was a Black Haven," *Washington Daily News*, August 8, 1969, p. 33.

"Exhibitions of the Month," *Independent*, 65 (December 31, 1908), pp. 1600-1601.

Fehrer, Catherine, "New Light on the Académie Julian and its Founder (Rodolphe Julian)," *Gazettes des Beaux-Arts*, 103 (May-June 1984), pp. 207-216.

Fish, Karen, "The Annual American Exhibition at the Art Institute of Chicago," *American Magazine of Art*, 17 (December 1926), pp. 622, 624-625.

Hoeber, Arthur, "The Art World: Pennsylvania Academy of the Fine Arts," *Commercial Advertiser* (New York), January 14, 1901, p. 5.

_______ , "The International Exhibition in Pittsburgh," *International Studio*, 27 (November 1905), p. xl.

Jewell, Edward A., "Work of Negro Artists on View," *New York Times*, February 17, 1931, p. 23.

Johnson, A. N., "The Greatest Pictures of the World," *A.M.E. Church Review*, 26 (March 1910), pp. 326-334.

L., F. A., "Our Art Exhibition," *People's Advocate*, 5 (October 30, 1880), n.p.

Lloyd, David, "The Exhibition of the Pennsylvania Academy of the Fine Arts," *International Studio*, 31 (March 1907), pp. xxii-xxiii.

MacChesney, Clara T., "American Artists in Paris," *International Studio*, 54 (November 1914), p. xxvii.

Maignon, Albert, "Le Salon de 1897," *Gazette des Beaux-Arts*, 17 (May 1897), pp. 353-372.

McCauley, Lena A., "Chicago Art Institute Exhibition," *Art and Progress*, 2 (December 1910), p. 47.

Murray, F. H. M., "'The Adoration of the Magi,' With Special Reference to Mabuse's Painting," *A.M.E. Church Review*, 29 (October 1912), pp. 89-99.

Pattison, William James, "Opening of the Hackley Art Galleries," *Fine Arts Journal*, 27 (August 1914), p. 530.

Paulin, Gabriel, "Exhibition of the American Art Association of Paris," *Brush and Pencil*, 4 (May 1899), p. 106.

Payne, Les, "Is It Black Art, American Art, or Just Art?" *The Post-Standard* (Syracuse, N.Y.), March 2, 1993, p. A-6.

Peckham, W. J., "American Art at Shepherd's Bush," *International Studio*, 53 (September 1914), p. lviii.

"La Peinture Américaine dans les Collections du Louvre," *Le Petit Journal des Grandes Expositions*, 139 (1984).

Perate, André, "Les Salons de 1897," *La Revue de l'Art*, 1 (July 1897), p. 136.

Redd, Penelope, "The Carnegie International Exhibition," *American Magazine of Art*, 14 (June 1923), p. 320.

Salmon, André, "Artistes Français," *Paris-Journal*, April 30, 1910.

"Les Salons de 1905," *L'Eclair*, April 29, 1905.

Shaefer, Francis B., "The Pittsburgh Exhibit," *Brush and Pencil*, 5 (December 1899), p. 136.

Smith, Lucy, "Some American Painters in Paris," *American Magazine of Art*, 18 (March 1927), pp. 134-136.

Stuart, Evelyn Marie, "Contemporary American Art as an Investment," *Fine Arts Journal*, 35 (April 1917), p. 257.

_______ , "Our Private Galleries: The Paul Schulze Collection," *Fine Arts Journal*, 32 (June 1915), pp. 256-257.

_______ , "The Twenty-Ninth Annual Exhibition at the Art Institute," *Fine Arts Journal*, 34 (December 1916), pp. 623-624.

Taylor, E. A., "The American Colony of Artists in Paris.—III," *International Studio*, 46 (June 1912), pp. 280-290.

Williams, Michael, "A Pageant of American Art," *Art and Progress*, 6 (August 1915), p. 347.

Wright, Melville E., "Philadelphia Art Exhibit," *Brush and Pencil*, 8 (February 1901), pp. 260-270.

Wyer, Raymond, "Art Collecting and Psychology," *International Studio*, 58 (June 1916), pp. cxxi-cxxvi.

Ziegler, Francis J., "Fine Pictures Galore: Brilliant Exhibition at the Academy of Fine Arts," *Philadelphia Record*, January 13, 1901, p. 4.

_______ , "Sixty-Eighth Annual Exhibition of the Pennsylvania Academy of the Fine Arts," *Brush and Pencil*, 3 (February 1899), p. 294.

_______ , "Sixty-Ninth Annual Exhibition of the Pennsylvania Academy of the Fine Arts," *Brush and Pencil*, 5 (March 1900), p. 268.

General Sources

Bacon, Edgar Mayhew, *Narragansett Bay, Its Historic and Romantic Associations and Picturesque Setting* (New York: G. P. Putnam's Sons, 1904).

Cooper-Lewter, N. C., and Henry H. Mitchell, *Soul Theology: The Heart of American Black Culture* (San Francisco: Harper & Row, 1986).

Cromwell, John W., *The Negro in American History: Men and Women Eminent in the Evolution of the American of African Descent* (Washington, D.C.: American Negro Academy, 1914).

Davis, John P., ed., *The American Negro Reference Book* (Englewood Cliffs, N.J.: Prentice-Hall, 1966).

Drimmer, Melvin, ed., *Black History: A Reappraisal* (New York: Doubleday, 1968).

Du Bois, W. E. B., *John Brown* (New York: International Publishers, 1962; originally published 1909).

_______ , *The Philadelphia Negro; A Social Study* (New York: Schocken Books, 1967; originally published 1899).

_______ , *The Souls of Black Folk* (New York: Dodd, Mead, 1961; originally published 1903).

Ferris, William H., *The African Abroad or His Evolution in Western Civilization, Tracing His Development Under Caucasian Milieu*, 2 vols. (New Haven, Conn.: Tuttle, Morehouse & Taylor, 1913).

Greenbaum, Susan, *The Afro-American Community in Kansas City, Kansas: A History* (Kansas City: City of Kansas City, Kansas, Department of Community Development, 1982).

Harlan, L. R., ed., *The Booker T. Washington Papers*, 14 vols. (Urbana: University of Illinois Press, 1972-89).

Harrison, Carter Henry, *With the American Red Cross in France, 1918-1919* (Chicago: R. F. Seymour, 1947).

Hartshorn, W. N., and George W. Penniman, *An Era of Progress and Promise, 1863-1910: The Religious, Moral and Educational Development of the American Negro Since His Emancipation* (Boston: Priscilla Publishing Co., 1919).

Kletzing, H. F., and W. H. Crogman, *Progress of a Race, or The Remarkable Advancement of the Afro-American* (Atlanta: J. L. Nichols & Co., 1901).

Lane, Roger, *William Dorsey's Philadelphia and Ours: On the Past and Future of the Black City in America* (New York: Oxford University Press, 1991).

Mitchell, Henry H., *Black Preaching* (Philadelphia: Lippincott, 1970).

Moore, Jack B., *W. E. B. Du Bois* (Boston: Twayne Publishers, 1981).

Morrison, Samuel E., Henry Steele Commager, and William E. Leuchtenburg, *A Concise History of the American Republic*, 2 vols. (New York: Oxford University Press, 1977).

Philadelphia African Americans: Color, Class and Style, 1840-1940, exh. cat. (Philadelphia: Balch Institute for Ethnic Studies, 1988).

Ploski, Harry A., and Warren Marr II, *The Negro Almanac: A Reference Work on the Afro American* (New York: Bellwether, 1976).

Quarles, Benjamin, *Blacks on John Brown* (Urbana: University of Illinois Press, 1972).

Revell, Peter, *Paul Laurence Dunbar* (Boston: Twayne Publishers, 1979).

Rhode Island, a Guide to the Smallest State (Boston: Houghton Mifflin Co., 1937).

Rogers, J. A., *World's Great Men of Color*, 2 vols. (New York: J. A. Rogers, 1947).

Scarborough, W. W., "Journalism and Colored Journalists," *People's Advocate*, 6 (November 26, 1881), n.p.

Simmons, William J., *Men of Mark: Eminent, Progressive and Rising* (Cleveland: G. M. Rewell & Co., 1887).

Tanner, Benjamin T., *Hints to Ministers, Especially Those of the African Methodist Episcopal Church* (Philadelphia, 1902).

_______ , *The Negro's Origins and Is the Negro Cursed* (Philadelphia, 1869).

_______ , *Theological Lectures* (Nashville: A.M.E. Church Sunday School Union, 1894).

Vincent, Theodore G., *Black Power and the Garvey Movement* (Berkeley, Calif.: Ramparts Press, 1975).

Warren, Robert Penn, *John Brown: The Making of a Martyr* (New York: Payton & Clarke, 1929).

INDEX

Photographs for this catalogue have been provided by the owners, with the following exceptions:

Ray Andrews: Plate 37
Gary Henderson: Plates 15 and 16
Paul Kennedy: Plate 51
Mike McKelvey: Plate 56
Robert Newcombe: Plate 1
Graydon Wood: Plates 2 and 3